THE CIRCLE GAME

BOOK 2

LIAM FARRELL

To
Malcolm

Merci
Love Liam Boz!

blaw
wearie
books

Published in 2017 by Blaw Wearie Books

ISBN Paperback: 978-0-9954905-2-9
Ebook: 978-0-9954905-3-6

Published with the help of Indie Authors World

ACKNOWLEDGEMENTS

My special thanks goes to Kim and Sinclair MacLeod at Indie Authors World, without whom this book would most likely never have seen the light of day.

Also a great gratitude is given to the Ordnance Survey open data for the maps, without which the book wouldn't be the same.

CONTENTS

Acknowledgements   3

Introduction   7

Basic Equipment   9

Following The Routes   12

Route 1 ⬤

    The Three Ferries Route Map   13

    Route Summary   14

    The Three Ferries Run   15

Route 2 ⬤

    Loch Fyne Route Map   39

    Route Summary   40

    The Otter Ferry Run   41

Route 3 ⬤

    Kilcreggan Route Map   63

    Route Summary   64

    The Kilcreggan Run   65

Route 4 ⬤

    Dunoon Route Map   91

    Route Summary   92

    The Dunoon Run   93

Route 5 ⬤

    The Clyde Coast Route Map   123

    Route Summary   124

    The Clyde Coast   125

Route 6

    Rowardennan Route Map   159

    Route Summary   160

    Rowardennan Run   161

Route 7

    Inversnaid & The Trossachs Route Map   183

    Route Summary   184

    Inversnaid & The Trossachs   185

Appendices   217

Local Training Runs   219

The Bike   222

Essential Equipment   223

Saddle Height   224

Cleat Position   226

Saddle Fore-Aft Position   228

Stem And Handlebars   228

Saddles   229

Heart Rate Monitor Info   230

Hypnosis Downloads   233

Injuries   234

Data   234

Photography   236

Workshop   237

Further Reading   238

About The Author   239

A most warm welcome to this, my first book, based around the cycle runs that I do from my home in Glenburn, South Paisley. These are trips that I do to anywhere I can reach and return from in a single day, without the need for assistance or overnight stops. The trips that I cover in the book are mostly old acquaintances of mine, and most have been done many, many times over the past 14 or 15 years, since I started my passion for road cycling.

Let me make one thing clear right from the start. I am no natural athlete. Nor one lucky enough to be born with the genes of a champion cyclist, or a champion anything for that matter. I have never won a damn thing in any sporting event in my life, nor am I of a competitive nature; far from it. I should have said I have never won a damn thing in my life. I am just a guy, that's how I regard myself, just a guy. I enjoy the outdoors, mostly on my own, and I only undertook the challenge of doing fairly long cycle runs for the sheer pleasure and personal feeling of achievement.

I came to the world of biking in adulthood by what is often regarded as chance, or more accurately adverse circumstances, when on a raw spring day in 1997 I was climbing a couple of remote Munros that lie to the west of the Linn of Dee, just south of the Cairngorms. At this point I had been climbing Munros for a good eight years, all on foot and without the assistance of pedal power. On that particular day the weather turned very nasty indeed and I was a long way from the car. For once I was slightly under-equipped and the trudge back to my vehicle was a very long one, of extreme cold and wet misery.

When I say misery, I mean bloody misery. In fact, I still rank it as about the worst day's walking in the mountains that I have ever had in 20 years, and that is bloody saying something. The vast majority of the approach to those two hills was along Land Rover tracks that I knew would be greatly shortened by the aid of a mountain bike. And, vowing never to suffer like that again, I went straight out the same week and invested in a nice wee GT Talera,

which was at bargain price as it was painted in the previous year's colours.

That was the start of it. I soon found that the remote hills in the Cairngorms and Grampians were now a pleasure rather than a drudge to approach, and I was hooked. Soon not only was I riding rough but also hitting the tarmac and regularly covering the Clyde Coast run, where the extra enjoyable exercise made a total difference to my weight and fitness level. Being a naturally wee stocky guy – 5' 7 inches tall – weight loss does not come easily to me. And having the bike meant that there was no need to do a long drive north to get a big dose of weekly exercise, now I could simply open the door and away I went.

For the first time in my adult life my fitness went up to a good standard and the remaining Munros and the following nine years of climbing the Corbetts were a damn sight easier than the first seven years of hillwalking. During that period I was a heavy smoker, easily doing in 40 cigarettes a day; this would rise to around the 50 mark if I was having a small carry-out (bevvy) in the evening after finishing work. This was occurring far too often, and I was getting close to slipping into addiction. So on a drunken night in October 1996, I decided that it would have to stop, as my lifestyle was not sustainable. I have been smoke-free and completely teetotal since that night.

The point I am trying to make is a very simple but important one to anyone reading this book and wondering if the cycle runs here are beyond them. If I can do these runs then anyone can, including you. A lot of guys who you meet on the road were introduced to the sport by their father or uncle or older brother, but if you have no-one to mentor you, don't worry. I didn't either. My old man's passions in life were Celtic and drink, but not in that order. I abandoned being a football supporter when I left school and became a passionate trout fly fisherman, which was enjoyable but very sedentary. When I finally took to the hills in January '89, I was only 24 and as unfit as a young man that age could be.

I struggled – and I do mean struggled – on for about seven years, before that fateful day west of the Linn o' Dee, which was when it all turned around. Often in life I have learned that the real blessings can come in disguise; the great energy of the Universe lends its guiding hand to steer you in the right direction. But only when you are ready, of course, there's no point in try to rush it.

Let me tell you something else I discovered: a lot of what you do or don't do is all in the mind. The law of attraction plays a major role in all our lives and the early conditioning we get can be very limiting and difficult to overcome, but it can be overcome.

"If you think you can or you think you can't, you're probably right." Henry Ford said that, and he knew what the hell he was talking about. If you have a negative mindset, or you don't value your self-worth, or lack confidence, or have any other negative program running your subconscious, including that major adversity of fear, then it can be difficult to accept challenges and embrace and get the best from life.

However, the early negative programing, with all its ills, can be overcome by installing a new program into your subconscious mind, much the same as you would do a computer. Computers and brains both work the same way at certain levels, and by using proven techniques like positive self-talk or confidence-building CDs, a lot of unwanted baggage can be gotten rid of. Constant, constant, constant repetition of the positive is the key.

Add to that the motorcar that just about every one of us now owns or aspires to own, and which a lot of us use for even the shortest of journeys, and it's easy to see why a lot of people would regard it as being nigh impossible to cover 100 mile runs or more on a bike. I can assure you that if the bike turns out to be your thing, it will be damn near impossible to stop yourself doing them, not the other way round. And this will take place in a fairly short period of time, which is good news if you are a human, as we are not a very patient species.

Bonnie Scotland is a most stunningly rugged, beautiful country. I rarely holiday abroad unless it's a cycle tour of the battlefields of France, but that's a different story. However, whenever I meet people in the remote highlands and islands, over 90% of them are from south of the border; very few people I meet are actually Scots. I don't have a problem with that per se, as there are so many of us heading south looking for work while they come north looking to escape the rat race, so it's a fair swap in my book. But what is disappointing is the fact that so many of us stay in the central lowlands and holiday abroad chasing the sun, so have no idea just how beautiful our country really is. That is a real crime, and one I'd like to redress.

I recently climbed Tinto Hill with a big mate of mine (Scotty Kirkland) who had travelled the world as a chef on board numerous sea-going vessels, including the QE2. But that day was the first time he had ever visited the top of the Clyde Valley, and he was struck by the serene greenness and beauty of the place. He'd no idea it was like that, and this was a man in his sixties.

I am in my late forties now and still going strong on both hill and bike. As I was taking a break on my last trip round the tough Arran run, one bike rider who flew by me turned out to be 72 years old and he was still in great shape. The health benefits of cycling are awesome.

I had to ask myself just who am I aiming this book at, as most established riders will know and most likely have done most, if not all, the runs in this book. They are, for the most part, either well-worn training runs or classic standards of long standing. So really I'm hoping to reach as many people who have either recently bought a machine and are looking for runs to do, or others who are thinking about getting fitter and don't fancy gyms or crunching their knees on concrete.

If the statistics are correct, then I might awaken the sleeping giant. For they say that there are as many bike owners in Britain as there are car owners, with the vast majority buying them with good intentions and using them once or twice before relegating the new machines to the back of the garage or garden shed, where they lie gathering dust.

So maybe if some clean up their hidden gems and get active again, it might help in some way towards us losing the unenviable tag of the sick man of Europe. This is despite the fact we are an undoubted rugged and hardy breed who, along with the Irish and Norwegians, have always had the toughest job in all of Western Europe in trying to eke out a living. Mind you, the weather doesn't help and I admit that it's easier to get motivated and look forward to a cycle in warm sunshine than it is in the rain and damp. But as Irish hardman Shaun Kelly once said, "You don't know how cold and wet it is til you're out there", as it often looks worse than it is.

Take it from me, the good days will come. And when they do, then boy, oh boy. Fancy it? Then just read on

Liam Boy.

If you are completely new to the game, here is some advice on what you need to get you started before we dive out the door for our first run together. Starting with clothing and starting at the top, a helmet is a very good idea. It's personal choice as to whether you wear one or not, and I know some guys who are very experienced road men who never wear one. Personally, I don't get out of bed without mine, and recommend you do the same.

Only once in a blue moon, if I am on a really quiet road round the back of an island, for example, will I take it off – and only then if it's a scorcher. In its place I will put on a cycling cotton cap, one of which I always carry to keep the sun off my head. The cotton cap's peak is also good under a helmet for stopping both hail and rain from battering into your eyes when it's so wet you have to remove your glasses to see where you're going.

The glasses themselves are also essential, and the ones with interchangeable lenses can be changed to suit the conditions. Some of these can cost the earth, but you don't need to pay top dollar for a good set. About £40 will get you a good quality pair.

Now although you don't actually need a cycling specific top, if you look the part, you'll act the part (or so they say). Cycling team jerseys do have the advantage of having three rear pockets, which are good for keeping essentials in. They come in short or long sleeves, and although most of us buy too many, probably two of each will be more than sufficient. For the short version, it's a good idea to buy a pair of arm warmers that go with them. I also have a couple of short-sleeved performance t-shirts that I wear under my cycling top on all but the warmest days.

You will also find most serious riders have more than one waterproof jacket – a heavyweight one for winter riding, and a lighter one for summer. The summer one can be rolled up and stuffed into one of the rear pockets, along with the cotton cap. Both rain jackets I have are yellow in colour to maximise visibility, which is a good

safety idea. My helmets are always yellow for the same reason.

Having a pair or two of track mitts (padded fingerless gloves) stops hands becoming sore when pressed against handlebars for long periods. On top of this they protect the ulnar nerve, which runs from your palm to your arm and becomes painful if pressured and damaged.

Next comes probably the most important item of clothing – the shorts. Don't skimp on price here. The one thing that can really put you off cycling early doors is saddle soreness. Get a pair that retails for around the £40 mark to start with; anything cheaper I have found doesn't quite do the job. I like the Campagnolo brand, but any reputable brand will do. You don't have to go more expensive than that at first, but if you start doing really long endurance then a really well padded top-end pair is recommended. A pair of leg warmers is also a good addition, particularly for spring and autumn; they're not required on summer runs, and for winter ones more substantial leggings are worn.

Cycling socks are basically just short cotton socks; some do claim to have beneficial properties like improving ventilation, but most just sport team logos or the like. They help you look the part, so it's good to have them, even if only to match your track mitts and jerseys. Cycling specific shoes are now mostly a must, with the cleat and clipless pedal system now in use, and some models go up to about the £200 mark. These are only needed by the top end racers, however, both professional and amateur. The level entry shoe that all manufacturers make will be more than adequate to get you going. Correct fitting and alignment of the cleats is real important, so I will give you the technique for that at the back of the book. If you get that wrong, your knees will hurt like hell, so it's important to get that one spot on from the word go.

So too is saddle height and handlebar stem length; again, I will give you an accurate and easy to perform technique at the back of the book to leave you millimetre perfect. Remember, it's very easy to spend every penny you earn on equipment, so at first just buy what you need and take it from there.

Next the bike itself, which is of course the main piece of equipment and the biggest outlay. Now you can cover a lot of distance on tarmac riding a hybrid or even mountain bike, but life will be easier and more pleasant if you're on a racing machine. Thinner tyres, less weight, the right tool for the job, will make it a lot easier and faster. What bike, or rather standard of bike, you use doesn't really matter on most of these runs, with the possible exception of the five ferries.

I started off back in 99 with a Lemond Reno. It was steel-framed, a Greg Lemond-made bike, which was the bottom of Greg's range. The Reno's group set (gruppo), was also bottom range, being Shimanos SRX. Nowadays they call it Sora (Japanese for sky). Despite being bottom range, Greg made a good bike and I did just about every run in the book with it, including Edinburgh and back in a day. On that occasion they actually refused to let me into the castle with a bike and even refunded my money. I vowed never to go back there again and, true to my word, haven't done that run since.

So to get you going, any half decent road bike will do. It can be a difficult decision as to how much you want to spend, as you don't know how far you want to take things. To be sensible about it, don't break the bank early on. You can get a lot of bike for your money nowadays, with a road bike in the £500 range being more than adequate for the job. The Government Cycle to Work Scheme is ongoing, which is a good idea in itself and you can get a machine to your liking for almost half price. You will have to source that one out for yourself to see if your employers do it, and if so, the guys in your local bike store will be happy to help on all matters, including sizing, and bargains.

Don't forget about Gumtree and eBay, where there are great deals to be had once you know what you're doing. But it has to be said that riding a real top-end machine is a pleasure and can make a lot of difference on a long run and also when hitting the climbs. It can even make the difference as to whether you can catch a ferry or not when doing the famous five.

The frame of the bike is the most important and costly item, and determines how a bike handles and performs. Next in line of importance are the wheels, then the gruppo itself. You'll soon learn that most serious riders have a good machine that they don't ride in the wet. For that, they have their training bike, armed with mudguards and a lower-end gruppo.

It's not always that easy to tell the standard of a bike by its frame; obviously the price is a giveaway, but so too will be the gruppo. They usually team up a top-end frame with a top-end group set. Shimano and Campagnolo are the two big name component providers, with Sram also now coming onto the market with a range.

Campag make some lovely gear, and a lot of guys like to ride with it. It tends to be more expensive than Shimano for two reasons. First, you pay for the Italian styling, and secondly, Shimano produce more so can do it cheaper. It's the same with a lot of Italian produce in general, including their bike frames.

I don't believe you get the same value for money from a Pinarello frame, than you would for say an Eddy Merckx or a Trek. If you start off by buying a lower-end machine and decide to further invest in a high spec model, that's great. Just put mudguards on your original and use it as your wet weather bike. My training bike is a Terry Dolan carbon fibre, with the Shimano gruppo comprising a mixture of 105 and Ultegra components. My top machine nowadays is an Eddy Merckx Cima with a Shimano Dura Ace gruppo. To ride the Merckx is a pleasure, despite the fact it's 11 years old and has a 9-speed set-up. The more modern have at least 10. It's all about justification here.

If you graft hard and want to splash out and treat yourself, why not? Some guys change their bikes every couple of years or so, but not me. I buy real good and keep it a lifetime if I can, that way I get quality and value for money.

Living in the west of Scotland will mean a lot of rain, of course, and a lot of wet weather riding. So having a good standard of training bike will be very beneficial as the majority of the miles you do, even in the summer, will be done on it. I then recommend having a bike with at least a mid-range group set. As for a real top-end machine? Well, only you can justify spending the money. Very few can justify Campagnolo top-end set, with some guys saying Shimano's Ultegra is the thinking man's gruppo, compared to the higher priced Dura Ace. You'll have to figure that one out for yourself.

Other on-bike essentials are a pump, saddle bag for carrying a spare tube, puncture repair kit, tyre levers, a multi tool, some dough, and your house keys. A more substantial track pump for blowing up tyres in-house will also shortly be required, as will some specialised cycle tools as you become more proficient in the art of cycle maintenance, along with your cleaning and lubeing kits.

The techniques required for correct saddle height (very important), correct stem length (nearly as important), and correct cleat positioning (helluva important), will all be given at the back of the book.

Don't let that lot jumble your brain. It will all come quite naturally to you in time. And with that, we are about ready to go. So it's on with the show.

The whole point of the book is to get people fired up enough to make them want to go out and ride the routes and enjoy the challenge that they present. So I hope that you will read the whole run through, and get in the mood to give it a real good go. I have, therefore, described the runs in great detail, much more so than most other guide books do. I also hope that the photos of our beautiful country and the history included will act as a spur to get you going and to keep you going.

To keep you on track to a certain extent when doing a route, I hope you will find the accompanying map and the route place names summary enough to guide you, for the most part. However some runs can become a little bit tricky in places, particularly when using country back roads for a few miles. Before you start out on any particular run, it might be worth checking with the relevant O/S map (if you have one) or even a large road atlas to give you a better idea of which roads to take, but that's only if you want to follow my way blow-for-blow, of course.

Remember that my route description may be only one way of many, and you might find a different approach road much more suitable for your needs. I am aware that everyone will be starting from a different location, bearing in mind that most people will begin the majority of the runs from their front door. Please don't forget that you are setting out on an adventure here, so a bit of trial and error on the road is more than acceptable and must be expected. If you don't get a route right first time round, that's fine, just check the map and correct your mistake the next time out.

Some cycling guide books give a brief description of a route and then provide a fairly long, though very accurate, set of instructions on how to follow the route. You know the sort of thing: turn left here, it's signposted such and such. However, I didn't want to do that, as it would mean constantly stopping to check you are on the right road, and that is the last thing you want to do on a bike ride. For me, flowing movement is the key to fun.

Just having the knowledge of your intended destination and some of the place names in between should get you there.

Bear in mind at all times that I personally just made tracks for any given place and made the route up as I went along, although I did use the O/S maps for guidance before I set out on most of them. So remember it can be done ad hoc and it all adds to the fun. Good luck to you all.

NOTE

Please note that when the idea for The Circle Game cycling book was first thought up and planned, it was my intention to produce only one book. It was not until it was just about finished that I realised just how big it was, and that it would therefore have to split into three books. Despite this, I have for the most part kept the original text for authenticity. Therefore, if for example you are reading about a run in book three and it mentions something that I have previously talked about and you have not come across it in book three, then it means that it is contained in an earlier book.

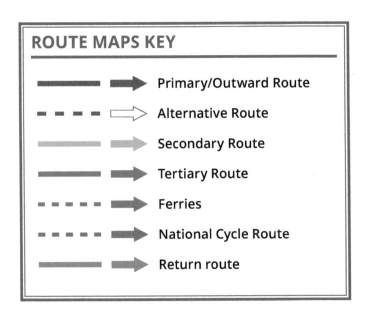

ROUTE MAPS KEY

➡	Primary/Outward Route
⇨	Alternative Route
➡	Secondary Route
➡	Tertiary Route
➤	Ferries
➡	National Cycle Route
➡	Return route

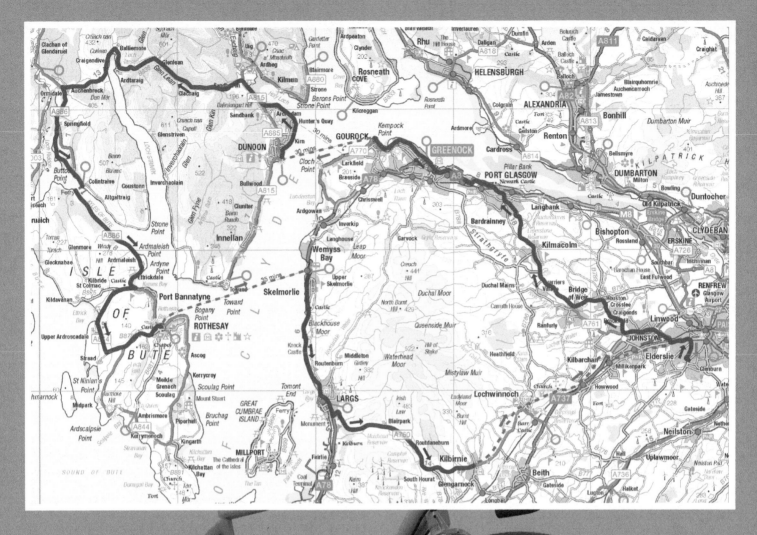

THE THREE FERRIES

FROM PAISLEY
84.6 Miles
5.33 Hours
Ascent 3500 feet
3261 Calories burned

FROM GOUROCK OR WEMYSS BAY
38.4 Miles
2.35 Hours
Ascent 2040 feet
1611 Calories burned

O/S Landranger Maps 64, 63, 56

Argyll Ferries Tel No 01475 650 338

Western Ferries Tel No 01369 706 020

Cal Mac Wemyss Bay Tel No 01475 520 521

ROUTE SUMMARY

Linwood
Crosslee
Bridge Of Weir
Kilmacolm
Clune Brae
Port Glasgow
Greenock
Gourock
Western Ferries

COWAL PENINSULA

Hunter's Quay
Sandbank
Glean Lean
Colintraive (Via B-866)
Ferry To Rhubodach (Bute)

ISLE OF BUTE

Rhubodach
Ettrick Bay
Bute West Side
Rothesay
Ferry To Wemyss Bay

RETURN ROUTE

Wemyss Bay
Largs
Kilbirnie (Cycle Track)
Lochwinnoch (Cycle Track)
Kilbarchan (Cycle Track)
Johnstone (Cycle Track)
Elderslie (Cycle Track)
Paisley (Cycle Track)

THE THREE FERRIES RUN

TREBLE TOPS

f you've enjoyed both the island runs and the Dunoon-based runs, then I've got a wee treat for you here, for I'm just about to string the two of them together. Also included is more of what feels like real back of beyond rural road riding, and another one of those Cowal weep-for-your-old-maw climbs thrown in for good measure. This climb, incidentally, hit me so hard the first time I did it that I can still vividly remember the first time I did it. That is saying something, as I am going back a good few years now. I can also still remember being enchanted by the old road running down the side of Loch Riddon, as I made my way towards the Colintraive ferry.

This rather shy hidden route has charm and surprises aplenty, especially, but not only, in its quiet backwater section between Glen Lean and Loch Striven. Now if my memory serves me right here, and I am going back a fair bit, I think I actually came up with the idea for doing this run when merely studying the old road atlas and

thinking it looked a goer. I'm pretty sure I got the idea from that alone and no-one else.

Sometimes you'll find that the advice from some old timer is invaluable to putting you wise to some cracking run you were unaware of. But, having done both the Dunoon and Rothesay runs, I simply realised that putting the two together would make a great run in itself (which it did).

Also, on paper it didn't look too long or demanding (how wrong can you be, well on one climb anyway!), and it only dawned on me when I began doing the writing for this run, that for the many, many times I rode the Three Ferries, it was always in the same direction, anticlockwise. Never once did I do it clockwise, even though it would be just as feasible and would take the sting out of the toughest part if I did. I don't even think I considered doing this one clockwise, which I'm pretty sure was due to the way that the ferries themselves were laid out in front of me. The Western Ferries from

Gourock's McInroy's Point are always more flexible than the Wemyss Bay-Rothesay, and therefore easier to get the ball rolling when heading out at the start.

However, and this is the tricky bit to explain, I don't think that was the main reason why I never went against the grain on this one. It was more to do with the way the route just seemed to lend itself better to the way I'd always ridden it. It's fair to say that about many runs, and no doubt you will come to learn that some of your regular outings will tend to fall into this category for one reason or another. They just feel better when done in a certain direction. With the Three Ferries, this was due in a large part to my enjoying a Largs Road finish and not a Largs Road start.

So the overall structure of the run, if you haven't already sussed it, is over the water to Dunoon, round through the Cowal hinterland, before jumping over the Kyles onto Bute. Then, more often than not, after a limited excursion of the old girl's west side, it's back over to Wemyss Bay, along the Clyde coast to Largs, then home. Not a bad wee day out, even if I do say so myself. It usually pitches in about the 90 miles mark, and switches the satisfaction setting to high.

So after that for an intro, there seems only one way to describe the run, but that's only what suited me best. For you, especially if you are driving down and starting from the coast, you can suit yourself. This preferably means to do it both ways (at different times) to get the best out of it.

I've met riders who have done just that, including a bloke I hadn't seen in about seventeen years, and who I just happened to bump into on the deck of the Cal-Mac at Rothesay. He (Bill Lawson) was an old climber of repute, and one whom I'd traversed the mighty An-Tellach in winter with, no less. After driving down from East Kilbride and parking at Wemyss Bay, he and his mate rode to Gourock before backing round to Wemyss again, while taking in a full traverse of the island. They had motored all the way down from EK and weren't disappointed; that's how far people drive to ride this one. You won't be disappointed either if you do, no matter how far the drive.

For me, as always, it's a Paisley start. And as I'm heading northwest for old Inverclyde, it means it's a flyer straight out the door, as down and across the streets of the north part of town I go. As always, I'm dodging the doctors' cars on the Corsebar Road, then negotiating the busy Ferguslie (main road), before gaining the ground

of Linwood. Now, as mentioned in the Loch Striven run, when warming up as you purr along Linwood's Kashmir Avenue (the A-761), the Clippens roundabout will be encountered and here it's time to make a call. Admittedly, it is shorter to turn left and make directly for Bridge of Weir on the 761, rather than go straight ahead and getting to the far end of Bridge of Weir via Crosslee and Houston.

But I tend to go for the latter route most times, as this way is quieter with traffic and less tight as well. Not all the time, I might add, for there's no doubt about it, as well as being shorter, it is also easier to turn left and if I'm doing the mighty Dunoon run clockwise (more of which later), then I usually opt for the more direct route. However, the sheer tightness and volume of traffic on the stretch between the Deafhillock roundabout and Bridge of Weir itself, normally persuades me that the gentle climb on the Clippens Road (one of my favourites) is too good to miss. And I'll head out on this towards Crosslee where, just for the record I'll have you know, as you cross over the River Gryfe when entering Crosslee Village, you are going over a stretch of the river known as the Mill Strach (straight). I know this because I was a member of the fishing club here (the Abercorn) in my youth, and I'm glad to say the old mill has been restored and is now an office block of sorts.

There once was a cordite mill in the village during the First World War, though I'm not sure if the revamped mill was that one. So, battering gleefully past old red phone boxes and older-looking council houses we go. Although they are a bit tired-looking, I much prefer them any day to the slick modern ones sitting across the road, positioned behind the inn and built on the river's old flood plain.

You then hit the Georgetown Road and get out the saddle for the tough wee climb that takes you past old Houston Village, which then levels out as the modern high school is reached before the remainder of the B-790 takes you pleasantly into Bride of Weir itself, on the Houston Road.

A great swathe of green conifers sweeps and covers much of the right ground before the large farm of Gryffe Wraes is passed. The fishing dam of Houstonhead, with its club hut and boats, sits prettily to the left, in among the flat fields and cattle. And this quaintly sums up the place, in my opinion, as a kind of huntin', fishin', shootin', green welly type of town. I'm comfortable with that sort of persona, though not part of it directly, being the outdoor sort myself.

Now the Houston Road meets the A-761 on the far end of the village, with a steel plate on the corner building actually telling you the B road's number (most rare).

The village was at one time known as Port of Weir, and this name continued for some time even after the place was officially known as Brig. Its initial cotton mills were to be superseded by its leather works, which still continues to this very day. The Bridge of Weir leather not only adorns the benches of Westminster, but also the seats in that American automobile icon, the Lincoln Continental (I am impressed!).

From the Houston Road junction, turn right and start to gain the green fields of the Kilmacolm Road almost immediately. As you do, be prepared for some real top drawer riding now, as you flatly, at first, purr along towards the start of the rise which takes you gradually up into splendid surroundings.

Be aware that this is you on the old main road which ran between the two major industrial towns of Greenock and Paisley, and which was constructed in 1794. Since then, only God knows just how much traffic and travel has used this former main artery. So with over two hundred and eighteen years of history rolling away from under the tyres, you climb, long and gently, up through the farms and fields of Renfrewshire, which wears its prettiest patched coat here. My, my, I always think. Whoever designed this part of the world was no amateur. They certainly knew how to put all the parts together just right.

Fields and farms with calves and lambs
Come all together with their charms.
Singing starts when climbing higher
Through the green of Renfrewshire.
Today she's donned her finest coat
As up the smooth grey road I float.
If I go too fast, it's soon all over.
I'll ease a bit and take it slower.

No exaggeration here, for to follow the slender slanting gradient that crosses into Inverclyde District on your way to the Clyde, is for me a real "How do you do" moment. In my book, no better destination could be on the cards, and the road through Kilmacolm is unsurpassed for

specialness. As height is gained, at a fairly easy grade, the right side closes in with its gorse and grass sitting slightly higher than the road, but the left flank opens up as it drops away from the elevated road position. The splendid sight of Quarriers Village, in its Gryfe Valley setting, is so soft and sensual. So, too, are the closer green fields, some of which are given an even softer surround by the deciduous trees that line their borders, then the eye is taken away from them by the points that top the Muirshiel Hills. These dark sentinels are always shapely and present, always providing the back canvas for the valley's sketching.

At this point, the road takes a bend at its highest point, and before you, as you descend slightly, is the village of Kilmacolm itself. It greets you with large, very large, white-walled and red-roofed dwellings, safely sitting behind their stone walls, some of which are too high to see over. Welcome to Scotland's millionaires' row (well, one of them), which has ivory towers aplenty. I speak from experience here, for I drive a cab at Glasgow

Am I in Bridge of Weir or Beau Geste? Neither. It's Kilmacolm, but this great-looking old church always reminds me of the fort in that old classic movie. You fly past it on the main drag when Port Glasgow-bound.

Airport and on numerous occasions have taken people home to this destination. I've lost count of the times they've said to me, "Just drive through the gates, driver" and found that these people live behind an 8 foot wall, and are a football ground's distance from their nearest neighbour. I would imagine it makes it difficult to get to know your neighbours under those circumstances.

However, I can also see why people would be drawn to this village, by its sheer setting in the moorland bracken of the high outer shire. The picturesque Knapp's Dam, that holds court on the right just before you enter, sets the scene for what's to come. The main road through boasts more walled gardens, more houses of grandeur, more leafy side lanes. It rises slightly on entering, before there is quite a marked dipping descent down and across the village centre crossroads.

Down the road on the left will be the old village station; the arrival of the railway in 1869 was what gave Kilmacolm the life-blood it needed to expand, and expand it did. Most of the houses in the village were built between the railway's arrival and the start of the Great War.

Up until then, the place had been nothing more than a small struggling centre for the agricultural hinterland that surrounded it. The end result was a splendid collection of Victorian and Edwardian dwellings that give the village a very luxurious and unique look.

As you leave on the Port Glasgow Road, you almost immediately pass the white shining old kirk, whose turreted tower always reminds me of the fort in Beau Geste. There is then, between the fields on the left and villas on the right, a bit of climbing and bending to be done, with the slight elevation giving

the householders splendid views across the fields and up to the higher moorland. You emerge from the village and once again it's magical moment time, for me at least, speeding toward the high threshold of land and rock that sits above the lower Clyde.

You know me well enough by now to know that I enjoy this area immensely, not only because of its rugged beauty, but because of what lies ahead just round the corner. Suspense is built up on this stretch of road by the way it dips then curves, all the while concealing the prize of the magnificent vista which heralds your arrival at the

The magnificent ship sculpture at the entrance to Port Glasgow tells of the town's links to all things seafaring. It is a most impressive work. You can either stay on the main road or go through the town centre, to gain access to Greenock.

top of Port Glasgow, through which you will descend at full speed towards sea level very shortly. But first you pass the wonderfully named Auchenbothie Road as it slips away left towards the cycle path, with which it runs cheek by jowl for a short section. Then it's round by the cottages of Craigmarloch, sitting above the wood-clad and semi-hidden Leperstone Reservoir, shortly after which the grey houses of the Port's Park Farm housing scheme appear on the horizon.

Their appearance is accompanied by the distant hills beyond the Clyde, where broad and bulky Ben Lomond (the Beacon Hill), lives up to its Norse name in particular. Now you bend and descend quite stunningly and swiftly into the schemes of the Port, but as you do so, exercise some caution at the new roundabout — built very awkwardly, in my opinion — that leads into the new school. Whoever designed the road layout here might have been a lopsided midget who drove a Reliant Robin, for the way the road now runs, that would seem to be the only person who could get through this roundabout without having to slam the brakes on very hard. After negotiating that obstacle, relax a bit now as the road ahead is straight and straightforward, as gleefully you plummet towards the top of the Clune Brae.

This takes you past the tough-looking filling station, which looks more like a West Belfast army post. Don't let that put you off, however, for things are about to get seriously good, as the road takes you on down through the houses and past another school. You also pass a red-bricked, cross-thrusting pineapple (chapel) on the left,

Looking back along Gourock's waterfront to Kempock Point, from the Western Ferries pier at MacInroy's Point. Gourock shorefront is always a pleasure to ride, what with the views and its busy persona. More akin to Brighton than a Clyde coast town, its striking yachting club building oozes middle to upper class character.

before the dive must be checked at the top of the Clune Brae. An enormous and thankfully sweeping roundabout greets you now. Unlike its previous smaller cousin, this one lends itself to movement and flow, and what movement there is. As you swing round full tilt, it's onto the top of the Clune Brae proper, then hold onto your hat, for you know what's coming. "Broad." I said, "Broad." And I mean it.

The first thing that hits you as you gather speed at the top of the Clune is how everything opens up wide, really wide. The brae itself is broad, but the blue and sand barred firth below is broader. It hits and stuns you into awe, as the initial top sweep of the road is covered. If you're lucky and the tide is out, before you will be

Just about to walk down the gangway onto the Western, which is always nice in the short term, for it means it's time to relax for a bit and rest up. It's also nice in the mid term, as the views going across are great; and in the long term, because you know what waits on the other side.

a patchwork of water and sand banks, sitting slightly submerged perhaps or just above the waterline. I always find it most interesting when the tide is out and the river reveals some of its secrets that stay hidden for at least part of the time. The hawk eye view you get as you scream falcon-like down the Clune, is fast, furious, and fantastic.

It allows, though only briefly, every natural sweep of the Clyde's inner channels and workings to be observed. Then, before you know it, the sign says that the road is about to drop at a rate of 8% (though it seems steeper), which means it's full concentration on the road surface alone. Don't forget the anchors too long or you might come a cropper on one of the lower pot holes before, with a bit of relief, a right swing deposits you onto the A-8 and the flat. We've ridden this ground before, as you know, so

After disembarking at Hunter's Quay, it's off round the side of the Holy Loch we go, and it's a brilliant swerving salty start beside this stocky sea loch. Today it looks cloudy and ominous, but I sometimes find there is a misty magic to these conditions.

you also know what to expect now. Occasionally you find yourself straining to look back up to where you've just come from, back up at the dark hillside which seems to hold precariously perched houses all along its seemingly impregnable face.

Fly round the waterfront on the dual carriageway and skirt the Clyde's edge, as returning inland slightly allows the A-8 to guide you straight and true into the heart of Greenock. All the time, the long road draws you hopefully and heartily westward, and eventually across and along the A-770 out further west to the choice of Gourock ferries that give access to Cowal and more. As always, when you clear the houses at Battery Park, the burst and sweep of the coast at Cardwell Bay never fails to inspire.

Now, which ferry I get will simply be down to timing. If I am near twenty past the hour, it's onto the Argyll and hit the coffee machine (morale booster). If I'm out of sync with that, then I plough on to the Western ferry.

Distance-wise, of course, it's the same, because the ferries cross over each other in mid-water, and therefore what you save on one side, you ride on the other, and vice versa. As I stated previously, the Western is more flexible and reliable, only rarely would bad weather affect this old workhorse, which was started in 1973 and proved a reliable success from the word go. This continued after a takeover in 1985, with an excellent service supplied in just about all weathers.

With one thing or another, chances are that the extra two miles would be covered to gain the red and white at McInroy's Point, then over to Hunter's Quay we go. The twenty-five minutes respite is always welcome, and the heaters in the passenger saloon have been a godsend on occasions.

After docking at Hunter's, the Holy Loch's side wall provides a most splendid banister to guide you in and around the bays of the loch's south shore. The road curves in sync exactly with the shoreline, taking you round a series of curvaceous corners, homing in on the pencil-like striking war memorial at the Italian-sounding Lazaretto Point.

Very modern and impressive houses hug the coast road, for the early part at least, before they start to give way to the older, and in some cases, gently decaying villas of old Sandbank. All the time, the view right up into the ever tightening and dramatic Glen Eachaig holds court with your distant vision, as fast and flat you take the bends on the lochside, before the very tight turn at Lazaretto Point itself forces a manoeuvre that tests your cornering skills. Beyond this, behold the long and grand old Ardnadam Pier — at 200 feet, the longest one on the whole Clyde, dating back to 1858. This one survived when many others didn't, due in part to the Royal Navy's reliance on the old girl during the Second World War.

The Yanks' requirement for a foreign submarine base, due to the short range of their Polaris missiles, meant that there was further need for the pier's services from the early sixties till the early nineties. The local economy took a huge hit in the summer of '92, when the

Heading up through Glen Lean on the B-836 in glorious autumnal sunshine, and the wall of the Tarsan Dam has just come into view. We're near the top of the glen now, having climbed up and through Clachaig. Despite its remote look, expect plenty of traffic.

Americans finally pulled out after Cold War hostilities finally thawed.

And so, after turning another tight left hander, it's up to the junction with the A-815, where it's right wheel and on up the glen we go. Some of the buildings here or hereabouts could do with a good bulldozing, as they appear to be well beyond repair. But, like a lot of our backwater communities, lack of Nelson Eddie's[1] means they will be around for a while yet.

Entering into the rough pasture land after clearing the loch head, soon brings on the left turn for the B-836, and it's Colintraive here we come. Things start off pleasantly enough on the flat and then the road rises through the woods. Fairly gentle climbing continues as the conifers are entered, though a lot have been chopped down now and the result is as ugly as sin. Once the bridge over the Little Eachaig River is crossed, you start to find yourself climbing on a hill that I have personally always found very deceptive. It always looks absolutely nought as you approach it, but will test you for sure. My computer says its 10% in places and, to be honest with you, its steepness can only really be appreciated when you descend it coming the other way.

Once up, though, it becomes very nice indeed, as the lower Glen Lean (Broad Glen) is entered. Right away, keep your eye open for an old moss-covered wall on the left, behind which lies numerous old moss-covered ruins, more of which in a minute. Rounding an elongated right hand bend, sandwiched between the aforementioned wall and rocks (the Broad Glen is not at its broadest yet), you come upon the white-walled and black slate-roofed homes of the hamlet of Clachaig. One or two of the houses are in need of attention, but most are very well kept indeed. So, too, is the quaint wooden bus stop, with accompanying interior bench, where a very informative board lets you know that Clachaig was once another one of Argyllshire's gunpowder mill settlements; hence its isolated position.

No fewer than five mills were operational here, along with just about everything else to sustain what was, in essence, a self-contained community. The cooperage at Sandbank provided the barrels for the finished product, which was where it was also transported from when ready. The whole operation was very carefully managed

1-Nelson Eddies (readies), rhyming slang for ready cash.

A dark striking view of the road running beside the Tarsan Dam, just before it drops long and dramatically down to the head of Loch Striven. Expect to be entertained.

able to support, but that doesn't detract from the riding. Far from it. It feels really remote and silent when you slip below the firs on the slope of Clachaig Hill, which steeply dominates the north side of the glen.

To the left there is a valley floor, though not even sheep grazing could be conducted on its marshy, reed-covered, and tussocky terrain. However, one or two houses sit way back from the road at the end of long tracks, isolated below the glen's southern hills of steep-sloped conifers, where the impressive shape of Leacann nan Gall provides the width to the Broad Glen itself. The 3 miles you cover from Clachaig up to the Tarsan Dam seems longer, but that's far from being a problem, for they are ones to be savoured. I personally really enjoy this stretch from here all the way down to the head of the Striven, as it has every pleasure you could wish and swish for — the riding is easy, smooth (for the most part), and stunning.

The narrow lane of the white-lined tarmac goes up the glen at a light gallop as you follow on expectantly, with the rounded muscle-bound dome of Creuch Neuran sitting dead ahead northwest. This dominates the skyline, till the taking of the long curving right sweep on the valley floor allows the dam wall to come into view. Sitting behind this, across its still high waters, is the left sloping steep face of Meall an Fharaidh, which totally overshadows even this highly perched pond. The road is still gentle climbs and quick curves, though it straightens up slightly as it glides through the almost-touching conifers, before it passes the farmstead of Glen Lean itself, sitting in its splendid isolation. The white stone farm building has only its barns for company, seen on the right, just as the final easy rise is taken up to the dam wall, known as the Col Dam.

This is the smaller of the two dams that had to be built to make this loch, which was constructed in 1953 as part of the Loch Striven hydro-electric scheme. The slight rise up to it allows a view back down the Lean, but that isn't where your attention will mostly be. Not only does the dam itself demand attention, but also the road ahead is very striking; the part that runs alongside the dam is pretty and eye-drawingly straight. All along this stretch, as well as the rest, are numerous passing places that give this narrow road some bumps and bellies, which is just as well. I say that because the B-836, although a quiet-looking back road, is relatively speaking quite busy with traffic coming from and going to God knows where.

and all more or less contained behind the mossy wall you first encountered as you approached. Despite their best efforts at safety, an explosion did occur — as happened in most gunpowder mills — and eventually production was switched to the mill over at Kames, the one you pass close to when doing the Five Ferries. It's hard to believe so much once happened in this tiny place, which is passed through in seconds if you don't stop.

The mills finally ceased trading in 1876, having been opened in 1838 by Robert Sheriff, who owned more than one such mill. There was a bit of a short-lived revival around the turn of the century, when the place reopened to produce sporting gunpowder only, but even that was over by 1903.

Just after you leave the hamlet, the road goes white-lined single track as you start to enter into the middle of the glen. From this point till it reaches the Tarsan Dam, it will very gently, almost unnoticeably, rise through a valley which couldn't be properly described as rough; rough just wouldn't do it justice. Nowadays, it seems that forestry is about the only thing that the ground here is

Still, this won't spoil your fun too much as smoothly you cruise the side of the dam, which itself is quite dramatic in appearance, especially the way it splits into three legs (or arms, if you like). On the map it looks like old Gandalf's hat in Lord of the Rings. The north running leg eventually becomes hidden behind the lower slopes of Sgorach Mor, the imposing peak that sits above the loch's east shore. The conifers that blanket the loch's west slopes almost come down to the water's edge, as other surrounding shapely peaks give this high dam a really wild feel.

Before long, you arrive at the Tarsan Dam wall itself. It's much larger and more imposing than the Col Dam wall, and it's here I must be honest and say that, despite all the concrete used in wild places to build these things, I really like remote reservoirs.

They do, in my opinion, have a really atmospheric look and feel to them, and the stillness they hold and keep has a draw on me whenever I'm in their company. So it is with the Tarsan, which is a classic-looking buttressed dam wall, and a look back over the water from this side will show the pointed and shapely Beinn Mhor sitting quietly in the distance.

From here, you are in for a real treat as the road now pays you back for all the climbing you've done, both hard and gentle, to reach this height. Look, then descend due west, down through open wild terrain at first, crossing the Glen Tarsan Burn by a solid stone bridge. Once over, your merrily drop into the woods for a real descent-and-a-half of flying twists and turns.

The early conifers soon give way to more mature and traditional woodland that signals your close proximity to the Ardtaraig Estate, as what feels like a roller coaster of a dive continues. The narrowness of the road and the hidden bends urge a bit of caution due to the chance of traffic coming the other way. Again, at its fastest, the road surface could be better in places, but it's still one helluva ride, which is long, great and long, but it's so fast. Before you know it, plonk! You've landed beside the Striven.

So here we are, at long last, finally at the head of the loch which boasts the magnificent Toward Lighthouse at its entrance. You'll remember it from the run where you frustratingly have to stop halfway up the lochside due to a lack of continuing tarmac, and then return the way you came.

At the head of the loch, it becomes even more apparent that a continuing road up would make for a beautiful and splendid circular run, as the bay at the top of the Striven is very isolated, tranquil, and as stunning a sea inlet finish as you could wish for. The white, fairly small power station building, which the Loch Tarsan Dam was built to support, is not too intrusive and neither are the numerous power lines, supported on wooden poles and not metal pylons, which run across the top of the tight bay.

The place has charm and plenty of it, with the passing places on the single track road being marked by the older and quainter black and white poles again, as opposed to the more modern versions that the road has been using up till now. Coming straight out of the trees so fast gives the openness of the loch an extra burst of freshness, and this continues as you bend round the top of the narrow bay. The wading birds on the small estuary's flats, which are fed by the Balliemore Burn flowing in from the north down Glen Laoigh, gives that seaboard feeling of calmness to put the icing on the cake of this rare spot. A spot that can also provide a glimpse of eagles, as they

After skirting round the head of Loch Striven, it's time for the pull up on the other side, and it comes in two stages. The first one (above) isn't too bad, and warms you up for what's to come. It also leads to breathtaking views down the Striven when you level off.

And here is Loch Striven in all its glory — a magnificent sight from this viewpoint, which is where the B-836 levels off after its initial steepish climb up from the head of the loch. You won't be complaining about the quality of the scene, that is guaranteed.

search and soar in the skies along the ridge of Cruach nan Cuilean, whose impressive steep slopes guard the bay's west side.

So flat and quickly comes the road that skirts the curve of the top, where flying round lets the rest of this classic fjord open its sea gate to your view. Being hemmed in tightly on its two sides only allows limited space for houses — most likely old workers' ones — though at least some deciduous trees have grown and survived here to add some softness to the stunning ruggedness. The large white impressive Balliemore House sits half a kilometre up Glen Laoigh in beautiful surroundings; its access track is passed as you cross the burn and start to come down the west side. The going is about to get more stunning but tougher.

The crux of the route is approaching, as a climb now starts at the solid grey house where the warning triangle

Another view looking right down the Striven and, despite the fact that the toughest climb of the day is just round the corner and you want to stay well warmed up for it, I admit that I often stop here and linger a while to enjoy the view.

tells you it's 12%. Up you go, and it levels out shortly with a view down Loch Striven that is truly awesome and then some. The O/S map shows two sections on this climb with a single black arrow, meaning the gradient is between 1 in 7 and 1 in 5. The first pull up isn't too bad, after which the road narrows again and you're into conifers and crash barriers. It stays fairly level for quite a bit as the road snakes away from you, disappearing into the trees then round a bend.

The first time I ever rode this route, at this point I actually thought all the hard work was done, for the real brutal climb doesn't show itself till you round the next bend. I actually said to myself on my first ascent, 'Liam Boy, I think you're out the woods!' No sooner had the thoughts entered my head than bang I was on the bugger, out the saddle, and puffing like an Olympic weightlifter.

The only good thing about this climb is it's short, thank God, or else I wouldn't recommend doing the bloody run in the first place. Just dig in for all you're worth and brutally force your way up. It's soon over, as on the plateau you get your breath back and your heart beat, which will be showing somewhere in the 190s, then you can take in the surroundings. To the right, greeting your arrival, is the shapely and rocky outcrop of Achruach — a most welcome sight. So, too, is the Tarsan Dam, sitting amongst its hills in the distance, which you would see from here if coming the other way.

With that over, it's reward time again, and you pedal along between the high rough meadows till in the distance the slender glinting of Loch Riddon, lying below the massive bulk of Cruach nan Caorach, signals the start of the second long glorious descent of the day. This one is much more open than the previous one, but again down on the narrow white-lined single track of the B-836. The An Leacan conifer plantation covers the left flank, but there's totally open moor on the right, as westward toward the sun you plummet, arm warmers rolled down, and not a bloody care in the world. With good clear forward vision, you can safely open the throttle on this one and totally enjoy it to the full.

It's a good one for getting the old descending technique polished up; you know the drill by now. Spreading your weight low again, covering the brakes by having hands in the hoods, feathering the brakes lightly when needed, not too much bite on the back brake to prevent lock up. Look where you want to go and lean the bike into the bend, but keep the body as upright as possible and all these

Things are just about to get seriously tough now, for the bend ahead is the start of the second part of the pull up from Loch Striven, and it is one that can shake you to your core. Expect your heart rate to go into the 190s, and dig in for all your worth. It is the hardest climb I do on a regular basis.

moves will get you down smoothly and safely. Flying down through the fresh air and rough stuff, undulating gaily over bridges and burns, you never want it to end. But then the end is upon you with a twist and turn in the road, and then halt! You meet the A-886. Wow! You think that was the business, no doubt about it.

Although you have those two great long wonderful descents when you are heading westward, having now done the run in the opposite direction, I have to say that overall it's probably easier to go eastwards; in other words, do the run clockwise. I say that primarily because you will then be descending the steep Striven climb, which is a bit of a white knuckle ride coming down. But on top of that, the two long descents aren't too taxing when reversed, far from it. They are very enjoyable, long, fairly easy-angled climbs, which makes the round trip clockwise a lot more relaxed overall. This is because the climbing workload is spread over a much longer distance and lacks the intensity of the tough westward climbs. But perhaps that's just the novelty factor talking here, as can so often happen when you try a run in a different way. So make your own mind up on that one.

As I was saying, you've now hit the more modern A-886 road, which as you know means you're turning left for Colintraive and the Bute ferry, now only a few short miles away. The A-road may be more modern, but after an initial small climb in between the trees, it drops down to the side of Loch Riddon and shows charm aplenty, enough to match any quiet back road. The start of the Kyles of Bute are reached and you know what's coming now. But hold on! Just when you think it can't get any better, it does.

However, once up and over the brutal climb from Loch Striven, it's a great easy-angled long glide down to the A-803 and Loch Riddon. It is a superb descent that takes quite a while to complete, which is just as well as you'll need all the time you can to get your breath back.

Ahead of you on the main road there is the long muscle-testing hill that we took doing The Five Ferries to reach Colintraive (that was the Jan Ullrich job, remember?). Well, no need to worry here, as it can be bypassed by taking the road signposted B-866 Coastal Route, just before the main climb begins.

Although the newer A-road is charming up to this point, it is totally blown away by the old one that follows. If you can find a more totally uninhibited, relaxing, and calming stretch of tarmac to ride, will you please let me know? I'm not holding my breath here or expecting to be inundated with replies, because for sheer quaintness and delight, you will have to go some to top this one. The sign is a bit misleading, in that the road only hugs the coast in its early stages before turning inland through the fields and woods, where at one point the loch is almost impossible to see.

But that's only a small matter, for it pleases all the way and none more so than at the start. After turning right, you follow the stone wall along the seaweed-clad rocky shore, where you may see hooded crows dropping shells to get at the meaty contents. The whole early stretch is duck-dabbling, sunshine-still, salt-shimmering waterfront. The backdrop of the far shore, steep-sided and wooded, does the near shore justice, as the red round marker buoys sit patiently in the blue bed of the loch, awaiting a boat's anchorage. Some yachts do sit motionless further down at Eilean Dearg — a small rugged isle just offshore — signalling this to be a bit of a picturesque playground for the sailors. I can't blame them, as I feel I'm riding through Shangri-La myself at this point.

I'm still by the shore, leaving the wall behind for a short while and passing some superbly positioned houses as I go. This, I take it, was the old main road that would have been bypassed in the late forties or early fifties by the new road, as a lot of road reconstruction went on in the area around that time. This left a slim strip of tarmac, a bit ropey in places now, to deliver you quietly round the side of this unique loch. I say unique because it has two names that seem to be able to be used in equal measure. I don't know any other loch where this is the case. Call it Loch Riddon or Loch Ruel, either one will suffice. Most strange! However, it is most pretty, and equally so when it climbs off the lochside and you find yourself sandwiched between fern-clad rock on the left and the guarding stone wall on the right, again all tightly enclosed by aged curving deciduous trees, windblown and battered.

When the fields open up on the right, the view across the Kyles to Tighnabruaich does also, at which point even the so-called coast road swings inland slightly, as it makes it way towards Dundarroch. Undulating, twisting, and turning among the trees, it allows only fleeting gorgeous glimpses of the loch and Burnt Islands between the leaves and branches. This whole section of the old road is just less than 3 miles long, but seems to go on for longer. Especially near the end, where it almost touches the main road but dives back into the trees again, before finally re-joining the A-886, where a much appreciated descent deposits you almost at the ferry slipway. Now don't forget the Colintraive cludgie here, where the water is cold and delicious on a hot day. When poured over an overheating head or down an overheated back, you sure do know you're alive!

Colintraive itself is a bit spartan nowadays, and the few houses it does have are mostly missed as you descend towards the ferry with your focus and attention on making it across. When going the other way, and not being concerned on making the boat, it's easier and more advantageous to take stock of the buildings (some quite splendid) in this sleepy backwater. Using the B-866 is also a bit more relaxed when travelling north. When heading south, you've often got one eye on the clock with regards to the ferry, because although the B-road avoids the long climb on the main road, it's slower and more meandering so a little bit more tension can creep in.

Looking across Loch Riddon, or Loch Ruel as it is also known, from the A-886 when you've turned left onto it and you're Colintraive-bound. If you stay on the main road, you have a big muscle-bound climb to get over to take you to the ferry some three miles away. But there is an easier alternative, and it comes up shortly in the delightful shape of the B-866.

And this is the aforementioned B-866 which, as stated, most delightfully contours the side of Loch Riddon in its early stages, and thus avoids the big pull up on the main A-road. Look out for hooded crows dropping shells to get at the meaty contents as you trundle down it. I say trundle, because it's not the sort of road you charge down.

Nowadays, there is quite a strict timetable applied to the crossing, with the boat leaving every half an hour, but in the old days it was (on the timetable at least) a lot more flexible and simply stated that it crossed at frequent intervals. The ferry itself spends the majority of its docking time at Colintraive, where there is also the Cal-Mac office, so there is plenty of shelter if needed. A lot of the day it leaves Colintraive every hour or half hour and returns from Rhubodach ten minutes later, but not all the time. More often than not the diesels will be ticking over quietly when you arrive, and you are treated to the splendid sight of the very colourful ferry sitting still in such a wondrous setting as the Kyles. The red, white, black, green, and yellow of the boat always jumps out at

This is further up the B-866, a bit closer to the ferry, and although we've turned in from the loch at this point, it is without a doubt still very pretty road riding.

you from the stunning but sombre green and blue hues of the backdrop.

The cost of the crossing can be kept down by purchasing the hopscotch 3 ticket to allow passage on both Bute ferries.

Colintraive itself is an anglicised version of the Gaelic place name, meaning swimming straits (or words to that effect), and goes way back to the time when the old drovers swam their cattle across the Kyle on their way to the lowland markets. There was nothing unique in this, as it was common practice on a number of islands. So that is where the name came from, and that will again give some idea about the shortness of the crossing. There have been numerous calls for a bridge to be built from time to time, but I'm glad to say that hasn't happened or I would have to rename a couple of my runs.

And at Colintraive it's once again the trusted Loch Dunvegan that waits to carry us over the Kyles of Bute, just as it did in the Five Ferries. It's always a welcome sight even if it's only a short break — as is the local toilet block, with its freezing cold water. Don't forget to fill up the water bottles here.

Once across, it's barren Rhubodach (Bute Headland) that greets you, where not even a bus stop provides shelter. So if it's a cold or wet day, try and time it well with the ferry (if coming the other way) or it might become a bit of a miserable wait. There's nothing miserable about the run down the island's inside road, though, with good flat tarmac to speed you on your way between the Kyle and the North Bute hills. We've been here before, à la Five Ferries, and follow the road likewise, always being drawn down towards the open sea till the entrance to Loch Striven is reached. This time, however, if you've done that run, you will be intimate with some of the landmarks and details of the place, which is always nice.

Looking across into the mouth of Loch Striven when coming down from Rhubodach, and on this beautiful autumnal evening the light couldn't be better. After all the upping and downing round the Striven, this mostly flat stretch down to Port Bannatyne is welcome respite, though it is no less beautiful as the above photo proves.

Then it's over past Ardmaleish Farm, with its wonderful lived-in look, and whose tough wee pull up I'm always glad to see the back of, before dropping down to tranquil Kames Bay. As the bay is skirted, it's always a marvellous sight to look across at the yacht masts nestled shoulder-to-shoulder in front of the town's rustic old shorefront. When we did the Five Ferries, we made straight for Rothesay and some grub, if I remember rightly. Well, that's where we differ this time. On this occasion, we aren't making a B-line for the island's capital. Oh no, this time we are taking our old mate the A-844 and heading over the west side again, to enjoy its charms once more. To be honest here, I actually think it's criminal to touch Bute and not hit the west coast, but due to hunger and ferry times and all, I usually give it a miss on the Five Ferries.

But not on this run, for it simply has too much to ignore. And this becomes more than apparent once you clear the pull up out of Kames and then break left for the south side of Ettrick Bay. Although I usually do this run from Paisley in the summer, it is more than doable on a good winter's day if you park at Wemyss Bay or get the train home. This gives you the added bonus that it will start to be twilight as the far end of Rothesay is reached, and as such the light will be at its best for scenery and photographs. To close in on the sands of Ettrick in the gloaming, trumps any approach in the midday light, when shadows become longer and scenes are softer.

The arrival of the modern, ultra-small, top quality digital cameras, now mean it's possible to take photos on your cycle runs, where before it wasn't something I fancied doing with the bulkier 35mm compacts. The winter landscapes, or even wilder summer day scenes on the coast, mean that good days are not needed to provide memorable runs; far from it. The wet misty ones will often delight and please just as much in their own way, as long as you are suitably attired. Keeping as warm and dry as possible is all that is required on such occasions, along with a good set of mudguards to allow the enjoyment to flow.

This is a great autumnal purple heather-clad view of the Striven hills, which you get if doing the Three Ferries clockwise when heading for Rhubodach. It goes without saying that no other season can provide the same colourful canvas that autumn can, and in the evening light the inner kyle becomes simply beautiful.

So once again the Sound of Bute's blue baize is encountered on another day when we just shave the south of Ettrick's sands and begin the long, easy-angled pull up to the ferocious bad bend near Straad.

By all means take the foot of the gas here and enjoy this most pleasant place. No matter how many times you visit it, the Rothesay girl never loses her charm. Never. Simply spin up through the fields and enjoy the view of the glimpsing blue westwards. After turning inland at the Straad junction, the undulating fast pretty descent finds us at that quaintest of junctions, manned most admirably by those old iron signposts that have long disappeared elsewhere.

No right turn on this occasion, though. It's straight on for Rothesay Town by the shorter B-878, which takes us through the centre of the island on a road we haven't cycled before. In doing so, the island shows us a side of itself that is somewhat different again, and it is quite remarkable that so small a place can have such a diverse landscape.

Although agricultural, the fields to the left — before and above small Greenan Loch — have a real barren

look to them. All folded neatly, they lie back clipped and spartan, surrounding their large farmstead. After this, the road takes a sharp turn right and starts a great descent into the town itself; a bit of a screamer to be honest. You're up so high that even when the first houses are hit, you've still got plenty more pretty descending to go before the town centre is reached.

The grey stone cottages that line the left hand side have a most splendid view across the fields opposite, which lead into the wilder-looking central higher ground. This view is better appreciated when actually ascending this hill in the opposite direction, where the detail of it all can be taken in at a much more leisurely pace.

At the bottom of the hill, there are more of ye olde treats waiting, most noticeably Rothesay Castle, rounded and stunning in its moat. Also take a slow trip round this part of town, which I dare say is the oldest due to the look of some the buildings, which are clearly of age and character. It is a good chance to do this, as the other runs tend to miss out this interesting and enchanting hidden quarter, which is very tight and compact and simply bursting with charm. At the time of writing, it's £4.60 for the castle entry and £3 for the museum. The ferry and front are just round the corner now, which we of course must return to in order to sail home.

And so again with another satisfying glow and sworn promise to return, we sit on deck, coffee in hand, and salute the Glenburn Hotel and all the other fine fellows of the front. We leave and settle in for a well-earned half hour break till the Tudor tower of Wemyss Bay station is reached. But not before we pass our guardian in shining

Looking across Kames Bay to Port Bannatyne and its marina, just after the slight drop down from Ardmaleish Farm. It was no hardship to skirt the sunlight bay on this evening, enroute to the far side of the island

A closer view of Port Bannatyne's marina with the town behind, again bathed in the soft evening light.

solid square homes, some of which were formerly owned by the tea barons who settled here in numbers. Skelmorlie is split into two, upper and lower, mostly because of the presence of a rather spectacular cliff, which sits just to the left of the road. Only on foot or on bicycle can you really appreciate its features, because it is so overgrown that it reminds me of the Burmese jungle.

A road called Long Hill breaches it to reach the upper houses, and that road runs west at a higher level than the coast road. It is one we shall take on a future run. Right in the centre of the cliff face there is a quite dramatic, almost square-shaped gash, which at first I thought was a natural feature — and a very impressive one, at that. Not so. Believe it or not, this was actually once a lift shaft, gouged out of the rock

white armour, Toward Lighthouse. It feels like an old mate now, and I'm sure it winked at me once.

On arriving back on the mainland, the Three Ferries tradition again kicks in and finds me, as always, taking the Largs (Shore Road) home without any hesitation. I always make this one an all-round trip and never consider returning via Greenock.

And so it is a right turn off the ferry, where the busy road takes us towards glorious Largs, sitting 4 miles away to the west. A few short yards is all there is before the bridge over the Kelly Burn is crossed, and that means you're into Skelmorlie and also North Ayrshire. The houses continue on the right for the next half a mile in the shape of mostly red sandstone Victorian

This view of Port Bannatyne's boats was taken just before the right turn was made to take you over to the west side and Ettrick Bay. The colourful boat makes this shot, as it stands out a mile when berthed beside the blandness of the plain white yachts and cruisers.

31

A fantastic evening view of Port Bannatyne's streets and pubs, and it does look so inviting on this bright autumnal evening. However, we don't ride through it on this run because we bank hard right on the A-844 and it's Ettrick Bay here we come. I really enjoyed the run round Bute this night, as I usually don't get to see it in such lovely late evening sunshine. I'd left it very late on this occasion, and it made for a most pretty and pleasing jaunt.

great road to ride and is in just too good a setting not to enjoy. From time to time, it bends and curves slightly to keep itself interesting, as it winds between the red sandstone rock on the shore and the fields and inner cliff of the land.

Riding here reminds me of the far shore of Millport, which is hardly surprising as they're so close, and I dare say at one time were attached. The land rises abruptly just in from the shore as it does on Cumbrae, but not with uniform distance, as it fluctuates greatly from the shorefront as you ride along. Shortly, you pass the German-sounding village of Meigle, where through the sparse Scots pine trees that line the road around Skelmorlie Castle can be seen the mound of an old fort high up in the Largs hills. One thing I noticed about the other trees in this area, even the rather taller deciduous ones, is that they seem to be less affected by the wind than the ones near Seamill. This may be due to the protection that is afforded by both Cumbraes and Bute.

The sea line on the horizon between the islands is, as always, a great sight to behold, as can be the light playing on the low lying green fields of Great Cumbrae as you near Largs. At this point, the ridge and trees of the mainland run right down to the water's edge and force

face to provide access to a hydropathic institution that sat on top of the cliff. Obviously the old Victorians placed a lot of faith in the water treatment remedy (how wrong can you be?). After passing the last of the right hand side houses, the sea appears again, this time through an open iron railing sitting at its nominal one metre height, and allowing all that glorious salt air freshness to reach you and your overworked lungs. Ah! Great stuff.

A sea level jaunt of 4 miles, with the shore and the railing almost ever-present, waits to take you to the Welcome to Largs sign, whose Gaelic name seems way too long for its anglicised equivalent. What's left of Skermorlie takes the shape of modern flats sitting on the left, as now you ride along a road that is pleasing in its situation and coastal scenery. The A-78 is busy and tight, but being a trunk road that is to be expected. Despite this, it's still a

As I said in the previous picture, I'd left this run very late and my reward was to get some great views over on the west side as the sun went down. This is one of them, it's of the sheep fields round Ettrick Bay. The fact that I stay so far away usually means that it isn't practical to still be on the island this late in the day.

Ettrick Bay as the sun goes down makes for a fine sight and a great parting shot, as the way back over to Rothesay Town now begins. What a setting, I must say. It put me in the mood for more late evening riding, to the extent that I went out and spent a small fortune on front lights, rear lights, and even one for my helmet. Good lights were something that I lacked as most of my runs were daytime; I work most evenings. However, after this run, I can thoroughly recommend leaving it late.

the road to make a slight headland detour. Rounding this, the entry to the town is soon made. As you do, the first in a long line of splendid bungalows greets you on the left, but ahead on the skyline, those two magnificent spires belonging to Saint Columbus and Clark's Memorial Churches, steal the show. The curve of the stony shingle bay draws your eye towards the shorefront, where you may see the ferry plying its trade to and fro on the water.

It's a bonnie and exciting ride into town, with delightful dwellings amassed on the left below the green rounded hills above. The town centre's bustle and colour means it's wakey-wakey time, as traffic queues have to be negotiated with care. Slowly — and if it's a good

summer's day, I do mean slowly — will be your progress throughout the next stretch. Well, it will be if you know what's good for you, otherwise there will be the chance of a collision — and not necessarily with a vehicle. Bear in mind that on certain days, half of West Central Scotland can be on the Clyde coast for a jolly, so along with a lot of fun-filled kids, stressed-out mums and not entirely sober dads, you've a lot to avoid. Be warned!

Now ahead is the mini roundabout, which means most of the madness is behind you, but it also means the start of the climbing as you've run onto the Irvine Road. OK, tough time coming up. Yes, the Haylie is about to rear its ugly head again, but joking apart, we've been here before and you know the drill. 6 or 7 minutes gets us up the

Returning back to Wemyss Bay on the ferry, passing that great landmark and old mate of ours Toward Lighthouse, and what a fine looking fellow he is. He doesn't show his age despite being born in 1812, which, as I said in the text, means we are talking Napoleon here. The small white building to the right of the lighthouse tower is the one that contained the foghorn.

steepest part, which is overlooked by heavily-wooded and densely-green steep slopes. Contained within, is a moss-covered stone wall almost unnoticeable in summer, when the foliage conceals all. And so round the modern wide sweep of the top bend, ever-steepening we clear our hill and make headway straight and gradient long.

Our entertainment, as we do, comes from rare glimpses through the right hand stone wall, where it has faltered with age, of the darkened islands brooding in the firth as the shining sunlight waters dance all around them. Then lo and behold, the high Fairlie Moors of the Dalry Road again. The all-encompassing green of the high laws and fields immediately has a soothing effect on my wee

When doing the Three Ferries anticlockwise, I always return via Largs. I love the approach to that town along the waterfront from Skelmorlie, and for the views it gives of Great Cumbrae on the run in. The town itself, with its church steeples and high ground behind, is a fine sight.

eyes, and away we go for the ride of a lifetime down to Kilbirnie. Fantastically flying, and I do mean flying, past Muirhead and Camphill Reservoirs — both favourites of mine — it makes for a summer's day sensation to pass them. Despite them being quite some distance away from my home town, they were actually built by the Paisley Corporation Water Works to provide water for the town.

Camphill — the older — was built in 1881, with Muirhead opening in 1942. They both have all the secluded still charm of their numerous counterparts, as they nestle quietly in the hollow of hills to the right, with between them quite a remarkable series of channels and workings. I particularly like the difference in shape and character of these two old dams, though no doubt my affection for them is helped by their location beside a road on I take particular pleasure in riding. Often boats will be seen bobbing in amongst the ripples, as fly fishers attempt to land some nice sized brownies and rainbows.

It's more of the same after they are passed, Kilbirnie-bound, still fast and full of curves and bends, with fantastic vista-filled straights in between. The broad base of the Garnock Valley, gentle hills beyond and quilted fields below, is the full finale before we begin the curving descent down into this old North Ayrshire town. We scream past its golf course, straightening in the streets below. As always, the chicane of the two town centre roundabouts can be speedily taken, if traffic allows, once you regain your composure after that brilliant but slightly hairy descent. The A-760 gives joy and always plays a blinder, but today we don't actually stay on this old stalwart. Just before leaving Kilbirnie this time, we turn right down Stonyholm Road and join the cycle path at that point.

This is you now onto another old rail line — the North Johnstone line, also known as the Kilbarchan loop — which unfortunately was an early victim of the Beeching report, closing in 1966. I dare say Beeching argued that the fairly close proximity of the modern day line was enough to ensure that this side line was not essential and therefore was expendable. It did, however, leave Kilbirnie and Kilbarchan without rail travel completely, and Lochwinnoch with a station about a mile out of town. The old Kilbirnie station itself was very close to the point where you join here, and the island platform is still very much intact. The station opened in June 1905, and closed almost 61 years later to the day, in June 1966.

A view of Hunterston and Little Cumbrae from the top of the Haylie Brae. I know I've included pictures from this viewpoint before, but I do so again not only because it is such a wonderful situation, but also to show just how much a change in the light can totally transform a scene.

The line itself would not have had very much further to run, as it joined the mainline just south of here between Glengarnock and Dalry. That is why, if you are following it in that direction on the modern day cycle track, you soon have to leave the old track bed and take to the back roads.

I turn left to take me home, of course, knowing that I am only about 13 miles from my front door, and immediately pass under bridge number 51. All the bridges have numbers allocated to them. The line, especially in the early stages here, is very closed in and lacks any sort of view at all. However, this can be used to your advantage when coming the other way, when there is a strong westerly wind blowing. For it is possible then to head as far west as Kilbirnie and enjoy a fair amount of protection from any headwind, the protection being provided by the steep sides of the embankment. They allow you to head into the wind without having to fight its full force and then, if you so wish, to return by a circuitous road route with the advantage of having the wind at your back. Also, what the track lacks in distant views, it to some extent makes up for by the marvellous bridges that span its breadth. They will come thick and fast at first, then fairly regularly after, as you speedily purr along beneath.

I know nought about civil engineering or building bridges, and usually when someone knows nothing about a subject they have no appreciation of it. However, even I can tell the quality and craftsmanship that went into the building and design of these almost one hundred-year-old structures, which to their credit are as solid today as the day they were first built. They add charm and character to the monotony of the Kilbirnie stretch. If you are approaching from the other direction, as you near the last bridge before the town, through its arch can be seen the roofs and chimney pots of the first

Looking back at the rooftops of Kilbirnie, after going under the first of many bridges on the cycle track back to Paisley. This runs along the former rail line that was known as the Kilbarchan loop. I am in awe of the bridge builders' skill.

down and continuing on. It carries on fairly similarly until you cross over the wooded gorge of the Maich Burn, the district boundary, from where it starts to open up a tad as the approach to Lochwinnoch begins. As you do so, Barr Castle appears on the left. This is a place I've mentioned before as being the ancestral pile of the Glen family, and despite its look of being a defensive structure was actually more of a show house for prestige than anything else.

The Barr Loch itself, lying below you at a field or two's distance away in the valley hollow, only reappeared again during the war, when the sluice system was destroyed and the water filled up again. The loch had been drained at one point to form the Barr meadow.

You shortly re-cross the A-720, called Newton of Barr at this point, on the River Calder viaduct. This is a fine arch bridge, whose height allows lovely views of Lochwinnoch and the rugged Muirshiel Hills above. Unfortunately, the next section of old rail line has been removed, which contained the town's main

houses, which makes for quite a pleasing finish. So steep are the embankment sides here, that two of the bridges had to be built especially tall — one a high curving stone arch; one a green painted straight iron job. But both elegant and impressive.

Shortly after this, there is a point where one — and I mean only one — bridge, which carries a small farm road, suffered from structural damage and therefore was filled in. The track now rises slightly off the old rail bed and crosses the road itself before returning back

station, so you must come off at this point by curving down through a playing field and ending up beside Castle Semple Loch.

Now you can ride along the Lochlip Road for a short distance, before regaining the cycle path with a short climb, or alternatively the cycle track itself actually hugs the loch shore proper, again for a short stretch, and can also be used. If taking the slightly more scenic second option, be sure to join the cycle path again at the start of the car park, as the lochside path beyond is more suited to mountain bikes than roadies, though it does join the cycle route further down. Either way, once the track bed and a bit of height have been regained, as you ride along the view of the loch is open and good where its true length reveals itself.

Just before the end of the loch, where the start of the River Black Cart is reached, the classic old relic of the Collegiate Church is passed, sitting half-hidden in the trees on the left. This is real Scottish history here. The man responsible for its building was John 1st Lord of Semple and the place was visited by James IV, our most able Stuart King. Unfortunately, both were killed at the Battle of Flodden in 1513, along with a lot of our nobility. The resident monks seemed to have been very self-sufficient, even having their own fish ponds, which I was told are still visible today.

A lot of the building is still standing, but it looks muddy round about (I'm surmising here). So to actually visit the site itself — and I've been advised it's worth a look — it might be best left to another time when you're down for a walk with the wellies on.

Coming out of the trees brings into view the high profile and highly puzzling Ellison Tower (commonly known as Castle Semple), sitting atop craggy Kenmuir Hill. This also goes back a long way, though not nearly as old as the church. It was built by the MacDowell family in 1758, during their lengthy reign in the area, which lasted from 1727 to 1810.

Most serious observers think it has masonic connotations, as the MacDowells, along with most other local powerful families, were masons. Incidentally, it was the MacDowells who split Lochwinnoch into two to form Castle Semple and the Barr Loch, with the plan to drain the Barr. When the now two separate lochs

were one, that was Loch Winnoch itself — from which the town took its name.

Just before you go under the Bridesmill Road (the Howwood cut-off) by a now enclosed white corrugated tunnel, there was, just for the record, a station that was meant to be built here. It was planned as Castle Semple station, but was, needless to say, never built. This doesn't surprise me, as I wonder who or what it was meant to serve.

So with that bit of history lesson over with, it's under the road and on towards Kilbarchan. This follows quickly after another enclosed stretch, followed by much more open fields. You don't see much of the village, even from up here, as the trees are thick at this point and the old station bridge sides are fairly high, allowing only brief glimpses of the rooftops. The platform is very much in evidence, as are the old station's access tunnels and approaches, which isn't always the case. Kilbarchan, like all the other stations on the loop, opened on the 1st of June, 1905 and sadly closed on June 27th, 1966.

The busy Johnstone bypass (the A-737) has to be crossed by a modern bridge, before Johnstone town can be entered. We do so at its northern-most edge, by crossing our old mate the Barrochan Road, near the

A couple of yachts are out to play on Castle Semple Loch as we ride through Lochwinnoch, still on the cycle track, of course. The tracks provide a safer and easier option back from the west, and although I usually prefer to stay roadside most of the time, they are a good plan B if you need one.

bottom of Mill Brae. This was clearly named after the now-closed Paton's Thread Mill, which sits empty and quiet, though with aged dignity, down by the riverside among the trees on the Black Cart's far bank. I sincerely hope they don't knock it down, because this was reputed to be the oldest machine mill in the world. It still looks a grand building, resplendent in its white garb, despite a major blaze and vandalism. Having opened in 1782, it ran till 2004, where it was in the business of making shoelaces before finally closing its doors.

When you do cross the road, by a helpful set of pedestrian lights, you now join the path which sits on an embankment just to the north, above the new Morrison's supermarket. This stretch was all recently landscaped when the large store was built and has a brand new look to it. However, look to the left and there stands an ugly big electricity pylon, which just happens to be placed right on the spot that contained the former Johnstone North station.

Unlike others on the Kilbarchan loop, this appears to have closed earlier than the rest, and from what I can gather actually shut on March 7th, to be exact, 1955. Now in all fairness to Beeching, if you look at an older map of the area, you will see that the Kilbarchan loop and the modern mainline ran almost parallel and very closely together. You can see the logic in closing one of the lines.

So now we head into the white, light birches of the Elderslie section, crossing the flowing Cart, where the cream colour of the trees contrasts against the blue of Malcolm's enormous goods sheds. The bustle of Elderslie Main Road is always guaranteed, but today the cycle track will be regained shortly, which is not that easy to do as you have to come off at the start of a long, straight, nice angled easy descent.

But it means we leave behind the vehicles to jostle and joust without us. The light smattering of birches are enjoyed again, as we go past the site of the old Elderslie station (another 1966 casualty, after 126 years' service) and on towards home.

The last stretch for me usually entails coming off at the Green Road ramp and winding my way through the Paisley streets of Lounsdale and quiet Meikleriggs. I'm shortly home thereafter. Tell me now, how was that?

Liam Boy

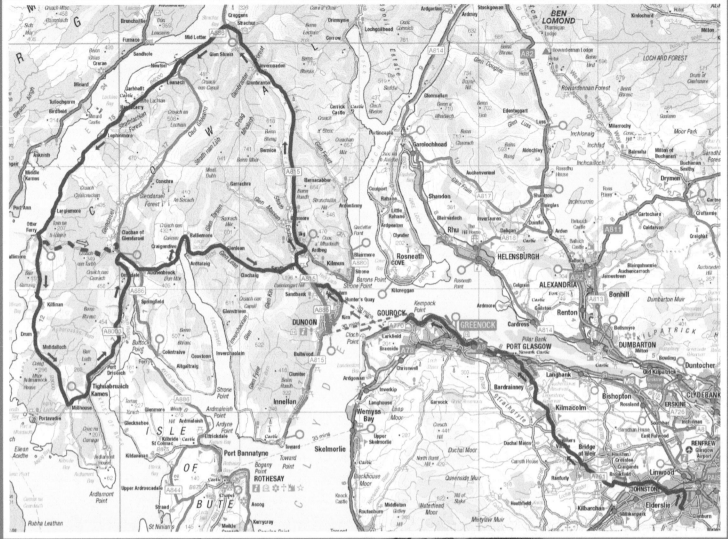

LOCH FYNE

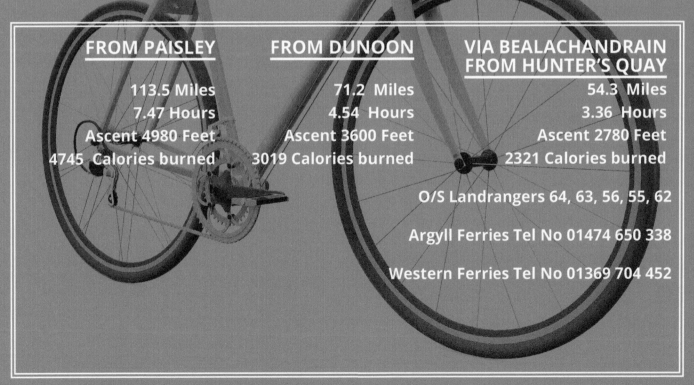

FROM PAISLEY

113.5 Miles

7.47 Hours

Ascent 4980 Feet

4745 Calories burned

FROM DUNOON

71.2 Miles

4.54 Hours

Ascent 3600 Feet

3019 Calories burned

VIA BEALACHANDRAIN
FROM HUNTER'S QUAY

54.3 Miles

3.36 Hours

Ascent 2780 Feet

2321 Calories burned

O/S Landrangers 64, 63, 56, 55, 62

Argyll Ferries Tel No 01474 650 338

Western Ferries Tel No 01369 704 452

ROUTE SUMMARY

Linwood
Bridge Of Weir
Kilmacolm
Clune Brae/Boglestone Ave
Port Glasgow
Greenock
Gourock Pier
Argyll Ferry To Dunoon

COWAL PENINSULA

Dunoon
Loch Eck
Strachur
Otter Ferry
Millhouse
Tighnabruaich
Dunoon Pier
Argyll Ferry To Gourock

RETURN ROUTE

Reverse Of Outward Route

SHORTER ROUTE

Bealachandrain
Dunoon Pier

THE OTTER FERRY RUN

A FYNE LOCH

Now, if you thought Loch Striven was big, or even Loch Long was long, then get ready to be blown away. We are just about to take a ride down the side of the big boy on the block, and by that I mean the mighty Loch Fyne. Of all the magnificent sea lochs that the Clyde possesses, none comes even remotely close to the sheer size of this monster fjord, as it brutally forces its way inland from the top of the Sound of Bute to the bay at the bottom of Glen Fyne. For 40 miles, she splits the land and is broad enough for a ferry to take 25 minutes to cross her breadth. You know the one I mean, our old mate that goes from Tarbet to Portavadie.

A lot of the miles on this run will be done on roads that we have covered already or on other runs we have yet to cover, but I want to include this as a separate run because of the situation and length that the side of the Fyne takes up in its own right. This is around 25 miles long if done all the way down, but there is a rather dramatic mountain road shortcut after 15 miles, should you so wish or need to use it. This can cut out the bottom half of the loch and takes you over a high mountain pass that reputedly provides the finest road viewpoint in the whole of Cowal (quite a claim).

I first became aware of this run when I was on the Western ferry at Hunter's Quay and met a group of five or six lads who had just completed it. When they first boarded, I assumed (wrongly) that they had just done the Dunoon run (still to come). But when one mentioned a distance in the region of 70 miles, I became confused, because none of the runs I do across the water come in at around that mark.

After chatting to the guys for a bit, they explained that they were parked at McInroy's Point and had come from as far afield as Troon and Glasgow, but all worked together and subsequently rode together. Their day out consisted of crossing to Dunoon, heading across Glen Lean, as we did for the Three Ferries, but then climbing over to Tighnabruaich (where they had breakfast). This was was followed by a jaunt up the side of Loch Fyne on the B-8000 to Strachur, before returning to Dunoon down the Loch Eck road.

Now let me assure you, that is one helluva run in its own right, never mind the additional miles that are required to get you from Paisley to the Gourock ferry and back. This run has been primarily (though not only) included for anyone who likes to drive or take a train to the coast, and start from there. It will simply depend on where you stay, as to whether you can begin any given run from your home or not. As the riding away from the main central belt is very beautiful and a lot quieter, I know that many of you will be big fans of starting your run from a Clyde ferry port and will be looking for something a bit longer than what we've already covered so far. Well, look no further, for you're about to get a full-on, in-your-face day out here, of length and toughness that should satisfy even the most seasoned rider.

After approaching Gourock by the most direct and easiest route, the plan is to describe the route taken by the guys, by starting and finishing at Dunoon; or Hunter's Quay, if you like. However, there are variations available on this run, not only on how you tackle Cowal, but also where you want to start and finish. It is possible to include the Isle of Bute, should you so wish, as you will run within 5 miles of the Colintraive ferry at one point, and can use it and include it if it suits your needs. In fact, you can begin at Wemyss Bay and finish there, which means four ferries instead of two, but that's fine if you fancy that.

There is also the option of starting via Dunoon and finishing via Wemyss Bay, or vice versa, thus missing out the tough Striven section. The best thing to do is get acquainted with the roads and the area, then after a while if you want to gig it, simply design the run to your specific needs or wants.

So once again, here we go now. After pumping up tyres (this should be done before every run), we're off again. And when I say the most direct and easiest route to Gourock, I am talking about taking the A-761 all the way to the bottom of the Clune Brae, after picking it up early doors when I reach Ferguslie (main road) shortly after leaving home.

I'm staying strictly roadside on this one, for information purposes mostly, as I want to provide you with another approach to the coast, and also because on the road – as opposed to the cycle track – there is less ducking and diving involved, along with fewer obstacles. This allows an easier time with regard to keeping momentum going, and therefore gives the feeling of getting there faster. It's very direct on the cycle path from Linwood to Port Glasgow and perfectly sound to take this way, even when starting out a mega run of over 100 miles or more.

But even so, I often stick to the route I'm about to describe, as it serves my purpose well and gets me where I'm going pronto. The big difference from previous runs is that after leaving Paisley and heading into Linwood, when I get to the Clippens roundabout I turn left, keeping me on the A-761 and making for Bridge of Weir directly. This starts off with a bit of a kick being required, ironically enough by having to climb over a bit of a hump bridge that spans the cycle track, no less. The old Johnstone ID (Infectious Diseases) Hospital stands on the left as you descend the bridge (it would have taken a brave bugger to work there), before a new roundabout and then a stiff wee climb up to the Deafhillock roundabout.

The new roundabout was purpose-built to provide access to the new school of St Benedict's, which was one of nine built, or should I say thrown up (banter), for the consortium of Amey, HSBC, and RBS in Renfrewshire. The three amigos then lend the schools back to Renfrewshire Council on a 30-year lease, so therefore it's education on the never, never. This is a very lucrative contract for the banks, hence the reason they were so keen to get involved and so many schools were built so quickly. I believe they call it PPP (Public Private Partnership). Anyway, we're through the Deafhillock and almost immediately skirting the edge of tiny Brookfield, with its three or four very well-to-do looking streets running off to the right, which are best known for being the former home to big Donald Malcolm, the haulage magnate.

We continue now into the wheat fields, as the road makes a big sweep right, passing the back road into Kilbarchan on the left, where just beyond on the right, the Kilbarchan cemetery ascends the hillside. I've mentioned before that this section of the A-761 can be busy and tight, which is true; however, if you hit it after morning rush hour, it's usually not too bad. It's helped by the view north over the fields. The view is actually quite dramatic towards the northern hills from such a low lying road, where the green of the dairy fields and the white of the wheat fields mean that even this busy road is not without its charms. As Bridge of Weir is approached, the cycle track comes alongside you on the right as, wooded and sort of wobbly straight, the road runs into the village itself.

On entering, you re-cross the cycle path on a classic old bridge that unfortunately needs a bit of support, then behold the great wee dive downhill into the centre itself, which finds you sandwiched between the old rail line wall and a great selection of buildings and businesses on the right. I love this small drop, always fast and furious, with the descent and the bustle and the alertness that comes with one half of this road always parked up with cars. The great arch of the Torr Road tunnel bridge is seen to the left, as you go through the first set of totally unnecessary traffic lights, as are the second set, which slow everything up at the Houston Road junction. Still, with the crossing of the Gryfe and enough quaintness

still attached to the place, the ride through is always enjoyed as will be the next few miles up to Kilmacolm and beyond.

The long easy pull up into Inverclyde is a good warm up as this will be your first hill of the day, and it couldn't come at a more pleasant place, as you well know by now. For the record, just before reaching the village, there is an area off to your left called North Dennistoun, and the name derives from the Dennistoun family who once held sway in this area. The Kilmacolm traverse is never dull, as there is simply too much here of quality and character for you not to see something new, just about every time you ride through. Ever since I starting writing the book, my powers of observation have improved. That wasn't difficult; I actually knew they weren't my strong point, but it now appears that I was a seeing blind man.

I'm not the best by any means now, as things still jump out at me from time to time, no matter how often I've

We're just about to draw level with, then pass, one of those reliable old red Westerns as we nip across the Clyde on the faster Argyll ferry, Dunoon-bound. Then we're off up the side of Loch Eck again, this time making for the mighty Fyne. Steel yourself for some serious endurance riding to come.

Today the Clyde's a millpond as we approach Dunoon pier, and it makes for such a calm and serene scene, with that most fine upstanding fellow – the Gantocks Lighthouse – standing guard, as always.

been to a place. So there is still room for improvement, though all the new discoveries keep things interesting.

The usual excitement hits me as I make my way between Kilmacolm and the Port; we were here only last run, so you know what to expect – the bracken and fir an idyllic tonic, before the flip over to the tight band of rough moorland above the housing schemes. But take it from me, the feeling of expectation never diminishes no matter how often you do this route, so great is what's to come.

It's all downhill from here on, providing you collided with nought at the new roundabout. Then travel speedily through the schemes to the top of the Clune, where – before you can say Screaming Lord Sutch – you're at the bottom of the Clune. In fact, you'll be lucky to have muttered 'Screaming', as that's exactly how you go down. With a sigh of relief, the sanctuary of the A-8 flatness is reached, which you know by now is followed west

The Holy Loch, like the Clyde, is a picture of serene tranquillity. And with no rainclouds threatening, it looks like we're in for a fine dry day on this run down the Fyne. For the purposes of the book, I am going anticlockwise and heading for Strachur, but most people would do it in the opposite direction and make tracks for Tighnabruaich to get the hardest stretch between here and Otter Ferry out of the way first.

with pleasure and expectation. However, there is an alternative descent route from the top of the Clune Brae, which misses out all of the early busy stretch of A-8 at the bottom.

When you reach the roundabout at the top of the brae, take the exit straight across from you and run onto Boglestone Avenue. This will carry you steeply in a couple of places and speedily down into the town centre via Springhill Road and finally Balfour Street, where you merge onto Shore Street, slap bang in the centre. A left turn lets you re-join the A-8 at the far side of town.

The busy main road, straight and long, exerts its usual influence as it draws you in, easily encouraging you into Greenock's centre, where the old East India Harbour still sits, awaiting a return to the glory days. The modern concrete structures, like the large cop shop on the right, don't entirely drown out the Victorian architecture from yesteryear, as there is enough of the old stuff around to make its presence felt.

Once you safely cross the large centre roundabout, you encounter the town's busiest stretch of road, with pedestrians that is; shoppers and the like seem to cross here in incalculable numbers. It doesn't last long, however, for once under the old rail bridge on Brougham Street, you find a bit more quiet, as you purr along the sandstone villa-lined A-770 and enjoy great glimpses of the firth. These are seen as you ride by and look down the access roads to the Esplanade; ones like Madera Street really whet the appetite for what's to come. Several streets provide these seaside insights, and that only adds to the quality and charm of the road you are on. Knowing that you are nearing the termination of this leg of the run and will soon enjoy a welcome rest, can lift the spirits no end.

The white elegant dwellings of the former fishing village of Gourock are always a glorious and welcome sight as Cardwell Bay is approached. It all hits you at once: the coast; the rising hill above the houses; the Cowal Hills across the water. And now it's pick-your-ferry time.

If I'm handy for the closer Argyll, then I'll grab it. Now, where is my change for that delicious coffee machine, I think I'll most likely go for the chocolate mocha. In fact, as it's a long run ahead, I think I'll have two. To be honest, if it wasn't a long run ahead, I'd still have two, but who's counting and all that jazz? On a really good day this will be drunk outside, with the marvel of the lower Clyde for company. It's simply too good to miss; the beauty and wonder of it all – some

natural, some manmade – is truly awesome.

Even if I land beside the old hallowed pier of Dunoon, as opposed to Hunter's Quay, I'll most likely take the slightly longer coast road, as I just can't get enough shore-side riding. So it's along the front I go, admiring the Clyde and all the old houses and stuff that have grown up and been built here over the years, which continues when I enter Kirn.

The vast fresh blue takes over you,
so open is the setting.
The cares have gone with bike and song
And now there's no more fretting.
The coasts delight, it's oh so light,
You're riding up in heaven.
Well, not quite there, but don't you care,
You're heading for the Striven.

A glorious shot down Loch Eck, which is the view you would get of this most classic-looking Highland loch when going clockwise. On this occasion, as we're going north, it would require a look over the old left shoulder from time to time just to enjoy the loch to the full.

The blue will play second fiddle, for a short time at least, as I ride into Hunter's Quay and pass the red devil of the Western ferry, its brilliant splash an eye-opener against the green firs of Strone Point. The Holy Loch now becomes your guide, taking you inside beautifully and gently, round its stonewall-lined bays, which remain remarkably unspoiled after all that has gone on here. Part of the reason is that, despite having an American presence here for over thirty years, the Yanks never actually built a naval base; instead, they serviced their submarines by a floating dock. This, on occasion, had to be towed over to Greenock for repair work to be done, and when they finally left in '92, the floating dock went with them.

Admittedly, they built some navy personnel houses along the shore in Sandbank, but nothing on the loch itself. This, I'm glad to say, was good policy, keeping the place as pretty as possible. Now we swerve and bend most gracefully up to the A-815, where we then spin alongside the loch's mudflats and out into the pasture land. After just clearing the last of the houses, you come to the point where you decide which way to do the bulk of the run, clockwise or anti. The B-836 to Colintraive is where it's make-your-mind-up time.

As always, wind direction will play its part, but just for the purposes of the book, I will describe the run anti, by heading up to Strachur first, but only because we've just ridden Glen Lean westward in the last run. If I'm being honest here, I would say that the hard climbing would be left to the end when doing it this way, so if you want to get that out of the way first, turn left for Colintraive. Choosing anti means it's fairly easy going for approximately the first 35 miles to Otter Ferry, after which it becomes more challenging for the next 9 miles down to Millhouse. Then, of course, the big pull up back over from Tighnabruaich is followed by the upping and downing round the head of the Striven.

As always, my recommendation is to try it both ways and see what grabs you most, for it won't be a disappointment either way. So we're heading straight up into Glen Eachaig on the glorious A-815 once again, and who's complaining? Ahead will take us alongside the magnificent Loch Eck and, as I've stated already, you will never tire of riding this piece of road, no matter how many times you do it.

The glen does show a fair bit of valley floor up till near the start of the loch, though both sides are steep and rugged. But after the sign displaying the whereabouts of the Uig Hall, sitting grandly alone in a field to the left, it starts to narrow appreciably. The road, almost flat till this point, does rise and fall slightly, as it passes the glorious Ben More Gardens, but it's still a real pleasure to ride all the way to Strachur.

If I don't stop at Ben More, I will at least slow down, just to be in awe of those giant sequoias and Douglas firs. Then comes the green baize of the Cowal Caravan Park, where you know the start of the loch is nearby, but that doesn't stop it sneaking up on you. Only after drawing level with it for a short while does it show itself through the trees and branches, after which the pleasure level rises quite noticeably.

She's 7 miles long, the old Eck, and what a 7 miles she is. The clear water lapping gently into the edge of one of its bays is usually what signals your arrival on the Eck, and from the word go your wee mince pie (eye) gets drawn across its water and up its full length, as the stunning open airy ruggedness is simply too much to ignore.

Unbeknown to the modern day traveller, not long after the loch begins, in among the early pines trees at Inverchapel, you can still see the wooden stumps that were once part of the pier there. Despite its now subdued and forgotten location, we are talking a serious amount of history here. Holiday traffic once boarded the Fairy Queen – an iron steam ship that looked like a yacht which would transport its passengers up to the top of the loch. This was just one of several stages, or legs, of what was billed as the World Famous Tour.

Now, as hard as it is to believe today, all that holiday traffic (and dirty laundry) that comes through Glasgow Airport from the main sun spots of Benidorm, Tenerife, and Torremolinos (sing it as you say it), at one time headed here instead. Thousands, and I do mean thousands, either came down for a week or two's stay, or just for a day trip from Glasgow. The day trippers arrived at Gourock by steam train from St Enoch's, followed by the ferry over to Dunoon. The next part of the journey was to be transported to the southern end of Loch Eck by horse-drawn coach, whose drivers wore scarlet coats and grey top hats. The guardsman would occasionally blow his horn for effect, making a most spiffing ride, as the excited travellers rode up Glen Eachaig to the start of the loch.

There, they boarded the Fairy Queen, which then carried them to a pier at the top of the loch near Glen Branter. It must have been a most splendid view of the loch and all its surrounding grandeur from the craft, which itself was sleek and cutting, with its two decks, along with a black funnel and double white stripes. She was built in 1872 and sailed every summer till the outbreak of the Great War, when sailing stopped, but it began again in 1919 till 1926. After that the introduction of the car and bus meant that the sail on the loch section could be cut out. Travellers then proceeded up the loch side by vehicle, then on to Inveraray by either vehicle or boat, before taking the steamer all the way back to

Once Strachur is reached, you turn left and it's off down the Fyne you go, and this is a beautiful shot of the loch in a mirror-like state. It's a real back of beyond remote feel to the riding now all the way down to Millhouse, some 23 miles away. The Fyne is looking her best here.

Glasgow. Nowadays, the pier ruins sit semi sunken and forgotten, hidden behind a thin curtain of sparse pines, where only a chance stop might bring them to your notice.

So now we settle in and get set to enjoy the next stretch of road, which is nigh impossible not to enjoy, so grand is the setting. I've spoken about the charms of the Loch Eck road already and don't want to repeat myself, but suffice to say the flat lochside wooded curves and rock-blasted bends will all be to your liking.

An old 17th century coach house, now the Coylet Inn – solid, linear and white, slate-roofed as you'd expect – is the next place of interest you pass. Small craft bob in the water out front, or more likely clutter the bay in front; with the quaintest chicken coop you ever saw stealing the show here. A large contingent of static caravans sits behind the inn and grows up onto the hillside. However, as they're painted green, you hardly notice them (if you believe that…).

The road takes you up the loch into more of the same top quality tarmac. More than halfway up, we pass our old marker on the Ardentinny run – the Whistlefield Inn – coming off the loch just slightly as we do, then back down among the bays and bends, where the red triangle warns of more bends to come. That doesn't bother us by any means, as it means more intimate dancing with our leading lady, Loch Eck. But the show has to stop sometime, and the end is signalled by the meeting of the River Cur as it meanders into the top of the loch through its rough flood plain, and the road runs us into Glenbranter.

Only the most haggard of trees line the banks of the Cur early doors, as the road initially runs through the conifers, where it passes the smart-looking new stone emblem that announces the boundary of the Loch Lomond National Park.

Another mile or so of trees, then the glen opens up and the ridge of An Carr makes its presence felt coming in from the left. It is balanced quite nicely by the twin hills of Creagan an Eich and Creag Dhubh on the right. These two have a similar geometry of lift and sweep that is pleasing and soft, and their greenness is highlighted by the orange roof tiles of the cottage that sits below the latter.

Just for the record, although he didn't come from here, that great Scottish entertainer Sir Harry Lauder was the Laird of Glenbranter in the first half of the 20th century. He, of course, was the man more than any who gave the world the image of the drunken Scotsman as he travelled the globe on stage. The crowds loved him, but the establishment hated him for the image he portrayed. He is still fondly thought of by many.

Also in Glenbranter, so-called labour camps were established in the mass unemployment days of the 1930s. These were officially known as instructional camps and were designed to 'toughen up' the unemployed and get them fit for work. They were brutal places by all accounts, to the extent that walk outs and mass meetings of the disgruntled men were organised in 1935 and 36. Glenbranter is also the traditional homeland of the Clan Ferguson.

Your speed is still good and tempo high, which will easily carry you over the small rise ahead, anticipating the grandeur that's waiting on the other side. At the top of the hill, you're looking down a long straight descent where the red splash of another Thames filling station grabs your attention. This one's a lot more welcome looking than its Port Glasgow counterpart, and for the record has a reasonably priced coffee machine and can be used as a pit stop should you be in need of some succour. So, it's spirits soaring as towards the Fyne you plummet, with the Argyllshire Hills as a backdrop. You don't actually see the loch till the road bends left and a road sign, half the size of the village, tells you to take next left for Tighnabruaich.

After obliging the sign, you find yourself right on the shore of the mighty one itself. A row of traditional Strachur (Glen of the heron) cottages, colourfully greets you to your left, as on down the A-886 you tentatively turn, knowing that an awesome jaunt into the quiet is now about to begin. It does so by starting off quite benignly, as one of the first things you pass is the Strachur Tearoom on the right. A snack or hot drink is available from there, but be warned, it's not cheap.

The road is followed southwest as you depart this former Clan Campbell stronghold, and as you do so, you will notice on the right a striking Celtic cross of a war

After an initial long gradual rise that offers great views of the loch, an equally long and marvellous gradual descent deposits you back at the lochside at a point that couldn't be more stunning, right beside the impressive Castle Lachlan. The loch itself has been obscured for the last mile or two, but now you stay completely lochside from here right down to Otter Ferry.

The view of Loch Fyne from Lachlan Bay, and it's from here – if going anticlockwise and south – that you will really start to appreciate the true size of our largest sea loch. Don't be too surprised if its scale and vastness catches you out first time down.

memorial to two local men who fell in the Boer War. It is the first time I have come across such a thing, as all others have been to the World Wars that followed.

No prizes for guessing that the usual array of modern bungalows and traditional stone homes line the shore here, taking advantage of the beautiful situation – and it is beautiful. But as you leave Strachur, these suddenly change to a uniform white series of houses that must all have been built at the one time. The view down the loch is truly awesome, and you will find it impossible not to have your gaze fixed and pulled in by the natural lines and length of the loch, supported by the hills either side as they jut in and cut the water. On the Cowal side, Barr an Eich – pointed and pyramidal – vies with the bulk of Beinn Ghlas on the Argyll side for your attention.

It's smooth riding on this stretch, which follows the Fyne's shore, long, flat and pleasantly wooded, continuing in this vein for about 3 miles till the A-886 starts to rise. At this point, the first of two cut-offs onto the B-8000 can be taken, now leading you onto the quiet single track that will guide you the whole way down to Millhouse. The cut-off is signed Newton Leached and Old Castle Lachlan, so you can't miss it. And once on it, continue to climb none too fiercely for a mile or so, all the time distancing yourself from the water's edge, till you reach a junction where the second cut-off from the A-886 joins from the left.

We are talking wild and rough here; the lower lying fields are just about able to support some sheep grazing, but not all of them. Conifer plantations use the higher ground on the hill slopes, and across the loch sits Furnace, with its massive quarry still going strong. I say

that despite it now being fully mechanised and employing a handful of men, when in its heyday it employed 200, who hand-cut the cobblestones for Glasgow. This is one of many small settlements that lie across the water, some of which you'll pass on the way down. You are sitting well above and quite a distance away from the loch at this point, a good half a mile at least, and are about to temporarily lose sight of it altogether.

You now descend into the roughness of Strathlachlan, where the broad shoulder of Barr an Eich separates you entirely from the loch. The roughness of the strath can at times be obscured by its wildness (boom, boom!), but the descent down the narrow road is a belter and it increases in speed after the red phone box is passed, before you skirt the edge of the large clipped rhododendrons. These lead you to a line of isolated white cottages and houses that belong to the hamlet of Garbhallt, where a smiddy and former inn once stood. A great wee chicane in the road is negotiated as speedily down and over the Lachlan Water you go, passing the white parish church, which dates from 1792.

From here the road glides straight, at a gentle angle, between the trees on the left and fields right, down to the shores of Lachlan Bay. First you pass a caravan park (would you believe?), but again don't let that put you off, because you are just about to encounter Castle Lachlan. Now it says on a nearby information board that the castle is one of the most picturesque in the country. It would be hard to argue with that, because it sits right on the lochside, round the far side of the bay, on top of a slight mound above the bay's mud flats and is sandwiched between a wooded hillside and the Lachlan Water's river mouth.

Expect some great swerving shore-side riding like this on the way down to Otter once you get through the initial wooded section. You've also got a great old damp stone wall for company to guide you down, into the bargain.

The curves continue for some time before things start to level off and straighten out as Otter Ferry nears. Just be careful not to knock over any scuba divers coming out of the loch after diving for oysters. You may actually meet one or two on the way.

church and graveyard you just passed, is where all the Lachlan Chiefs now lie buried.

The nearby, equally quaint Inver Cottage serves grub in the summer months. A navigation beacon sits offshore here in mid-water to warn boats about the dangers of the nearby Eilean Aoghainn, behind which and above Minard, the Argyll Hills run ridge-like southward. The very good news is that from now on, you are right on the side of the Fyne again and the riding from here to Otter Ferry will be at its best.

You start off through the woods, nice and flatly, then onto the shore, where the metal crash barrier keeps you out of harm's way, as the road curves and bends with the loch shore. This it has to do from time to time, as the

On the final run in to Otter Ferry itself and its main building, the Oystercatcher Bar/Restaurant, can be seen in the distance. That's all the easy riding over if you're going south; for now it will be tough all the way back to the Tarsan Dam at the top of Glen Lean. However, if you do the run clockwise, it means all the hard work is over for the day on this side of the water at least. That is why most guys do the run clockwise.

This square tower house, dating from the 15th century, is green leaf-covered to a magnificent extent (though in summer the trees almost totally conceal the castle). The backdrop of the Fyne and Beinn Ghlas beyond is the icing on the cake. The area had been a Clan Lachlan or MacLachlan (either will do) stronghold ever since the 13th century, when Lachlan Mor made his mark in these parts. Over the centuries the clan became aligned with both the Campbells and Lamonts by intermarriage, thus having a foot in either of those two warring and neighbouring clan camps (good thinking, Batman).

To their credit, the old Lachlans were staunch Jacobites, and again to their credit were out in the '15 and out in the '45. Unfortunately, their chief Lachlan MacLachlan was killed at Culloden leading his men and some MacLeans into battle on horseback; he was hit by a cannon ball.

The next year, a government warship sailed up the Fyne and blasted the castle for good measure. The castle itself was finally abandoned in the 18th century and now the clan chief lives nearby in the new castle, which is a white and rather ostentatious (showy) affair. The mossy old

high ground to the left will cut into the loch and force the road out in places.

It's round about here that you will start to realise the sheer size and scale of the Fyne, Britain's longest sea loch. Not only does it stretch so far in front of you, but as you look across the loch and see the natural harbours on the other side, it's easy to think, 'Oh, that must be Tarbet across there'; not yet, no, not by a long shot. You're not even level with Loch Gair. Shortly, you pass the red and white cottage at Barnacarry where you witness the first and smallest of four alluvial fans[1] that you'll meet on the road down to Otter.

---

1 - A geographical term for a flat fertile plain formed round a river mouth

Continue meandering along through the trees down by the lochside till you cut in at the second larger alluvial fan at Lephinmore. There the road rises before dropping back down to the shore line and once again back into the trees. Occasionally the protection of a stone wall is a welcome companion in places, before flat safe terrain makes even that guard unnecessary, and then there's nothing between you and the water except for a few trees and stones.

The Fyne around here seems to be an absolute hotspot for divers, and I often wondered why. When I once met one, he explained that the waters were crystal clear at this point and, although a lot of his contemporaries went down to admire the reefs, he was after the scallops. So now you know.

Continue on down the large loch in similar style, till the next alluvial fan at Lephinchapel allows another cut in; the farmouse here is a very modern-looking one, and

After a very steep and unwelcome pull up from Otter Ferry, the second main decision of the day has to be made when you come to this Y-junction. It's left to take you over the Bealachandrain, or it's right for Millhouse and Tighnabruaich. Going over the Bealachandrain is the sort of opt-out short cut route, but it's no picnic, that's for sure.

is more like a wee detached hoose sitting right below the Campsie Fells. This can be a very welcome sight among all this roughness, and can cheer you up if you're feeling a bit homesick. The flat green fields here also look out of place in this wild and remote setting, though their flat baize is easy on the eye. Again, it's back down through the trees and onto the loch, where the big broad blue sits on your shoulder, seemingly never moving; it's easy to feel you are making no headway down this maritime monster.

On rounding the jutting bulk of Carn an Tilgidh, you find yourself on classic single track loch shore road. No crash barriers here, no siree. This is the real McCoy. The barrier is a well crumbled stone wall, moss-covered and bracken-lined, with the passing places marked by black and white poles. And all the time, the elegant curve of the near shoreline carries your gaze down and distant, where… Oh, somebody stop me! I could go on for hours here. It means that the headland of Otter Ferry is now in view, and shortly the fields of Largiemore will guide you along to the old pier and pub. The hills on this side now start to lie back more permanently as Otter is approached, though they have done so intermittently on the way down.

Other than the Oystercatcher Bar, this is about all that makes up the rest of Otter Ferry. It is a very still and calm spot to stop and enjoy for a while, however, with the weight of the Fyne's heavy salt water helping to suppress any worries. The classic-looking old direction sign tells you it's 15 miles to Strachur.

First, though, Largiemore itself has to be passed, where the sturdy old large farmhouse is now surrounded by wooden holiday chalets and a nearby fish farm that specialises in halibut, I'm told. I hope it provides more than just low paid menial work for the locals. After this,

natural-looking harbour that sits directly across, and which would have appeared as you came down, might also have been Tarbet. Again, not so. It's Port Ann.

As the name Otter Ferry suggests, a ferry did ply the Fyne from here, going over to Port Ann. But it was not named after the otter which, admittedly, you will find in the loch. No, the name otter comes from the Gaelic 'An oitir' meaning shingle bar, which still runs out into the loch to this day. It goes for over a mile at low tide.

This is as pleasant and picturesque a spot as you could wish for; well, what there is of it. It mostly comprises of the Oystercatcher pub/restaurant – a beautiful solid white house, with black trim and grey slate roof. This, I assume, at one time must have been the ferry house. The old stone quay finished in 1773 is a splendid specimen, as is its counterpart sitting across the loch at Port Ann.

The ferry was to aid the re-aligning of the hill road over to Dunoon, which took place in 1769. The house and quay are joined by the exquisite trimmings of red phone box and old road sign, sporting an iron warning triangle and Strachur 15 miles arrow.

From here on down, it starts to get tougher and cuts inland, climbing straight away, which is a bit of a jolt to the system after all that lovely flat easy going that has just filled your tank. The pull up inland is no picnic, though it does pass the exquisite old school house sitting on the left. Very quickly you then come to a rather striking Y-junction.

If you take the right fork, on the road down to Millhouse you will pass Paddy Rankin's well, a welcome watering hole. This comes just before you drop down and cross the River Auchalick when going south, or have just climbed up from it when heading north.

some more flat road, the last for a while, leads through the trees, then follows shallow shingle bays into Otter Ferry itself.

Now, if you're unfamiliar with the settlements across the water, you may be forgiven for thinking that the

Now, this is a chance to cut the run short, if you so wish, or if there is a need to. Taking the right fork will continue to take you on the main run, where the signpost shows it's 12 miles to Tighnabruaich. Don't forget at this point, if you do carry on, you are going a long way down to double back on yourself, by having to come a long way

Both Arran and the Holy Isle come into view as Millhouse draws near, and this is a good position to be in because it means you now hold a lot of height in the bank and a very tough section is behind you. It will be a most pleasant high gentle rollercoaster ride from here over and across then down to the Kyles of Bute and Tighnabruaich.

back up. This is highlighted by the fact that the left sign shows the same distance all the way to Colintraive (12 miles) as it does just to Tighnabruaich.

Taking the left fork over the hill to Glendaruel (6 miles away), will cut out a big chunk of the run, should you want to for any reason. This may be shorter but it is certainly not easier, not by a long way. A very direct, fairly brutal road – known officially as the C-11, but locally as the Bealachandrain (the pass of the thorn) – will prove a test for most riders[2]. This is the one that the ferry was supporting the upgrading of, and if this is the upgraded version, I'm glad I never rode it before then. This is also the road that I mentioned in the intro that claims to give the best view in the whole of Cowal, especially when coming from the opposite direction. That, I dare say, is true. You will be up high enough to see over the hills of Knapdale towards those unmistakeable Paps of Jura which, take it from me, always stand out grandly when seen from any west coast mountain.

The only problem is that the conifers are now so high that you will be bloody lucky to see them. The loch itself cuts a fine dash from there, too, with the jutting headland directly across the loch providing Lochgilphead with a natural harbour. Tarbet is still some 10 miles further down the far bank.

The road itself starts off fairly easy at first, cutting through the conifers that are, needless to say, the dominant ground covering for the most part. The road inevitably steepens, hitting two points of single arrow 1:7

that are more than manageable. The second one is taken as you force your way round a crash barrier-protected bend, whose clearing reveals a rather splendid craggy gully on the left with a burn crashing through it.

Still we climb, the road twisting and rising between firs and electric telegraph poles, meandering quite continuously through the high ground, till in the distance the bulk of Sgorach Mor appears, along with the other Loch Tarsan hills. This signals you've crested out, and it's dive, dive, dive time.

From the Loch Fyne side, the road may meander quite a bit, but not from the Glendaruel side. Not a bit of it. On the way down, you will descend three single arrow sections 1:7 to 1:5 and also a two arrow section of greater than 1:5[3]. You feel like you are looking down into an Alpine valley the way the road sits high above the slender strath of valley floor as down you go, grabbing the brakes for all you're worth.

On this descent, it helps if you have forearms like big Arnie Schwarzenegger, or perhaps if you are a fearless descender with acute suicidal tendencies, then you could find yourself in your element here. For the rest of us, it's time to hang on for dear life and keep yourself and your speed under control as best you can. As luck would have it, the road surface on the way down isn't quite as good as on the way up, so that also has to be watched. As if you didn't have enough on yer plate, mate! With mucho relief, you hit the valley floor, re-joining the A-886 at the grand old Glendaruel Farm, after crossing the River Ruel in some style. From here, after turning right, you very quickly pass the cut-off to Tighnabruaich and, shortly after, the meeting with the B-836 gives you the option for either Dunoon (left) or Rothesay (straight ahead). So that is the get-out route taken care of.

However, if no quick exit strategy is required, then bear right at the Otter Ferry fork and climb up through rugged conifer terrain heading south. Once the road bends right, the climbing's over for now, thank God, where the slanting slopes on the left have had their conifers chopped. In places, the landscape is so tree-bare and destroyed that it looks like Ypres after the Third Battle. Straight ahead shows a rise that appears as straight as it does tough, but don't worry, it's nowhere near as

---

2 - It climbs for approximately 1080 feet in 2½ to 3 miles

3 - Small single or double arrows are used on the Ordnance Survey maps to indicate the steepness on certain minor roads.

And it's Arran's high peaks that welcome you to the end of the long stretch on the B-8000. It is a lovely flat section that allows an easy wind down to the crossroads at Millhouse, where a right turn will take you to Portavadie which would put you on the Five Ferries run. We, however, want to go left for Tighnabruaich and some more stunningly scenic riding. It will actually top what has gone before, believe it or not.

fierce as it looks. Neither, it has to be said, is the rest of this road all the way down to Millhouse, apart from one 1 in 7 section at Cela Cottage.

For the most part, the long gradients to be taken are nothing to fear and the surroundings and distant views of the Fyne (loch of the vine or wine?), can be appreciated without too much grind or huff and puff. After clearing the bolt straight rise ahead, you encounter some real rugged upland, as you'd imagine. But the climbing doesn't stop there, for there is another gentler curving rise into a corridor of very tall mature pines. After firing straight through these, the right flank opens up and the old girl can again be spied glinting away in the distance. Soon you sit high above Kilfinan, from where it is obvious why a settlement sprouted here, as you can

clearly see that the ground around this pretty white hamlet is a lot more fertile than what has gone before or is yet to come.

It is a very picturesque setting, aided by the way the road curves and dives down its steepest drop (1:7) on its way towards the Kilfinan Burn. When crossed, it signals the start of another long pull up, which continues right through the village and well beyond, beginning by curving and swaying beautifully and gently past mature woodland, and guided by a most exquisite moss-covered stone wall. All buildings within are uniform solid white-walled, black-trimmed, slate-roofed. This includes the hotel and the old kirk (1759), along with the old post office, which signals you're on your way out the place, but still climbing long and easy.

Welcome to Kames and its great wee crossroads, which is not only very quaint but very useful as it does possess a well stocked wee store – the first one since Strachur, so you may well require its services. Take the left turn here and drop most delightfully and fast down onto the Kyles of Bute, right on Tighnabruaich's shore front.

As you climb out, take a look at the stone wall to your right, which is God knows how old, but was clearly built by craftsmen. A more impressive specimen I doubt you'll see in a hurry. The climb does, of course, mean that height is again gained, and with the elevation comes the Fyne, always good to see. The land at first is actually quite fertile and broad on the loch side, supporting some sheep, but then the road leads into more rugged moorland, before it dips down and over the River Auchalick.

Just before the road drops down, you come to a well of sorts that was put in place to commemorate local man Patrick Rankin (1880). By all means, fill the water bottles here; just for the record, they have even left a mug for anyone to use, should you be out walking or just driving past.

I met an old bloke there once called Mickey. He came from Tighnabruaich and had walked round. He informed me that one of the mugs that used to be there was a West Ham United one. I was so surprised by the set-up here, I almost belted out I'm Forever Blowing Bubbles.

As you look across the Auchalick valley, you see the road snake upwards and away, the hillside ahead. Again, don't worry too much, for the bulk of the climb isn't too frightening despite its length. Dive down around the bends and joyfully rise through the bends on the other side. Get into a good rhythm for the long straight pull up in front of you, which will be fairly easy till the brightly coloured Cela Cottages are passed, and then the 1 in 7 has to be taken.

Ouch! But never mind, only one more rise to go and then we're into easy street. This climb comes almost immediately as you pass the bonnie wooded, secluded Loch Melldalloch. Grittily dig in and grind your way over the next rise, where the craggy lump of Creag an Fhithich greets your arrival. Ahead… well, savour what's to come, for the floor is all yours for the next few miles at least. A slight chink from the Kyles of Bute is seen far ahead to the left as the road drops then leans right, levelling out. And just as it goes into a dive through the woods, look

What a scene awaits as you meet the waters of the kyle just before you skirt round the bay in front of Tighnabruaich's villas and bungalows. If it's a scorcher, you'll think you've died on the road there and are riding up in heaven; it really is that stunning. It will be a blue heaven at that, as the water and sky encompass all around. The biggest climb of the day is just round the corner, however, though I wouldn't have it any other way.

On one of the early sections of single track road on the climb out of Tighnabruaich, and thankfully it's a level stretch. The initial steep ramp as you leave the coast is a real shock to the system, and you're glad of the respite on this stretch. Don't forget it's four miles of climbing to the top, and you've been in the saddle a long time, so pace yourself well for this one. Fortunately, it isn't sustained the whole way, by any means.

ahead and marvel the sight of the Holy Isle, which stands out boldly and sentinel-like in the distant firth.

The curving drop down through the trees is a belter, including new tarmac (in places) and an old iron railing thrown in for good measure. You then arrive onto the final straight down to Millhouse – a telegraph pole-lined straight, whose jagged backdrop of Arran peaks make it a fitting finish to this superb stretch of coastline. 44.4 miles to here from Dunoon, I make it, and we turn left to head for Kames, of course.

The white houses here are, not surprisingly, replicas in many ways of their Clachaig counterparts; some have a bit of a rundown look, but most are in fine fettle. This you

It may be a tough climb up from Tighnabruaich, but it has its rewards, like this view right down the western kyle where all the sailors are making the most of the weather. The white sails of the yachts always make such pleasant dots on the blue canvas

will notice as you trundle down what is, I suppose, the main drag, where Gunpowder Cottage steals the show, with its exquisite clock set high in its wall and its position just before the Craignafeoch Burn.

After crossing the burn, climb slightly left, before swinging right and ahead you go. In the distance you see a ridge, barren and rugged, where another higher one runs parallel behind. The first one is North Bute, showing the wild and desolate side of the island; the second is Beinn Bhreac, running behind Colintraive and still a long way off from here.

Dip into the Kames crossroads now with its war memorial, road signs, and post office, all packing a lot into this one small corner. Turn left and, with the greatest of pleasure and expectation, descend the bend and then

Now it's the turn of the inner eastern kyle to provide the views, as you climb higher on the A-8003. Colintraive pier can just about be seen, though not the ferry, so it's safe to assume it's berthed over at Rhubodach right now.

fire straight towards the 'Kiss me quick' Kyles of Bute.

Kames itself is quite funny in the type of housing it has. There are the stone villa types, as you'd expect, but also what I think are some bloody ugly-looking concrete council squares, and even some wooden jobs. How this lot came together, I'll never know.

A lengthy crash barrier finally leads you down to the coast road itself and the shinty park between you and the Kyle (the local team are quite successful), and now just purr along the flat for a while and take in your surroundings. Two very good reasons are now presented to you for taking your time here. One is the very obvious sheer splendour of the setting, where the long elegant sweep of the bay road, with neatly-lined villas, draws

If you elect to take the left fork when you leave Otter Ferry, it will be a long, long pull up towards the high pass that is the Bealachandrain (the pass of the thorns). This is the view looking back from fairly near the top, on an evening when I left it very, very late. To use the pass to get to the Fyne and Otter Ferry is a run in itself, with many preferring to use it and then looping back either north or south to complete the run. Be warned, however, for although it is shorter than going all the way down and then back up to Tighnabruaich, it is an arduous ascent no matter which way you do it.

The best views you will get, if you decide to go via the Bealachandrain, will be to go from east to west. This will allow you fantastic views of the Fyne, like this one, as you descend down to Otter Ferry. Once there, you have two options on which way to return. Turning right for Strachur will be the easier of the two, with mostly flat riding; turning left for Tighnabruaich may be harder, but the scenery is drop dead gorgeous.

This gives you some idea of the steepness involved when ascending the Bealachandrain from the Glendaruel side. When you see the electricity wires, it means you're near the top, but this is only one of several ramp-like sections you encounter on the way up. The way they come at you, one after the other in fairly quick succession, can really sap your strength, especially on a really hot day.

Once the flatness and safety of the A-886 are met, whether you came via Tighnabruaich or the Bealachandrain, take a right turn to return to Dunoon. A Colintraive and Rothesay return is also an option. Although the A-886 is a more modern and busier road than what you've been riding on recently, it does afford a wonderful view right down the impressive Loch Riddon.

Not Loch Riddon this time. No, this is the head of Loch Striven after descending the ferocious brae on the B-836. The short swerve round the top follows (always a delight), then the long pull up to the Tarsan Dam. After that, it's easy street all the way back to Hunter's Quay.

Another view of Loch Riddon from the A-886, looking dark and enticing

Coming down the side of the Holy Loch into Sandbank and looking forward to a good rest on the ferry. As no provisions are available on board the Western, if you come back on it as opposed to the Argyll, don't forget to grab something from either the store in Sandbank or the wee Coffee Ahoy bar across from the ferry at Hunter's Quay.

your wondrous eye full tilt right round onto the top of the Rothesay ridge in one continuous movement.

High ridges on every side, along with the great flat blue of the Kyle, give a feeling and setting of true Highland remoteness and isolation that this old timer of a village contains. So there's no hurry here to get out too quickly, regardless of how far you are from home.

The second reason is more tactical, and that is to allow as much recovery time as you can before the inevitable big pull up out of Tighnabruaich begins, and it's one you're always glad to see the back of. Just before you turn left at the Royal Hotel, take note of the local filling station on the right, which appears to have been an old barn converted for the job. A quainter specimen I've never seen.

So, left turn onto the ramp-like start of the A-8003, past stone-walled homes and up its stone-walled street, where its hope-to-God time you are still hydrated. If not, this is when you will notice it big time.

A very welcome stretch of flat single track follows quickly, taking you just above the houses on the shore road below, before the next section of single carriageway signals the start of the longest and hardest part of the entire 4 mile climb up to the kyle viewpoint.

Here is as good a place as you'll get to talk about a part of the cycling game that we all come across sooner or later, and that is suffering and the ability to suffer. Fear not, we all face and get through it, making us a better person and character for it. When on a lot of endurance runs, or shorter ones when the weather is against you, or you are out of nick and battling a strong headwind, then suffer you will.

The hardest part of the A-8003 is a common place to hit the bonk (runners call it the knock or wall); it's just dig-in time. Often, you will be dehydrated and/or tired, so it is to a great extent a physical problem. To keep this to a minimum, try and stay hydrated for all or at least most of the run, which admittedly is easier said than done. A sensible build-up of miles, rather than a kamikaze long run early in the season, will also help in minimising the worst of the suffering pains. However, despite the best laid plans of mice and men, the problem will still rear its ugly head, and fairly regularly at that.

The holy loch from the western ferry shortly after leaving hunter's quay.

Despite it being a physical problem, the best way I have found to tackle it is through mental toughness. I've mentioned positive self-talk and all that already, but also a useful thing to do is to imagine and picture in your mind your favourite riders and climbers and how they tackle the big mountain routes in the Tour de France and the like. Watching them on TV or YouTube, then following their example, can help tremendously in getting over any hill. I'm a big Greg Lemond fan (the real Maillot Jaune) and it's from Greg I take my inspiration. So remember, when the going gets tough, think Lemond. I repeat, think Lemond. Sermon over.

After the tough, arduous, long climb on single carriageway, another welcome flat stretch of single track provides a dramatic respite, chiefly because of the way the road goes close to the edge and the crash barrier is a necessity, giving a sense of being on a real mountain road. All the time, the glorious kyle sits below, where its slender sides pull away down to the Holy Isle, which puts in its third appearance of the day. The two jagged peninsulas jutting into the West Kyle from the top end of Bute, provide some maritime drama as you are immersed in your own world, still fighting your way up to the top of this outstanding meandering summit.

Time and again the road levels and you think 'thank God it's over', but no, round the bend another rise, followed time and again by another. None of these are as tough or sustained as the early sections, so after getting pumped up and into a rhythm you should be motoring quite well by now. After 4 miles of ascent, the latter part mostly through conifers and crash barriers, the very welcome sight of the viewpoint is passed and it usually screams at you to stop and linger a while.

The bonnie Kyles they stretch for miles.
Blue waters sparkling brightly,
The soft green slopes protect her boats,
When sleeping still and quietly.

The descent down the other side is less than half the length of the one you've just come up and, with that fact in mind, it's no surprise to learn it's a screamer-and-a-half, to tell the truth. And, other than a bit of slightly dodgy road surface, it's a great reward for all the previous suffering you have just endured. It is scenic enough in itself, though admittedly you won't see much of it, as the road swings swiftly and slenderly between rocks and trees, carrying you safely down to the edge of Loch

Riddon and into the flat of the valley floor and all the prettiness to follow.

Enjoy here to the utmost, as the woods and walls that border the curves of the River Ruel are a rarity in the Highlands (the woods that is), so systematic was the clearing of the land. Now only small pockets of them remain, and here is one of them, where Ormidale House, with its moss-covered stane dyke and all, doesn't let the side down.

Keep twisting and turning and still running north for a good bit, till at last the main A-886 is hit. The wee rise that comes immediately after turning right feels a bit of a pain at first, but the view it gives far outweighs any effort involved and is most definitely worth the toil. Particularly good is the view back down the length

Just one final look back. See you again soon, promise!

of Loch Riddon, and keep your eye open for a most impressive piece of large stone dyke wall that acts as an archway to the adjacent farmhouse of Auchnagarrron, which has a small post box built in. Really charming.

The meeting of the B-836 means the cruising's on hold for a bit, as the climb over towards the Striven starts the second you turn left onto it, and just happens to be the most taxing part, to boot. So dig in again and just force that old machine between your legs up this unwelcome intrusion to your Cowal canter. Only half kidding here, for it's not so bad after the initial stage, and it's just a case of keeping your eye on the craggy peak of A'Chruach, as experience tells you that when you draw level with its lower slopes, you're up. One or two bits in the middle of the climb test you – oh yes, they do! – but the finish is fine, as you slowly gain height between conifers right and real rugged moor left.

From there, the brake-holding begins in earnest. It's time now to descend the brutal one to the top of the

Striven. The warning triangle (1:5) shows what's to come, but you're helped by the fact that the road surface on the very steep descent is more than decent. The tightness of the situation, with the close proximity of the ever-present, almost-touching trees, adds to the feeling of acceleration and exhilaration. The road here has all been re-tarred, so at the steepest point it's fine; so, too, the second drop leading down to the lochside itself.

Mind how you go here still, though. But, once down, it's the usual bonnie skirt round the bay, narrow and classic as always. Now the final rise before Dunoon starts, just as you pass the white, though unobtrusive, power station on the far side. Again, the early stages prove the toughest (it's another Greg Lemond job) just as the entrance to the Ardtaraig Estate is passed.

The deciduous woodlands lend charm to this all-out effort, with the knowledge that it's the last climb of the day (if you're parked in Gourock) helping to make it a lot more bearable. The pull up almost mirrors the previous one in character, where once out of the trees, then over the Tarsan Burn, the single track snakes its way up through open heath, where the going gets easier till the dam wall is finally reached. Congratulations! All the hard work is over now, and the going to Hunter's Quay or Dunoon itself is flat and friendly. Start off with a smooth purr along the Tarsan's side, all birches and bracken, till the swing right and drop into the Lean means tally-ho! Through the rough one we go.

It appears just as rough and wild going this way as it does the other, where the steep flanks of the glen wickedly impress with their carved faces. Faces carved by the great forces that have gone before, a long time before, as they show the scars of the Ice Age handiwork.

Again, the 2 miles or so down to Clachaig always seems longer, with the usual high amount of pulling in to be done to avoid on-coming vehicles. With the white walls of the cottages passed, it's out of the single track and before you know it, you're flying down through the trees and over the wee River Eachaig and out the glen to Sandbank. Phew! Or words to that effect.

The tranquillity and softness of the Holy Loch's water always have a calming effect to ease you back into civilisation, and it's a welcome sight to any tired rider who knows a rest is just round the corner.

If this is a winter's run and you're parked across the Clyde, then you may be arriving back in the dark, with lights flashing to signal your position and safety. When cruising along the shore front, this is a very special moment as the darkness of the water helps highlight the lights of the bay houses. It makes for a fitting end to any Argyllshire run.

Your circumstances will dictate which old tub you choose; sometimes it matters, sometimes not. Sometimes pot luck, if a Western is waiting; or if coffee and grub are considerations, then it's an Argyll job.

On a long summer run, the road back to Paisley will still need to be ridden. I've mentioned before if, for any reason, you feel you need to jump on the train, then jump on it. It's no disgrace. Hopefully, that won't be the case, and on arrival in glorious Gourock, I will ease myself back into my stride along the purringly perfect A-770.

In Greenock I'm faced with the old choice of going home via the Kilmacolm Road or continuing on into Port Glasgow and taking the Clune Brae, which is probably the easier option. After all the hard climbing, I would usually, though not always, plump for the Clune.

And so as we've ridden both these return routes before, I won't go over old ground, but suffice to say that another great long day in the saddle is starting to draw to a close.

The Fyne is one of the hardest routes to do, but don't let that faze you. Remember, it's only a case of building up and planning. Then, before you know it, it's another mega you can add to your collection.

Till the next time.

Liam Boy

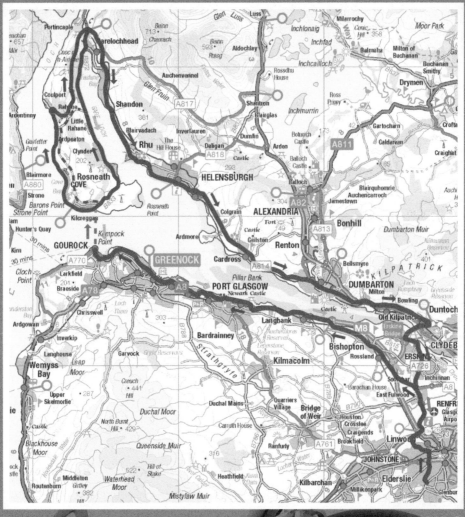

KILCREGGAN

RET BISHOPTON
64.4 Miles
4.01 Hours
Ascent 1500 Feet
2997 Calories burned

FROM GOUROCK
21.6 Miles
1.26 Hours
Ascent 1120 Feet
1062 Calories burned

RET HELENSBURGH
59.1 Miles
3.39 Hours
Ascent 1500 Feet
2763 Calories burned

O/S Landranger Maps 64, 63, 56.

Clydelink Tel No 0871 705 0888

ROUTE SUMMARY

Bishopton
Langbank
Woodhall
Port Glasgow
Greenock
Gourock Pier
Ferry To Kilcreggan Pier

ROSNEATH PENINSULA ROUND

Kilcreggan
Rosneath
Garelochhead
Coulport/Barbour Road
Kilcreggan Pier
Ferry To Gourock Pier

RETURN VIA GOUROCK

Reverse Outward Route

RETURN VIA HELENSBURGH

Garelochhead
Helensburgh
Dumbarton
Erskine Bridge
Paisley

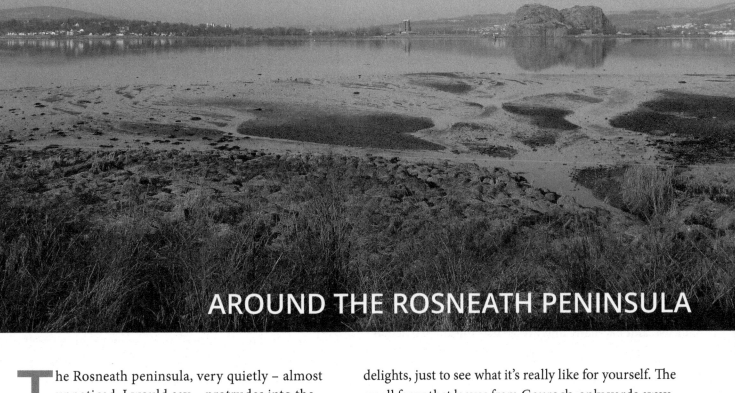

AROUND THE ROSNEATH PENINSULA

The Rosneath peninsula, very quietly – almost unnoticed, I would say – protrudes into the River Clyde from the north, flanked by Loch Long to its west and the Gare Loch to the east. Approximately 7 miles long, with a breadth of 1 mile at the top, it gradually fans out to 3 miles breadth at the bottom, with a rounded ridge for a spine running most of its length and only just clearing the 200 metre mark at its highest.

The front of the peninsula is guarded by the transmitter-topped Gallow Hill that oversees all maritime traffic criss-cross the Clyde below it. From time to time, as you've ridden along several sections of the runs we've already covered – particularly the Greenock Esplanade, and the Ardentinny to Strone road – you may have noticed the soft green hues and gentle rising fields that leave the water's edge and slope above the houses of Kilcreggan and Cove.

So inviting does the peninsula itself look, that it's hard not to feel drawn towards it and want to sample its delights, just to see what it's really like for yourself. The small ferry that leaves from Gourock, only yards away from the Argyll Ferries pier, also plants the seed firmly in your mind that a jaunt over to Kilcreggan is well within your grasp. In fact, it is a much shorter crossing than the Dunoon one – a 12 minute sailing, which is less than half the time it takes to reach Dunoon. Now it is perfectly feasible to reach Kilcreggan from Paisley or numerous other places by skirting the north bank of the Clyde and accessing the peninsula by Dumbarton, Helensburgh, and ultimately Garelochhead.

Unlike Dunoon, there is nowhere near the amount of distance to be covered to reach this neck of the woods. So with the ferry and the north bank route at your disposal, it is most certainly an option to make this an all-out round trip, should you so wish. It's great to have the option of the boat here, which brings the place within such easy reach. At the time of writing, the service has just been taken over by Clydelink and, after a few teething problems, things have settled down and the service seems to be running smoothly. The ferry's clientele is made up of about 50% locals and 50% workers from the nearby MOD base at Coulport. Between the two, there seems to be enough business to keep the wee steamer going, and I for one am grateful for that.

It gives the wandering cyclist the option of popping over for a jaunt round this quiet backwater, before returning to Gourock and then home. Or, as previously mentioned, you can also gain the peninsula by the boat and return home via Helensburgh and the Erskine Bridge, or do the route in the opposite direction.

As great a bonus as the ferry is, therein lies, to a certain extent, the Achilles heel of the run, especially if you do most of your riding on a Sunday. There are actually no sailings on the Sabbath at all. Three sailings a day were tried for a while on a Sunday during the summer, but proved to be financially non-viable, and so no further ones are planned at the moment.

When I first read the timetable for the ferry, I noticed with some trepidation that not only were there only 13 sailings Monday to Friday and 12 Saturday, but there was no real pattern to the crossings, with regards to either departure times or frequency. But it transpired that this lack of regularity seems to have a focusing effect, on me at least, and I actually find myself making any particular ferry I aim for with more time to spare than I would do with the more frequently crossing Dunoon boats. I find I plan better and am more punctual, knowing that if I miss the one I am after, then it's a fairly long wait of about an hour (sometimes more, sometimes less), till the next one. So I have tended to be more on the ball, so to speak.

If I can do that, then anyone can. The timetable is available on board or from the CalMac office at Gourock pier. There are two types at the moment, a leaflet and sheet version[1]. The sheet can be folded up and carried in the saddle bag for reference on the move.

The timetable for Monday to Saturday is the same all year round. It's cheap into the bargain, with an adult single at time of writing of £2.50 and a return £4.80 all year round. Kids are about half that price, with wee bambinos aged five or under getting a freebee.

It is, therefore, possible to get the kids across very reasonably and ride the 5.5 flat miles to Coulport, then back, where you can try and explain to the weans the benefits of nuclear warheads. This should prove quite a challenge to even the most articulate of parents!

So now that the aquatic leg of the journey is well and truly covered, it's onto the road run itself. Despite the fact that we are heading for Gourock, if we decide to do the run clockwise, we will be taking a different approach route from previous runs, not only to add another string to the bow, but also to provide a useful Clyde coast approach route for some riders, depending on where they stay, of course.

However, I find that the way in which you approach the Rosneath peninsula can have a major bearing on how you tackle it. Despite having few roads, there are quite a number of options available to you, and again it might take a few trips over there for you to figure out what is your favourite way to do it. This can include, if you're up for it, probably the hardest climb to be found on the whole of the Clyde. For as well as great coastal riding, there are three high roads into the bargain, with one definitely not for the faint-hearted… Read on, if you dare.

So I mount ye olde trusted steed and steel myself for more action. Action of the highest calibre, for the Rosneath peninsula contains the Barbour Road, whose view down the Clyde just about kicks the arse of all others. But that's only my opinion; you judge for yourself. On this occasion I am going to approach the coast by contouring round the back of Glasgow Airport and, after turning left at the Red Smiddy roundabout, head through Bishopton. This route, from the Smiddy onwards, will be beneficial to any rider who resides between Renfrew and Southwest Glasgow – places like Ibrox, Hillington, and the like – and that is the main reason I include it. So Northwards from home means one thing for me, and that is the charge down the old Corsebar Road.

I often decry the Corsebar in a way, due to the amount of parked vehicles per se, but that is doing the old girl an injustice. For it is a real flyer and joy to ride down nonetheless. To actually get to the top of it, I first have to ride along the tree-lined and also mansion-lined Moredun Road. Three very visible mansions line the right hand side of the road and, to be honest, I don't actually know if anyone stays in them. For all the times I've ridden, walked or driven past them, I've never seen a single person – or car, for that matter, in any of their surroundings. Most odd.

1 The Kilcreggan ferry timetable is also included at the back of the CalMac timetable brochure.

Anyway, enough of my nosiness, for it's down the Corsebar we now descend, then level and descend again, where up on the right sits the big house – the RAH (Royal Alexandra Hospital). Only once was I in need of the big yin's assistance with regards to a cycling injury. I hope it's the last, though they took good care of me, so *merci*.

Across from it, on the left, stands a row of Coronation Street-type houses, most rare for Paisley and our only ones of that ilk. They are followed by the Ferguslie Cricket Club ground, and I've been known to stop the

When going down the Barnsford Road behind the airport, I always like to check out the windsock just so that I know what the old airflow is doing. As it's good to have the wind at your back on the home run, it helps with planning if you can see a flag, or better still a windsock, early on in the run. As the sock here shows a gentle breeze coming from the Northwest, then it's a perfect day for Kilcreggan.

machine here and watch the action from time to time. Howzat! No heading for Ferguslie (main road) this time; oh no, I'm purring north, down through the Maxwellton lights and west end streets, before shortly passing the new St Mirren Park on Greenhill Road. Being built in Ferguslie Park, it has earned itself the nickname 'the San Giro stadium'; my apologies to all those hard grafters who come from the scheme.

Next it's the usual dice with death at St James' interchange, which is followed by a rather serene

curving descent down onto the start of the Barnsford Road, (the A-726). There, the first thing that hits you is the sheer flatness and scale of the airfield as you look across it through its bonnie barbed wire fence – quite an unusual sight in such a hilly country. Although the road is now dead flat it is completely open, so any wind that is blowing will be affecting you full blast. At the end of the back straight, you come to one of the airports windsocks and, take it from me, this can be a great aid to any plans you have. As a word to the wise for any new or inexperienced rider, it is never that easy to judge wind direction and strength from the bushes and trees alone; far from it. It is always better to view a flag, or better still a windsock, to give you a much more accurate picture of exactly what the wind is doing.

Why is this so important? Well, I suppose I should have mentioned this sooner, but it is always better to head into the wind at the start of any run, so that you are wind-assisted on the way home. This is as big an advantage mentally as it is physically.

As I have mentioned previously, I drive a cab at the old airport and it's only from this angle that you can tell how much the place has expanded in recent times. The planes stand safely and still, sheltered by the protruding arms of the docking terminals, which run out northwards onto the tarmac. Basil Spence, the original designer of the terminal building, the 1966 vintage, would be amazed to see just how big the place has grown. For the check-in desks nowadays actually signal the front of the former building, and they are quite some distance in from the modern front doors.

Taking our leave of the airfield's boundary, which we do shortly after passing the swaying orange sock, it's over

As we purr along the Esplanade in Greenock, our destination town Kilcreggan shows well across the water. The views from the Esplanade make the slight diversion onto it worthwhile every time.

the River Black Cart on the Barnsford Bridge. The river is wide and slow here; real pike water this. Passing through as we go:

Scatty old fields with scatty old trees.
Full of scatty old grass.
Coming up to your knees.
Nothing grows or is seen in these,
Save a scatty old dump full of disease.

Speeding straight towards the Red Smiddy roundabout, gained in half a mile, there we turn left to Bishopton. Just for the record, the roundabout was named after the large, red-bricked kennels that at one time stood on the site just to the left.

If you are intending to do this run in a counter-clockwise direction, you would continue straight ahead towards Erskine at this point. And, as previously mentioned, any riders coming from south west Glasgow or Renfrew would join the route here. But we're Bishopton-bound for the moment; where the landscape that we cut through is flat and broad, save for the bulk of a rise that sits above the sprawling farm of Nether Southbar, to the right. Bright red bricks, just like the smiddy's, give some antiquated charm to the farm's front. The whizzing M8 draws near on the left, just as a bend and a rise over the motorway are taken, before the long leisurely straight into the large village – all on the former main Greenock Road, the A-8.

Bishopton's most famous feature is now undergoing a major change of land use, evident almost immediately as you pass a very large new roundabout, still unfinished at the time of writing, which will assist the new development's residents to gain access to the motorway. The new housing will be on the land formerly occupied by the old Royal Ordnance Factory, the ROF. So large is the site, formerly occupied by seven farms, that it would easily more than double the size of Bishopton, even if it wasn't developed fully.

The rest of the road through the village continues almost dead straight ahead and then right out the other

Is it Alcatraz? It's not stunning scenery on the Clyde all the time, as a look into the old back doors of the Woodhall tenements shows here.

end. Contained in between are some new and not so new houses, giving the game away that this is a real commuter town now. The road passes the Holmpark rugby ground, with its old sort of white Nissen huts on the left side. There are a few really old rustic, again red-bricked houses and barn-style working buildings at the start and elsewhere, as a reminder of the village's former quaintness.

Another new roundabout – this one called the Chestnut – now marks the spot where you leave the village on the far side. It starts to get a lot more interesting when you do; after a taxing wee rise that is fairly hemmed in by trees, it's tally-ho!

Over the top and a great – and I do mean great – long, easy-angled descent finds you flying down, facing the might of the Clyde and all its partners in crime at this point, most noticeably Dumbarton Rock and Castle. This twin-topped volcanic plug steals the show in what is quite a deck of cards; as always, the first sight of the coast, even this far upstream, is a memorable one. The speed gained on the way down freshens you and your spirits, as does the openness of the air and the water. Sometimes it's all bright blue, other times sea haar and mist, making it a most mysterious subtle scene.

The castle itself was once the seat of the Kingdom of Strathclyde from the 5th to the 9th century, though Strathclyde is a misleading title, because the kingdom went as far south as Morecambe Bay. Legend has it that even the mighty Merlin himself spent time in the castle. How's that for hosting an A-lister? The rock itself was at one time known as Alt Clut (the Clyde Rock) and you can see why it would gain this title, as it has such a striking pose.

When the gradient has run its course on this stretch, you find yourself turning left at the old West Ferry roundabout and picking up the very busy dual carriageway of the A-8 trunk road which has just ceased being the M-8 motorway only yards before. So the traffic flying past you is doing just that, flying. It can be a bit intimidating riding along this stretch of road, though it is possible and helpful to sit inside the white line to the side and use it as a sort of unofficial cycle lane.

Respite is soon reached, however, at the Langbank roundabout, and it's then possible to come off the dual carriageway for a bit and ride parallel to the A-8 along the pretty village front road (recommended). Langbank is a very well-to-do place; its name coming from the old Scots word for long bank. The well-to-do-ness is evident by the quality and character of the housing that lines not only the front of the village, but also up on the slopes above. The slightly rising, slightly curving Main Street, oozing charm, guides you round past the perfect village

The small plucky MV Island Princess returns to Gourock pier, and it will be all aboard shortly for a great wee bouncy jaunt back across the Clyde. Taking only 15 minutes to cross to Kilcreggan, it feels as if you are there in no time.

store and under the church steeple. Like many other places, Langbank blossomed with the arrival of steam trains, in this case in 1841. And the railway line and village station are still doing the job to this day.

As the Main Street is ridden, notice if you will, some wooden stumps sticking out of the Clyde just offshore, which can be reached at low tide. I used to think that they were some sort of basic fish traps, but not so, apparently. It seems that the shipyards used them to store wood for their boats there; why this was done in this way, I don't yet know.

The respite lasts for a mile, if that, before the busy stuff must be re-joined – and, again, sitting in the gutter is a good option – until the entrance to Finlaystone House provides another bit of breathing space. The former ancestral pile of the Dennistoun family, going way back to about the 1390s, may even have seen John Knox preach there in 1556. So another A-lister was in this neck of the woods, albeit at another time and place.

The majestic hall and gardens are well worth a nosey, if you ever take a notion when riding past on a quiet day. And for the record, the house is now home to the chief of the MacMillan Clan.

Inverclyde District is entered shortly after Finlaystone, and again this is another mile or so of very fast dual carriageway. But fast will be your progress to the Woodhall roundabout, where just like Langbank, taking the inside road will relieve you of the traffic to have some quiet time again. That is where the similarity stops, however, because the two settlements are of completely different character, something that has always been a way with Scottish housing.

There is probably somewhere in the region of a 10-year difference of life expectancy between Woodhall and

And once across, the piermaster secures you safely to the side of this picturesque old jetty. There is definitely a hint of days gone by here the moment you dock, with the old pier building and what stands behind. The silence and tranquillity will also be apparent right from the word go.

Langbank. That is how much a few miles can make to the quality and length of people's lives in Scotland today. In fact, that's always been the case. The contrast is almost immediately noticeable. Soon after dipping into the area, you will see on the left – standing isolated and alone – a corrugated iron shack, which on closer inspection turns out to be the local store and post office; it couldn't be further in appearance from its quaint Langbank counterpart.

No houses surround this old Alamo, the former Dino's Café, in the former Woodhall Square. These have already been pulled down. Nor are the houses on the hill anywhere near the splendour of their near neighbours. Not even close. They, too, are earmarked for demolition. These were the dwellings of Parkhill Avenue – the ones we rode through on our way to Loch Striven. Their

If a left turn is taken once you disembark from the ferry, then the road to Peaton and Coulport will shortly provide views like this down the Clyde. It is a fantastic scenic ride all the way, with no climbing involved, and is therefore ideal for the kids if a simple return to the ferry is made thereafter. Quiet, safe roads make it even better for the little ones.

windows are boarded, standing in the sad greyness of their final days, awaiting the final blow. A whole different world is now entered, or so it seems, as you climb gradually and gently up between the large sandstone blocked wall of the cemetery on the left and the railway line on the right, passing Woodhall's station as you go.

The Fyfe Park Terrace tenements are a reminder of the past, as now the long descent down to the bottom roundabout of the Clune Brae begins. At this point, it is still possible to feel the weight of dark grittiness and social oppression of the place. Only on nearing the end are the old tenements encountered again; looking into

their backyards gives a real insight to an age goneby – the 1930s era, I believe. Three sides are high white-painted walls, with the fourth side open to the north, and they look like Alcatraz's exercise yard. One of the Sunday tabloids actually reported that the cheapest flats in the whole country are to be found in this area. That puts as much daylight between here and Langbank in economic terms as is humanly possible.

So there you have it, as you negotiate the bottom of the Clune and return onto the A-8, there's plenty of food for thought.

As we are at the start of Port Glasgow and heading for Kempock Point, Gourock, there is no need to tell you what comes next, because this is a road we have covered already numerous times. But suffice to say, mark my words here, you will never lose your joy of spinning down this one. The draw and expectation of what awaits across the water will always get your juices flowing, and the amount of hustle and bustle from here to the ferry will keep it interesting every time. That is right all the way down the long slender corridor that is the way out west; that corridor, of course, being the dynamic duo of the A-8 and the A-770.

Although I've already said that the timetable for the Kilcreggan boat is a bit erratic, there is a pattern to three of the morning ferries that leave Monday to Friday from the Gourock side. These at 9.18, 10.18, and 11.18am. It's down to two on the Saturday – the 10.18 and 11.18am – but that gives you something to aim for at least. There's no cludgie on board, so if you need to go, the waiting room WC will be handy. If you arrive a little bit before sailing and fancy a coffee, then the Bluebird Café at the top of Tarbet Street or the snack bar outside Gourock station will attend to your needs. And if you've planned well enough, you should actually see the wee *Island Princess* cutting through the water coming towards you.

The pier is well signposted in this old sheltered haven. A skipper and one of two experienced crewmen will dispense the gangplank and allow you access to the comfortable craft. Steel-hulled and robust, the *Princess* is actually better suited to the changeable conditions on the Clyde than the larger glass fibre Argyll ferries. Coloured white on top and black below, with a bright aqua blue stripe at the water line, she is a well-equipped slope, with two former fishing fleet men of repute manning the gangway and ropes. White twin liferafts and orange lifebuoys surround the decks, so you're as safe as houses

This is another great view down the Clyde and out to sea from Kilcreggan, as you head round Barons Point. The Cloch Lighthouse is visible on the left, and Goat Fell is prominent dead centre. The shoreline of the Rosneath peninsula is all like this – flat, fabulous, fun-filled and uplifting riding every single inch of the way

and it's off we go. The good news is, it does rock about a bit, which is great and the kids will love it if you're going over with them.

There's hardly time to get settled in the warm lounge, with its rows of beige benches and heat coming from two small vents above, before the pier master is securing the ropes on the famous old Kilcreggan jetty on the other side. Its name is displayed loudly above on the pier waiting room, which is an odd-shaped building of two halves – one part slate pitched roof, the other a mini square tower; both white with blue trim.

The grey erect tenements of the village stand in line behind to greet you, all sombre and solid, above which the greenness of the hills look pastoral and unthreatening. These are seen through the front glass of the boat as she approaches. Tiptoe off the pier, and shh! Quiet, or you'll wake the baby. No Brodick or Dunoon clamour here!

It's just you and the bike strolling off and onto the B-833, the shore road round the peninsula. The cludgie is to the left, if you need it. All's well with the world as you arrive in Kilcreggan. Take my word for it.

One of the old shops contained within the tenements is a second hand furniture store called Rustic Charm. And I couldn't have put it better myself. Needless to say, it's closed. The pierside café is still open, I'm glad to say, and seems to be doing well. It's particularly handy when waiting for the ferry, of course.

So far the route has been fairly straightforward, but at this point there will be decisions to be made, kind of on a par with Millport. For the way the roads run round and over the peninsula, there has to be some doubling back or redoing a bit of tarmac if you want to cover all the roads in a oner.

There's no need to do them all in the one go, however; much better to save some for another day, in my

This is round about Cove, heading up the side of Loch Long on the B-833 still making for Coulport. Being such a beautiful ride makes the finish at the barbed wire-clad base all the more of a shock to the system. The good news is you don't see Coulport until the last minute, and even then it's only briefly.

opinion. If you intend to return or arrive via the Clyde's north bank, then that can also have a major bearing on which road you ride into or out of the peninsula on, and in which direction you ride it. As always, my recommendation is do them all at your leisure; different ways on different days. No rush, they're always going to be there. Suss out what is your personal preference. Needless to say, I'm about to give you the benefit of my substantial experience here (blowhard, blowhard) in the hope it will give you a few pointers to get you going, and then you can then take it from there.

Most likely, the easiest decision will be for any mum or dad who has taken the kids over for a day out, because the only serious option for anyone with youngsters will be to cover the flat shore section from Kilcreggan to Coulport and back. This is a great ride in itself, covering 11 miles, and is good enough for any adult recreational rider who wants a pleasurable run without any serious exertion. Fair enough, enjoy.

And enjoy it you will, from the minute you turn left and almost immediately leave the solid grey stone structures that adorn the pier head. This is followed by a gentle sway downhill between rhododendrons and head-height grey walls, which shield and protect their stunning shacks on the one side from the ever-opening coast on the other. Pick up the bending banister of the sea wall and railing that invites you to follow it round the shore front as it goes enticingly out of sight.

Then follow, follow you must, like any good Teddy Bear[2] would, before the full flat of the big blue blast of the firth hits you all at once, a bit like the Copland Road stand in full voice. For me, it's a case of hush my boyish heart, for the place comes alive with the dancing sunlight on the water's floor. Not even the impressiveness of the dwellings of the former rich merchants, whose permanent and summer homes line the shore here, can steal my view away from the aquatic side of the show. This is despite the fact that they were men of means whose houses would stick out in any other setting. They certainly left their mark on the place, and in a most elegant fashion.

We ride in front of these houses, flatly and fast, as the road continues softly and smoothly. At this point, the coast and sea lochs play tricks with your eyes. It's nothing to do with the glinting sunlight this time; oh no, it's just the way that Strone appears ahead of you, sitting approximately 2 miles across the mouth of Loch Long, but it does so in such a way as to fool you into thinking it's on the same side. Only when you swing further round toward Barons Point does the true lie of the land become apparent.

At the same time, the view down the Clyde is even more impressive, by the way the eye is drawn towards Arran through the narrows that slip between the Cloch

---

2 - Teddy Bear is rhyming slang for Ger, short for Rangers supporter. *Follow Follow* is the club anthem.

Once I reach Coulport, I like to then double back and climb up the Peaton Road briefly before turning right onto Barbour Road and head back towards Kilcreggan, only this time sitting much higher on the hillside. I think that the Barbour must rate as one of the finest, if not the finest, road on the whole of the Clyde coast. This is especially so for the views it affords, particularly round about Knockderry Lodge, one of which can be seen above.

lighthouse and Dunoon. It is a true natural funnel that shows off the island's skyline to its best.

The sheer width of the Clyde here is its strength, expanding out in all directions. Its blue blanket stretches back upstream to the east, as well as away towards Arran to the south. West, even the mouth of Loch Long is over 2 miles wide. We now swing up into Loch Long itself and into the village of Cove, which continues where Kilcreggan leaves off but in a more dramatic fashion in places. And the houses! If you thought Kilcreggan's were good, wait till you get a load of this place. Baronial piles queue up to meet your acquaintance, one after the other, and about a dozen of them were built by the great Alexander "Greek" Thompson himself, no less. The rather misleadingly named Cove Castle is one of the grandest, but it's got plenty of competition, that's for sure.

The Cove shoreline itself is long, slender, shallow, and of shingle, naturally drawing you and your eye further up, which is no problem as we are going that way, anyway. Behind and across Loch Long, another old mate of ours puts in an appearance – the ruggedly striking Creachan Mor, sitting right behind Coulport and dramatically adding to the scene with its pyramidal lines drawing up to a sharp point. Across the long one sits Blairmore Village, at an often flat, calm distance, while the hills above her show their ridges and complexity; rough terrain for any walker.

Back on this side, as we skirt round Cove's cove, we pass under Knockderry Castle, built by the Greek boy's own fair hand, and probably the grandest of the grand. Complete with its turrets, clifftop position and all, it's not easily upstaged. Then we start to clear the last of the houses, leaving the Rosneath suburbia for the wooded domain of Ardpeaton. This part of the route in many ways tops what we've just done, for it is the northern part of this road and the Barbour – running parallel and above – that have all the specialness that woods and wildness can bring to the proceedings. It has a much quieter feel, if that's possible, and to add to the pleasure, right on cue the road will meander in concert with the shoreline, just to move you into a higher zone. This is especially so when returning back.

Crags and woods take over the right side now, before giving way to rough fields as Peaton is entered. We pass the start of the challenging Peaton (hill) Road, just before arriving at the Coulport base's large roundabout, signalling the end of this leg of the journey. It has to

be said that for the size of the place it keeps a very low discreet profile, and you only see it when you arrive right at its front gate. Having said that, it is a barbed wire-shrouded monster, brown and bulging, brutal in the extreme. Miles of the barbed stuff run up the hillside in coils, to deter any would-be intruders who might want to break in and steal a torpedo or nuclear warhead and perhaps break it down to sell as scrap.

The base itself is on the site of the old Duchlage Farm, where building started in 1963 as a result of the Cold War and finished in 68. It holds 16 reinforced concrete bunkers, where the goodies are kept. The base then got an enormous upgrade in the 80s to facilitate the coming of the more modern Trident system, the expense of which has only been surpassed by the Channel Tunnel. With the base came more modern access roads, because from time to time the warheads have to come and go between Coulport and Aldermaston in Berkshire for refurbishment.

One of these roads presents itself to you now as a way of getting over to the Whistlefield roundabout, which sits above Garelochhead on the other side of the peninsula. These roads had to be built, as the original road infrastructure simply couldn't cope with the needs of the large military bases.

As a general rule of thumb, the modern high roads are longer, less steep, and more mundane than the older roads, and lack the sharpness and charm of the originals. If you do decide to take this one, be prepared for a long, long climb, in the range of about 8%, up through the conifer trees, before another 4 miles or so of undulating riding in similar terrain brings you to the Whistlefield.

This road's main saving grace is the superb view you get down the length of the Gare Loch and into Faslane naval base as well. From up there, you will notice that at the mouth of the Gare a shingle bank (an oitir) runs out from Rhu on the east bank towards the protruding headland of Rosneath on the west bank. This makes for a protected sheltered loch, which is obviously good in military terms, but doesn't leave a lot of room for a bloody great big nuclear sub to manoeuvre in and out of.

When you do reach the Whistlefield, there are two options facing you. One is to stick to the new military road system and go straight ahead to the next big roundabout (you're now on the A-814), sitting above the Faslane girl herself. From here, it's payback time for all the climbing out of Coulport a few miles back, because a long banshee-like descent now begins, right down to the naval base's north gate and thus bypassing Garelochhead completely.

Just for the record, from the roundabout above Faslane, there is the option of turning left up the A-817 and descending down Glen Fruin to Loch Lomondside. This way provides a wild way down, with a couple of tough climbs to start with. However, it does provide splendid views of Loch Lomond and its islands as the A-82 is approached. This is the way the nuclear warheads take when being transported.

The other option from the Whistlefield roundabout is to turn right and dive down the double bends for a mile or so into Garelochhead, then along to Faslane that way, or return to Kilcreggan along the west side of the Gare Loch, thus making it an all-out trip round the peninsula clockwise. That is just fine, if you fancy it, or you can do the round in the opposite direction.

Returning to Coulport for the moment, as I mentioned earlier, the way back along the shoreline is the best option if you are out with the youngsters or just fancy an easy flat day out. The way back will surpass the outward run, as it is assisted by the fantastic view of the Clyde as it heads for the open sea. This is especially true of the early stages at Peaton and Ardpeaton, which are uncluttered and sublime. However, shortly after leaving the Coulport roundabout, you pass an old red telephone box, followed by the Peaton Road. To maximise the effect of the sea-bound view of the Clyde, it is actually advisable to take this road, to let you gain access to the star of the whole shooting match – the Barbour Road.

The start of the Barbour is actually signposted, where it sits right across from the really old outbuildings of Peaton Farm. This near relic reminds me of French farm buildings, with its rounded walls and open slits for light.

Another view from Knockderry Lodge, this one is of the shimmering Clyde with the Inverkip power station tower visible. Expect to linger here a while every time you ride the Barbour Road, as there is a very high chance it will stop you dead in your tracks.

The roof has so much vegetation on it, I actually thought it was a turf-roofed job the first time I saw it.

You only have to climb on the Peaton for a very short distance, 200 metres or so, before turning right onto the peninsula's only stretch of single track and prepare to be entertained. It is 4.4 miles long, not long enough, and starts off fairly steeply through the trees, but the effort is well worth it.

A calm and serene look out to sea from the Barbour Road, and I put this in the top five viewpoints anywhere on the firth. That includes Pladda Lighthouse from South Arran, and the Kyles of Bute from the Tighnabruaich road.

75

Having ridden the Barbour back to Kilcreggan, I like then to head up the side of the Gareloch where there are several options open to you. You can climb the Peaton Road back over to Loch Long, and either head back to the ferry or reclimb the modern road from Coulport up to the Whistlefield roundabout. Or go all the way up to Garelochead itself and then return home via Helensburgh, or climb up to the Whistlefield roundabout and head back over to Loch Long and the ferry that way. The above photo is taken heading up the Gare just after Clynder.

Then it opens out onto the rough fields, where a long meandering climb takes you up to the wonderfully crumbling Barbour Farm, complete with caved-in roof and a clapped-out old green Land Rover that won't be seeing action any day soon.

There's still a bit more pulling up to be done, but I repeat it's all well worth it, for as you take the bend at the outstandingly positioned Knockderry Lodge… bang! The scene really stops you in your tracks. What a bloody view. Mama Mia! Holy Moses! Or how about a belter, a brammer, a stoatir (read *Only an Excuse?* here[3]), because in any language, words won't really do the whole scene justice. Knockderry Lodge itself, unlike the castle, is really just a normal house, painted pale pink and of traditional design.

It's what it looks onto that makes it so special. The adjacent telegraph pole has a weather cock on top; I've never seen such a thing before. But it is the shimmering light on the Clyde, particularly the way the lanes of light draw your eye towards the tower of Inverkip power station, that holds your stare and keeps it there. If you haven't already guessed by now, I've stopped the bike, which is a rarity, if I'm being honest.

Once we get mobile again – and it really is hard to pull

3 - *Only an Excuse?* is the satirical football comedy show on BBC Scotland, starring Jonathan Watson. I was using one of his quotes on this occasion.

yourself away from this place – the rest of the Barbour rolls over the moors to the south, and a roller coaster ride on pretty good tarmac begins.

It's just as well that the road surface is up to the job otherwise there would be a high chance of a crash in a pothole, because so much of your attention is diverted by the sea view. It shows itself splendidly all the way along, as you dip and climb past the very old farm of Knockderry, which is more knocked down than Knockderry.

The road reaches its highest point above Cove at North Ailey, and then descends swiftly to the houses above Kilcreggan, where at this point they resemble Erskine, looking ever so slightly out of place in the process. The fields are finer and sheep fill this end of the Barbour. It is a most fine road to ride in either direction, but coming from the north shades it… just. I think so, anyway.

Sweep left now and ride above the rest of the village, getting great views right up the Clyde, passing the last farm at Little Aiden, and down through the trees to the junction with the B-833. A right turn takes you speedily downhill back to the pier. Going out along the shore and returning on the Barbour makes a great day in itself – only a short one admittedly, but if that suits your needs, it's a most splendid one. If you want to do a circuit of the whole place, I would say that it is probably best to tackle it anticlockwise, principally for two reasons.

The first being that it is arguably more enjoyable to ascend both hill roads from the Gare Loch side, one of which you have to do. Second, as previously mentioned, it means you finish off by heading south on either the coast or Barbour Road, and therefore maximising the view.

So with that to look forward to, we make a right turn after disembarking from the *Island Princess* and it starts with a fairly testing wee rise up through the trees and passing a house which, for some reason, has quite a sizeable yacht up on blocks in the garden. Perhaps the bloke couldn't afford his mooring fees. The climb doesn't stay steep for too long and, as it starts to level out, keep your eye open for a Rosneath gem – one of its three way milestones. It's on the left, not long after passing the start of the Barbour, and informs you it's 7.5 miles to Garelochhead, 23 to Dumbarton, and 1 to Kilcreggan.

Now you're up among the sheep fields and conifers as the road crosses the high point of the pass, where the transmitter mast on Gallow Hill stands out prominently. Shortly into view comes the Gare Loch itself. Then it's a flyer down, bending and descending long towards the loch and Rosneath Bay's mud flats, with its swans and waders. Easily a 30 mile an hour job this descent, but it has to be said that despite this being an exciting part, it is one of the few disappointments that the road itself does not run right round the front of the peninsula, taking in Portkil and Rosneath Points. Instead, it cuts inland here.

When you arrive at Rosneath Bay, there is a road to the right that appears to run towards the peninsula's nose, but it only leads rather disappointingly into an enormous caravan park,

Looking across the Gareloch to Faslane submarine base, and it's only when seen fairly close up that you realise just how big the place is. It houses about 5000 personnel, and you can't help but think that's a lot of guys for a few wee submarines.

which just adds insult to injury, in my opinion. But that's only a minor blip in the overall standings, because in front of you, patrolling the picturesque sheltered flats of the bay, will be an array of wildlife from graceful white swans to noisy red-beaked oystercatchers. The curlew, with its slender beak and mottled colouring, is my favourite to watch, as elegant in its movements as the swan. Rhu sits across the Gare from this wooded and low stone-walled haven, where the masts from her marina's yachts can just be made out.

There now begins an almost unnoticeable rise up towards Rosneath itself, through the trees at first, but followed by an enormous works yard for boats and yachts. A jagged iron railing protects row upon row of expensive craft, chocked up and dry. Beside this, two massive corrugated iron sheds, painted red, beige, cream or whatever paint was available at the time, stand blighting the landscape. An old CalMac ferry is berthed alongside, for either fixing or scrapping. I suspect the latter, but I hope I'm wrong.

Now it's into Rosneath Village proper, which was a bit of an eye-opener for me personally. It wasn't quite what I was expecting, not in the least. I was very surprised

to see a settlement more akin to a council estate than the usual set-up of older houses which normally adorn the shoreline in these parts. White-built homes for the working class predominate here and sit below a conifer clad hillside, reminding me of Patna in Ayrshire. There are some remnants of the old village, however, in the shape of a street named Clachan that consists of low white-walled cottages for the most part, running up beside the magnificent St Modan's Church. This grey-stoned, broad, and brilliantly built house of the Lord, was named after some travelling missionary, who also built a place of worship here, some 600 years ago.

Soon comes a cheeky wee curving descent down to the loch again, and this crash barrier-lined stretch now signals the start of Clynder. The more football-minded of you may have noticed earlier in this run that I made some references to the glorious, glorious, glorious, Glasgow Rangers – the good old teddy bears (read *Only an Excuse?* again). The reason for this was because Clynder was once home to Moses McNeil, one of the founding fathers of the club. He died a pauper incidentally, and his death in 1938 went totally unnoticed by the media. He lies buried in Rosneath old cemetery, where apparently there have been plans by the Ibrox-based side to honour him in some way.

Taking a look back down the length of the Gareloch over its mudflats, once Garelochhead village itself has been reached. Here it's make your mind up time as to whether to recross to Loch Long for the ferry, or return home via the Clyde's north bank.

Heading over to Loch Long from the Whistlefield roundabout that sits high above Gareloch on the newer road designed to service Coulport. This is no country back road, but it has its benefits nonetheless, like its final screaming descent down to the armaments base and great views of the Gareloch itself.

The Gareloch in all its glory, from the modern high road. Notice how narrow the mouth of the loch is with a large sandbar (An Oitir) jutting out far into the loch. I wonder how they manage to negotiate a big nuclear submarine in and out of the place. Can't be easy.

For us bikers, however, it's business as usual as we charge up the lochside, where Clynder contains the more upmarket type of housing that you would expect. The view goes right up the Gare Loch from here, and from now to the top there is great shoreside riding. Faslane is already showing prominently and will do more so the further up you go.

We leave the village behind, and have trees and the hillside for company now. No problem with that; I'm in my element in that sort of terrain. The Arrochar Alps now dominate the distant horizon, which does the scene no harm at all. Soon, beside some swish-looking wooden houses at Rahane, we meet the Peaton Road again. It is an option now to flip back over to the Loch Long side using the Peaton, if you so wish. Attacking from this side will be a bit more meandering and less brutal than coming from the opposite side, I may add.

The climb up behind the Swedish-style houses is fairly easy managed, though it gets to 1:7 when the higher bends are met. The steepness of the road does mean you're up fast, where the road snakes pleasantly enough across the high plateau. But not for long, because then the Kamikaze descent down the other side begins. Hold onto your hat (or words to that effect), for even if you have climbed up the brute from the Coulport side, only now will you truly appreciate its gradient and length. It's times like this you wonder if you should carry spare brake pads, because the old fingers will be wondering what hit them as you plummet down, past Peaton Farm, glad to level out by the side of Loch Long again. The view is good this side for the few seconds you see it, but it could be argued that the view is better of Faslane as you come the other way.

Now, should you be up for the Peaton that way, then take it from me, it will bloody test you – no two ways about it. Coming from Loch Long, the real climb starts after you pass the farm, where the warning triangle shows that an 18% gradient is what you're up against, but what it doesn't tell you is how long it lasts. This is the killer punch of the old Peaton, for the sustained gradient of about half a mile or so is what makes it so tough. It is wide enough and quiet enough to allow you to zigzag, should you have to. And if it's early season and you're on the old training bike, or you're carrying too much weight, or are out of nick, or – like me – it's often all three, then it's no disgrace to do so.

The sting in the tail is that when it does start to lie back, it does so slowly, dropping only to 15%, then a little bit less and so on. But being tough blokes, we get over it and then, after getting the old heart rate down pronto, fire down the other side where the beige buildings of Faslane are unmissable. That's the Peaton taken care of. It's not your only option when doing a round of the place, though. When coming up the Gare, you can choose to ride past that and continue along to Garelochhead, where it's then up the Whistlefield Road and over to Coulport on the new road.

From Rahane, this starts off by riding through the woods and undulations of sparse Mambeg, before starting to pick up more housing as the village of Garelochhead is approached. Round the top of the bay and a gentle drop down takes us to the junction of our B-833 and the B-872. Now it's right for the village and left up to Whistlefield. Turn left. The double bend triangle and 15% warning signs let you know what's coming. But it's all good stuff. The bends make it feel a little bit Alpine, only a little, but it makes this climb enjoyable as it steepens in two or three places, levelling out over the West Highland rail line and among the MOD's birch trees.

The approaching roundabout signals your arrival at Whistlefield, where just beyond is the famous Green Kettle tea rooms. No time for tiffin now, however, for we're left onto the new road, up among the high stuff. The going on the new road consists of about five rises and one dip, with each rise being less sustained and shorter than

Returning back from Ardpeaton towards Kilcreggan on a glorious day, and it's perfectly fine to make directly for the ferry or skirt back round into the Gareloch if you want to return home via Helensburgh and Dumbarton. However, as far as I'm concerned, no visit is complete to the Rosneath peninsula without a climb on the very tough Peaton Road.

Looking back at the start of, what is in my opinion, the toughest climb on the whole of the Clyde – the Peaton Road from the Loch Long side. Maybe not the steepest, but certainly the most sustained. The sign, if I remember rightly, says it's an 18% gradient, which is hard enough in itself but it feels like it goes on for about half a mile. Could it be I'm just imagining that?

Now, if I am coming back via the ferry, I would most likely return to Paisley not by the outward route but by the Kilmacolm Road, Greenock, or the Clune Brae, Port Glasgow. The busyness of the A-8 beyond the Port would usually deter me from taking that way, but it may be the best option for you.

Woodhall can be used to keep things quiet for a while, but the Langbank stretch isn't available to you when going east. It's not long to the West Ferry roundabout, however, where the ride up into Bishopton is very pretty and pastoral. The sheep fields with their silence are appreciated even more, now that the busy stuff has been left behind.

If you intend to return through Helensburgh, then Garelochhead will be the gateway to that route. Regardless of whether you gain it by coming down the Whistlefield road or along the B-833 from Rosneath, it's a great entry either way. Fly down the bends and undulations from the high roundabout, or enjoy the long sweeping bend of the top bay as you approach from Mambeg; the choice is yours. The bay arcs round grandly as the hills behind sweep with it. And on the shoreline, the white dwellings follow the sweep in concert. Coming in along the lochside road is oh so mellow, and once in

its predecessor. The long view right down the Gare Loch to the Rhu narrows, is best seen coming this way, where it takes about 4 miles to reach the point where it starts to descend to Coulport. At this point, there is a link road leading across to the Peaton, which allows you to jump between the two, should you so wish.

The 4 miles of climbing are cancelled out in about a mile of descending, as the road drops, and drops, and drops some more. Sweeping to the right as it does, allows the shapely Creachan Mor to come into view, as frighteningly you plummet to Coulport. A real good descender could get to 50 miles an hour or above here, easy. I'm not one of them. Thank Christ, we've hit the bottom. From there, make your way back along to Kilcreggan pier any way you like. As for the pier itself, it really is an old wooden classic piece of architecture and long may it continue to work and serve. The Clyde would be a poorer place without it.

On top of the Peaton and just about to descend steeply down to Loch Long, which can be seen glinting in the distance. Like a lot of steep hills, you can really only appreciate just how steep it is when you are actually descending it. Hold on to your hat now.

Cresting the Peaton Road when heading towards the Gareloch, and note just how much snow cover there is on the Luss hills, which shows that these runs can be done in winter as well as summer. There now followed a very cold descent, of course.

the village, contour round the head of the loch through its picturesque pretty streets.

This leads onto the east bank of the loch, where one of the local stores sells hot drinks and grub if you need some. It's a bonnie wee ride down between the white buildings and the water, looking back across to the Rosneath side; just as the village stops, then the barbed wire fence of the submarine base begins.

For the record, Garelochhead was another old holiday resort for the Victorian Glaswegian, but again changes in transport modes saw that era come to a close. The place made a couple of revivals since. One was during the war, when about 22,000 US troops trained here for D-Day; God knows where they stayed! And the other was during the building of Faslane itself. Now that those two heydays are over, things have quietened down again.

Where was I now? Oh yes, the barbed wire fence. Yes, we've arrived by the side of our country's nuclear deterrent, not what you'd call a sight for sore eyes – but whether you are for it or not, it ain't pretty, that's for sure. If you weren't aware of that fact up till now, then you soon will be. You roll along the side of the fence, with its highly visible double – no, make that treble – rolls of bad-assed barbed, ready to stop you in an instant. The old place started in '64 and was built to house the Polaris system carried by the Resolution class of submarine, which was superseded by the Vanguard class subs carrying Trident warheads.

Two types of sub are based here now: the previously mentioned Vanguards, of which there are four carrying the nukes; and the more conventional Trafalgar class, that are currently being replaced by the Astute class and

The Peaton Road at the point it starts to tilt down to the Gareloch and Faslane naval base, can be seen through the trees. It is a great descent; not technical, nor as steep as the Loch Long side. This is some reward for all the effort to get up here, which is just as well as it is a very short plateau when you do get up.

will number seven in total. The *HMS Astute* is already in service and is the most advanced sub in the world, they say. Not cheap, mind, but no matter what way you look at the higher than expected build costs, you should still get change from £1.5 billion per sub. And as any used submarine salesman worth his salt will tell you, "You won't get a better one at that price." It's just a pity they don't do three for the price of two.

So on making your way up to the big roundabout at the north gate, you will notice through the fence that most of the work gets done at this end, while the south end is mostly taken up by accommodation. To get there, there is a long gradual pull up, over, and down beside the rest of the base, passing all the numerous beige housing blocks that were so prominent from across the Gare

Firing down to the Gareloch on the Peaton Road before making for home. It's right at the bottom for Kilcreggan and the ferry, and left for Garelochhead and Dumbarton. Take your pick.

Loch. Shortly after passing the slip road to the south gate, you'll see the rainbow caravans of the peace camp sitting in among the trees on the left. They have been there since 1992, mounting an ever-present vigil and protest.

I obviously don't have the time or scope to go into all the right or wrongs of nuclear weapons, and everyone knows the arguments for or against anyway. Suffice to say that I admire the peace campaigners for their dedication alone. Apparently it's well organised inside, but certainly looks like a bomb site from the outside.

After clearing the base, you ride along the shore front towards Rhu, where I can safely assume there is a helluva lot of money in the area, judging by the houses and cars that are sitting to my left. You then purr along the old A-814 in the Shandon area.

Approaching Kilcreggan pier from Cove, and it's time to wait for the ferry. If you arrive a wee bit early, there is a great wee cafe across from the pier, which is always handy for the caffeine – and that won't go amiss on the run home.

I assume this is Shandon, but I'm not 100% sure, for every few yards it seems there is a signpost telling me a different place name. The Gables, King's Point, Queen's Point? Rosneath itself is your opposite number across the water, as you take the rise up into Rhu. The jetty out into the loch gives the game away, as does the quality and age of the homes here, that this was also an old bolthole for rich Glasgow merchants of the time. The twin stone-walled climb over and down past the parish church is as elegant as it is rewarding. The church, with its striking rounded tower and clock, has in its graveyard the final resting place of Henry Bell, builder of the Comet and the first successful steamship company.

Two other famous sons were Peter Campbell and

Reboarding the Island Princess at Kilcreggan, before returning back to Gourock across a glinting Clyde on this occasion.

Peter McNeil (brother of Moses), both of whom helped found the Glasgow club. And with that mention, you can now relax, for there breaks this run's association with anything Rangers and no more associated corny comments.

The marina is skirted round next and also some small type of Navy base, but the shorefront and bay are pleasant and undamaged by the presence of more barbed wire. We batter on towards Helensburgh now, where the initial stretch of road seems like a re-run of the Shandon stretch. But it's all quality here, for as we pass the tip of Rosneath Point, the Clyde really widens and Greenock appears far across.

With it comes the wow factor, as the big blue opens up all again. So now in the full fresh of the front, the clock tower by Helensburgh pier appears and beckons us near. There's no doubt this is a pretty and wealthy town. Built in 1776 by Sir James Colquhoun and modelled on the Edinburgh New Town district, he named the place after his wife, whose name I forget. He actually started a ferry service over to Greenock to encourage workers from there to settle this side of the water. That ferry service used to run till fairly recently, and could have been used by any cyclist wanting to include it as part of their run.

This option is not available at the moment, as the ferry has ceased running and the boys on the *Island Princess* have told me that there are no plans in the pipeline to restart it, due to lack of demand. No such problems for thee aforementioned Henry Bell, as his paddle steamer Comet was highly successful in bringing in holidaymakers from Glasgow. From 1812, Helensburgh and Craigendoran piers were very busy places indeed.

Now the 13th of August, 1888 was a very special day for the world, because in this very town was born one John Logie Baird, the inventor of the gogglebox itself, the television set. Yes, this is the man who brought into all our homes quiz games, soap operas, and shows such as Big Brother, the X-Factor, and Sir Jimmy 'howzabout-

Looking back at Kilcreggan as the Island Princess pulls away.

that-then Saville. He's got a bloody lot to answer for, actually.

Continue in on West Clyde Street, where ahead the high slope of Ben Bowie's downward sweep continues to run right out and into the Clyde in the shape of Ardmore. The long elegant draw of the Helensburgh waterfront

Heading for Greenock on the wee Island Princess, and a grey look she gives. Not long till we're over, and then you can pick your route back. For the purposes of the book, we're returning via Bishopton this day to cover as many routes as possible.

keeps your eye in the far distance, as the sheer openness of the whole situation is just so wide and wonderful. Then it's through the crossing at the pier and on along East Clyde Street, catching glimpses of the water in places between the shore-side buildings, before you go under the rail bridge of the North Clyde line that terminates at Helensburgh Central. Going right at the bridge will run you, dead end, down to Craigendoran station and its now dilapidated old pier. This old relic (the pier that is) is not entirely forgotten, because it gets a mention by Kenneth McKellar in the *Song of the Clyde*.

Heading out of town and continuing on the A-814, we pass the final well-to-do suburbs and also the new academy as we go, before entering into the fields between here and Cardross. The road sits low down at first, among some fields of rough machair, before it starts to rise and takes us up above the jutting, rounded headland that is Ardmore. It's quite a scene at this point so turn and look across the fields and firth, and be charmed by its prettiness. It is particularly pleasing to drive this stretch of road at night in the opposite direction, and admire the lights all along the far bank. A testing long pull brings you above Cardross, where the payback is the shoot down into and along its main street.

It runs approximately about a mile through this large village, passing some nice touches. The old Coach Inn and, in particular, the old derelict church tower provide the charm. This was apparently destroyed by the Luftwaffe.

You leave by the fields right down beside the rail and the river, where everything here is mostly equestrian (horsey). Horses, ponies, painted poles for jumps clutter the small fields all around, before the road rises to test you a little before it enters Dumbarton. It's a bit of a Langbank/Woodhall scenario here. For Dumbarton is no millionaire's row, not by any stretch of the imagination. The barren white tenements and white council houses that you first encounter are in stark contrast to the opulence of neighbouring Helensburgh.

This pattern is very often repeated throughout the country. But the home of The Sons (Dumbarton F.C.s nickname) isn't without its saving graces. One of them comes on you quite quickly, as you go down past Dalreoch station before crossing the River Leven on the modern and fairly charmless bridge. This is positioned beside some modern high rise flats, but don't let that put you off, because the view downstream of the small

The Clyde at Langbank, and isn't she still and soft?

moored craft, sitting mid-stream in the river, with the elegant spanning arches of the road bridge behind, is a most serene sight. John Brown built this one in 1765, on the site of the old ferry crossing; he made a first class job of it.

Behind this, the dramatic view of Dumbarton Rock is enjoyed above the bend of the Leven, where the red-bricked tower of the former Ballantine's Whisky grain distillery and the local church spire are always prominent on the right side. A busy big roundabout, a busy wee roundabout, then a street of tall grey tenements of character follow next. Off down one of the side streets to the right lies the castle and rock. Dumbarton itself actually means Fort of the Britons, and that's exactly what the rock was. All is grey and imposing here before escaping away under the railway, and then the long, long straight out of town begins.

About a mile or so of the straight stuff, cutting through the semis of the town's more upmarket side, takes you up to the lights and junction with the mega busy A-82. But not before passing that old white stalwart that is the Dumbuck Hotel on the left, behind which stands the imposing bulk of the Milton Quarry, a sort of mini Dumbarton Rock. Then Ballantine's grey warehouses will follow. These are no longer protected by the famous flock of Chinese geese, but by modern CCTV.

Despite the fact that it's only about another mile to the cut-off for Bowling, and therefore sanctuary from the fast stuff, I still avoid that stretch of the A-82 by jumping on the conveniently-placed cycle track here.

Just before the lights on the left, there is an unofficial way onto the track – a mere break in the trees, but quite noticeable all the same. It's worth your while to slow down and look for it. I advise you to take it and speed

Dumbarton from across the Clyde at Langbank, as we make the return to Bishopton on the busy A-8. Not my favourite road, but it becomes still after the majority of traffic has gone off down the motorway. As it climbs up to Bishopton, you're back into the pleasant, quiet sheep fields.

along the track in safety, beside the rail line. But if you miss the impromptu entrance, don't worry, as the proper one is just round the corner, though it is on the other side of the road.

Once on the track, it is flat and birch tree-lined, till a slight rise brings you up to the road again where the A-814 is re-met at the large Bowling roundabout. Directly across the road, the cycle track continues and I again advise you to take it, for it is a beautiful, tunnel-assisted, wood-lined stretch, where the tarmac is silky smooth and will be much to your liking.

A gentle quiet climb up through the mature trees sees you go under a bridge, then the slight rising continues till you meet and pass under a most ornate and exquisite tunnel of a bridge, which appears to have bored through by a precision burrowing machine. Even a coat of arms,

showing the year of construction, adorns its castellated ramparts, making it a most striking-looking fellow. You're actually on the bed of the old Caledonia railways line that ran from Lanarkshire to Dunbartonshire, and provided Bowling with a second station before closing in 1951. It had run since 1896.

From the tunnel, the track stays high and passes some striking rock clad embankment, with equally impressive man-made support in amongst it. Thereafter, it drops back to the road.

When you return to the road, there is the option of crossing straight over and continuing towards Old Kilpatrick on the cycle track, which now runs on the towpath along the side of the Forth and Clyde Canal. The Bowling basin quite simply is chocolate box pretty, and the money spent recently on this stretch was well worth

A closer look at Dumbarton Rock and Castle from across the Clyde.

If returning along the north bank instead of the ferry, you may find numerous serene scenes such as this one, as you ride through Helensburgh. Although coming down the Gareloch is nice, it's only when you swing onto Helensburgh's waterfront that the whole Firth of Clyde hits you full-on – and what an overwhelming blast of blue air and open space it is.

outlying bungalows. The solid sweeping line of the expansion bridge above dominates the skyline as you come in, the way it has done all the way from Bowling. It cuts a fine dash, I must say; particularly the way it spans the river so grandly, in such a high and mighty fashion. It's impossible not to be in awe of the thing, and to admire the designer William Brown for what is a truly impressive structure.

The Old Kilpatrick square church tower, with its blue clock face, regal and old, makes a nice contrast between it and the modern structure towering above. The red sandstone tenements you pass enroute to the village centre, easily outshine their modern concrete square counterparts found nearby.

it. After about a mile, you can cross on a delightful small black and white lifting bridge to take you into the village via Gavinburn Street. Or if you prefer, make your way out of Bowling on the A-814, bending through the trees then rising, as you bridge the small distance between the two villages. Halfway there, you pass the cut-on and off from the northbound dual carriageway of the A-82.

Now the Erskine Bridge is approaching, and must be crossed to get me home. However, it can be a little bit, not too much, of messing around to gain its cycle lanes from Old Kilpatrick itself. So for sheer expediency, I have been known on occasion to ride up the pavement beside the A-82, starting at the Bowling cut-off, till the last countdown marker to the Erskine Bridge is seen on the other side. At this point, there is a break in the crash barrier, allowing any nimble-footed rider to dash across when a break in traffic allows, then remount the old steed and fly into the curving cut-off and onto the bridge pronto. This can be a good way to save time and effort if you are in no mood to faff about for any reason. The cycle lane is quickly gained, and away you go.

If you prefer to play safe, then by all means continue into Old Kilpatrick itself, descending into the village after curving between its very respectable-looking

This is a real trip down memory lane in the shape of Craigendoran pier, which lies at the east end of Helensburgh. Admittedly, it does take a slight dead end diversion to get down to it, but I have visited it on occasion just to see what it was like after I heard Kenneth McKellar sing about it in The Song of the Clyde. It you want to view it, just follow the signs for the railway station as you make your way out towards the east end of town. Like all Clyde piers, it's hard nowadays to imagine the throngs that once used it in the bygone days, especially Craigendoran which is a bit dilapidated now to say the least.

Crossing the Leven at Dumbarton, and it's a beautiful scene. The grand old Bridge Street bridge behind is a delight to ride across, and easily puts its modern counterpart (from where this photograph was taken) into the shade.

cable-yielding masts. Looking upstream from this side, the view shows the sprawl of Glasgow in the distance, with the closer Clydebank sitting just below. The Clyde is slow and statesman-like at this point. Unhurried and out of concert with the speed of the modern vehicles passing above it, the river flows unnoticed and unconcerned westward.

From the high point on the bridge, start your belt down the other side. Always glad of the free wheel to save time and effort, you can nip down the side of the bridge on the doubling back cycle track, rather than follow the road proper to reach the same destination. That destination is the A-726, which is followed back up towards the airport, through a series of scrub-lined and tree-lined roundabouts. There is no great scenery here to take the sting out of the slight rises that draw you up to the Southbar roundabout, going through the new town-like road terrain of this very old low lying land. Tired legs again feel the benefit of the long gentle drop that takes you down to the Red Smiddy roundabout, and with that we find we've come full circle on ourselves.

After passing the row of village shops, break off left and follow the cycle track signs up and around the bridge access roads at first, then round the side of the bowling green. This gives access to both cycle lanes; it actually passes under the bridge itself to get onto the south bound one. A fairly plodding ascent takes you up to the structure's high point, between its two double

Some flat land lies between here and Saint James' interchange, which is a good place to ease up and let the old legs wind down and clear out the lactic acid

Going into the very skilfully built and ornate rail tunnel on the cycle route at Bowling, which is a lovely – albeit short – alternative to using the road once you reach that village. After the tunnel, you soon drop rather dramatically back down to the road. Although it is only a very short stretch of track, it is definitely worth using from time to time. You can't fail to be impressed by the efforts of the men who built and blasted for the track.

If coming back via Dumbarton, then it will be the dramatic-looking Erskine Bridge that will be the alternative to the Kilcreggan ferry to get back across the Clyde. And she makes a splendid sight from the pavement beside the busy A-82. She is no eyesore, that's for sure.

from hard-worked muscles, following the airport's perimeter fence as you go. Looking through the fence, you still see rather old airfield paraphernalia, brightly coloured wooden steps, and such like. Real Biggles-type equipment. It amazes me how the ultra-modern electronic navigation aids are used side by side with these old relics.

A sharp intake of breath and a charge across the hectic one – St. James' – soon sees us within the sanctuary of North Paisley's streets' and with regards to Paisley's streets... follow to Glenburn.

Liam Boy

N.B. The Gourock ferry terminal can make a most convenient starting point for a great run that will include both the Dunoon and Kilcreggan ferries. I did not treat this as a separate run, as all the roads involved are covered in both this and the next run, which is the Dunoon run itself. It can obviously be done in either direction, but due to the Dunoon-Gourock service being much more frequent than the Kilcreggan-Gourock service, it is probably more convenient to do it anticlockwise. This would mean there would be less waiting for a ferry and less anxiety about missing one if you were making for the Argyll ferry at Dunoon Pier, as opposed to the much less frequent Island Princess from Kilcreggan Pier.

So, a very brief description going anticlockwise would be to catch the Island Princess to Kilcreggan, then gain the A-814 running up the side of Loch Long by either Coulport and the big climb up to the Whistlefield roundabout on the newer road, or go round through Rosneath on the B-833 and gain the Whistlefield by the climb up from Garelochhead on the B-872. At the top of Loch Long, you will join the A-83 at Arrochar, and you follow this round and over the Rest and Be Thankful before breaking off left in Glen Kinglass and heading for Dunoon and the Argyll ferry on the A-815. It gives a helluva run coming in at just under the 60 miles mark, along the side of classic-looking fresh and salt water lochs, as well as all the mountain grandeur of the Arrochar Alps and Cowal Hills. Enjoy.

Liam Boy

KILCREGGAN-DUNOON
57.7 MILES
3.40 HOURS
ASCENT 2240 FEET
2611 CALORIES BURNED
(FROM GOUROCK PIER)

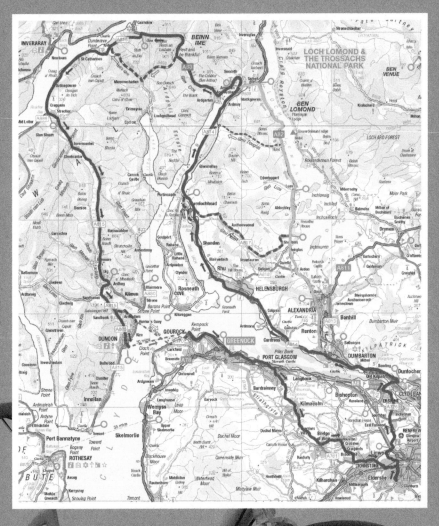

DUNOON

VIA LOCH LOMOND
97.4 MILES
6.16 HOURS
ASCENT 3400 FEET
4440 CALORIES BURNED

VIA HELENSBURGH
100.6 MILES
6.34 HOURS
ASCENT 3700 FEET
4724 CALORIES BURNED

ARGYLL FERRIES TEL NO 01475 650 338

WESTERN FERRIES TEL NO 01369 704 452

O/S LANDRANGER MAPS 64, 63, 56.

ROUTE SUMMARY

Erskine
Erskine Bridge
Old Kilpatrick
Bowling
Dumbarton

A-814 HELENSBURGH ROUTE

Cardross
Helensburgh
Rhu
Garelochhead
Whistlefield
A-814 Loch Long
Arrochar

A-82 LOCH LOMOND ROUTE

Renton
Alexandria
Balloch
Old Luss Rd*
A-82 Loch Lomond
Tarbet
Arrochar

BOTH ROUTES

Rest And Be Thankful A-83
Glen Kinglas A-83
St Catherines A-815
Strachur A-815
Loch Eck
Hunter's Quay
Ferry To Mcinroy's Point

ALTERNATIVE ROUTE

B-828 And B-839
(Gleann Mor/Gleann Beag)
St Catherines

RETURN ROUTE

Gourock
Greenock
Auchmountain Rd
Quarriers
Bridge Of Weir Or Cycle Track
Linwood
Paisley

ALTERNATIVE RETURN ROUTE

Gourock
Greenock
Port Glasgow
Kilmacolm
Bridge Of Weir
Linwood   Kilbarchan
Paisley   Paisley

* Please note the Old Luss Road will take you onto the cycle track/pavement before joining the A-82 road proper.

THE DUNOON RUN

LOCHS, BENS AND BENDS

No need to introduce this one to anybody who has been riding a bike in the Greater Glasgow area for more than five minutes. For this run has a pedigree umpteen times that of any Crufts champion. Done by all, at one time or another, and a firm favourite of many — including myself — this grand loop does have an air of initiation about it. But forget about that and do it for the pleasure alone. You won't be the first to get great enjoyment from it and you won't be the last. It has been done by famous faces, too. If you read Pamela Stephenson's excellent book about her partner Billy Connolly, she describes how the Big Yin would do it regularly and then, after returning by ferry to Gourock, 'have to make the long way back to Glasgow'.

Well, if it's good enough for the Big Yin, it's good enough for me. You're sure to find it good enough for you, too. Funny thing about the Dunoon run is that I always find it a bit of a morale booster. For no matter how tired I get whilst doing it, or how wet I get, I always seem to stay upbeat and my spirits remain high. Very rarely, even in the middle of winter, have I found myself wishing I hadn't taken it on. This, despite the fact it was often done in freezing conditions, even to the extent that on one occasion I found myself having to de-ice my feet on the heater in the Luss toilets. After that, I continued on my way back to Paisley in the dark freezing fog, singing all the while as I went.

The snack bar at the top of the Rest and Be Thankful[1] is great to stop at and have a break in the warm summer sunshine, but I don't recommend it in winter. For you'll find you've cooled right down and then have to descend for quite some distance through the freezing air, where it can take quite a few cold and miserable miles before you warm up again. But enough of all this winter weather talk, as all that lies in the future. Most likely, you will be attempting this through the summer months, at least until you get your hand in.

---

1 - It may no longer be there.

If you're going clockwise, the bare bones of the run entails catching the ferry over to Dunoon from Gourock, running up the side of Loch Eck, then Loch Fyne, before going over the Rest and Be Thankful to Arrochar. From there, you return via the Erskine Bridge by either coming down Loch Lomondside or taking the Loch Long road and then through Helensburgh. If going anticlockwise, the decision where to make the main split will come when you are in and around Dumbarton.

Most guys you speak to will have a preference on which way they do this one. Me? I find that there is one major pro and con, regardless of what way I do it. If going anti-clock, it means that I have a tough pull up out of Inverclyde when I've got around 80 miles in my legs, but it does mean I get the awkward section of negotiating the Vale of Leven out of the way early doors if I'm going via Loch Lomond. The Erskine Bridge finish is less testing for me. But again, if I've come down the A-82, then I've got to bugger about a bit round the likes of Bonhill and Alexandria at a time when I would much prefer to keep the old momentum going. You know what I'm going to tell you now, don't tell me you didn't see it coming: yes, try it both ways yourself and see what suits best.

So here we go, here we go, here we go... out on the old El Classico. No finer run do we have, and one that is looked forward to with the anticipation it deserves. Just one little word to the wise before we depart. The first few times you do it, particularly if this sort of distance is fairly new to you, then do your damndest to pace yourself well. The old Rest and Be Thankful can take so much out of you, that you're never the same man after it that you were before. As it comes roughly in the middle of the jaunt, then it means that you have somewhere in the region of 45 miles to pedal home, and if you're not feeling exactly at your best, that's a long way to suffer. So hold something back, if in doubt.

We're going anti on this occasion, and that will entail the exact same start as the Kilcreggan run up to the Red Smiddy roundabout. Meaning for me, it's down through Paisley's west end and north end, to gain the old A-726 behind the airport, the Barnsford Road. I elected not to mention St James interchange this time, in case it put you off cycling altogether.

After giving the old wind sock the usual once-over, we go on our way merrily merrily to the Smiddy and beyond (Buzz Lightyear-style). We don't turn left for Bishopton this time, however, but plough straight on into Erskine.

Just about to start over on the big grey whale back of the Erskine Bridge, in the safety of the cycle lane (going anticlockwise). Remember, there is a long way to go today, so nice and easy does it; no need for kamikaze tactics early doors.

This former old hamlet, which had a ferry crossing the Clyde for yonks, was designated ripe for development in the early 1970s by some plonker, who decided to give the place the new town treatment. As a result, we are left with what I call the modern monstrosity that is today's Erskine.

The hamlet and ferry, incidentally, were in existence from the late seventeen hundreds, with the ferry supplanting what had been a ford there, believe it or not. It's quite difficult to imagine fording the Clyde at Erskine nowadays. The place name itself goes much further back, to about the 1220s, and most likely it took the name from one of the time's major landholders, the dashingly named Henry de Erskine, whoever the hell he was.

The roundabouts and roads are quickly flown through, as you drop down towards the river. It's hardly surprising, as Erskine actually means 'high marsh', hence the reason that the roadside surrounds have rather a less than chocolate box-pretty look to them, being more a thicket of close-growing trees.

They do act as a shield to hide some of the housing developments, and as you descend to just after the centre, the sight of the Erskine Bridge with the Kilpatrick Hills beyond does make quite a serene and striking sight.

Now the bridge is approaching, and after some recent reconstruction it is better to gain it by using the official start to the cycle lane rather than using the road proper, which would entail a big looping jaunt to get up there. That is because the new crash barrier on the bridge actually blocks off the cycle lane from the road, forcing you to lift yourself and the bike over it now[2]. It's easier to go up the path, despite its steepness and awkward tight switchback. Once on it, however, there are no such problems, and away you go, safely separated from the traffic and climbing gradually ever upward.

A fantastic view down the Clyde from the Erskine Bridge (anti) and what a show-stopper she is. The distant hills give some idea of what is to come today, as they will be reached and ridden in a couple of hours' time.

Take note that early doors you pass a phone box, which is strategically positioned along with another three others, one at each corner of the bridge, so to speak. These have been placed there deliberately to act as a last chance saloon to any suicidal jumpers who are literally heading for the bridge to throw themselves off. In fact, there are even billboards displaying the Samaritans' number, should anyone require their assistance. I've actually witnessed this sort of thing first hand as it is a fairly regular occurrence, with around 15 jumpers a year. The Old Kilpatrick side seems to be more popular than the Renfrewshire end for some reason; I don't know why.

---

2 - You can gain the cycle path by jumping on the pavement well before the crash barrier is reached, therefore avoiding the need to lift your bike over the barrier that way.

An attempt was made to curtail the jumpers by installing a new higher fence all along the entire length of the bridge's sides. However, it now appears that people are actually carrying up ladders to get over the side. Where there's a will, as they say.

But it's not all doom and gloom for the rest of us, because the scene is rather spectacular as the early trees are cleared, and when the high point of the suspension bridge is reached there is a monumentally great view looking right down the Clyde to the sea lochs and mountains afar — and that's exactly where we're going. Those green serene Kilpatricks actually act as a natural draw the way that they slant away from your right side, down into the Clyde, ending at the Dumbarton Rock no less.

The fun is added to by the way that the bridge will bounce every time a big articulated lorry goes by, or at least it used to, and it's then that you can fully appreciate the engineering feat that the big girl herself truly is. A cable-stayed box girder design, to be exact, it was opened in 1971 by Princess Anne. The initial tolls were only supposed to be charged till the bridge paid for itself, but these were kept in place till March 2006, by which time the bridge had paid for itself three times over. They've gone now and all the motorists are pleased, but it didn't make any difference to traffic volume as was hoped, with the bridge still carrying the same amount of vehicles per day as it's always done, about 35,000.

The great high-perched open airy view accompanies you on the way down, as you fly into West Dunbartonshire, avoiding any debris that's been knocked onto the cycle track from all the nearby traffic running beside you. Right below you, the houses of Old Kilpatrick look cute in their miniature scale. At the bottom of the drop you have quite a difficult decision to make, because by this point you have gathered a fair bit of momentum and it is very tempting to join the road and follow it onto the very fast and busy A-82, at least as far as the Bowling cut-off. No doubt about it, this is the quickest way to continue on your way, and I've been known to use it myself often enough. But I do find it scary the way the top speed motors almost take the paintwork of the bike frame, and therefore I'm very glad when the aforementioned Bowling cut-off is reached and there's a big sigh of relief when I take it.

On the plus side, the view down the Clyde opens up grandly, and looking back over your left shoulder

Funny wee place, I must say, as there must have been a lot going on here at one time.

What with the old docks, now ripe for redevelopment, and the old rail bridge that you go under from the old Lanarkshire line, now running onto the modern cycle path. This is one I usually take when coming the other way, preferring to stay on the road when heading west. And then at the far end is a former Shell fuel dump. It's now closed, but only fairly recently, compared to the village's other old industries. The meandering Main Street, dotted with old tenements and houses of such character and age,

Having dropped down into old Kilpatrick via the cycle lane, it's onto the A-814 and away we go (anti). The main Loch Lomond road, the A-82, sits above to the right, but this road that you are on was the main road north at one time. It's hard to believe that now, as it's all quiet as we purr past the old church with its lovely blue clockface. Shortly comes Bowling, at the end of which will be the main make-your-mind-up time of the day. Which way for Arrochar? Will it be Loch Long or Loch Lomondside?

shows the bridge off beautifully, too. The other safer choice, when you reach the north side of the bridge, is to continue to use the cycle track down into Old Kilpatrick Village, but this entails losing all your momentum. It's suddenly all quiet again as you manoeuvre gingerly around the perimeter of the bowling club, or a bit more quickly on the track round the football park, before dropping down Station Road and onto the A-814 again.

The place is as pretty as a picture, just the way that the old kirk and red sandstone tenements sit below the Kilpatricks. Yes, Old Kilpatrick — Phadraig's Church, in old Scots, but the place was known as Clotagenium to the Romans, meaning Clydemouth. For here was the western end of the Antonine Wall, which ran all the way for 36 miles to the Forth and signalled the northern extreme of the Roman Empire. A very large fort also occupied the town, which is why as you rise up and bend out of the village, the aptly named Roman Crescent is passed.

Then onto Bowling we cruise, and I do mean cruise, as it's downhill curving along the tree-lined road and accompanying rail line and nearby canal. Real boys' own stuff this, what with the craggy Kilpatricks sitting above. The welcome sign means what it says, you're in Bowling.

also contains quite a lot of new flats, as it still has its rail station on the North Clyde line so the place will now appeal to the modern day commuter.

As you come out at the other end, the A-82 is met again, and also the cycle path leading into Dumbarton. Now some roadies will elect to use the road, but I always

If deciding to go via Helensburgh and Loch Long (anti), then Dumbarton must be ridden through first, and its great old grey tenements make a splendid avenue to fire down.

Crossing the Leven on the old splendid Bridge Street Bridge gives a great view of Dumbarton Rock. Normally you would use the modern bridge carrying the A-814, but occasionally I like to go across on the older one — not just for the views, but also because it's so grand and ornate. It's also part of the official cycle route.

use the path. It's getting near to make-your-mind-up time as to whether you go up Loch Lomondside or go via Helensburgh. If you want to take the most direct route for Loch Lomond, then the A-82 is it, but it's not the most pleasant. Even if I am going that way, I will just about always use one of numerous permutations involving Dumbarton, Bonhill, Renton, and Alexandria.

If you've decided to do the run by using the A-814 along the Clyde's north bank and then Loch Long, it is much more straightforward, though surprisingly slightly longer. You would imagine without the aid of a large road atlas that going inland as opposed to the coastal route would be the lengthier choice. Not so, even though both routes actually come together again on the coast in Arrochar at the head of Loch Long.

When you do examine a map, it becomes apparent that the A-82 is in fact much straighter and direct, with the A-814 actually bulging out like a belly, before going back in; hence the added mileage. But as it is the more straightforward route, we will handle it first, before returning to tackle Loch Lomond.

So skip down the cycle track for starters, and you shortly pass under the arch stone bridge which carries the A-814 above, before quickly jumping onto it, by using the unofficial exit on the left through the trees. Watch out for the thorns. Start rolling into Dumbarton, through its numerous outlying grey warehoused whisky bonds, overlooked as always by the striking and towering height of the Dumbuck Quarry's high rock face.

Pass the Dumbuck Hotel as you go, where at the time of writing two can dine for £9.99. This done, it's into the busier, older, and even greyer centre. Keep your wits about you for a while as it is always busy-busy here, and tight into the bargain. An occasional left glance will show off the town's most dramatic feature: the rock and castle, of course. Even the high tenement-sided streets add to the effect, all covered in their damp grey garb.

Once safely through, cross over the Leven and as always enjoy and admire the classic lines of the Bridge Street Bridge slightly downstream. Now things start to open up and quieten down a bit, as you first pass through the bungalows and then the housing schemes of the town's west side.

You've probably sussed that we are doing part of the previous run in reverse now, as we shortly leave Dumbarton, but not before I mention that this was also an old ship-building town of repute and the birthplace of the famous *Cutty Sark*, no less. It was one of the last of the old tea clippers to be built, constructed in the Scott and Linton yard. The last big players in the ship-building game were William Denny and Bros, who finally shut up shop in 1963. This was a bit of a loss, as they were renowned innovators who had come up with an early hovercraft design and even an early helicopter prototype, would you believe? So with some serious Clyde-built pride in our gut, we take our leave from the Sons of the Rock and head into the fields above the Clyde.

The road's straight lines soon drops down to the flat of the near riverside, where it continues to run straight with the rail line, till it then turns into the village of Cardross. An old lane on the left is Ferry Road, though little trace exists now of a pier or quay, so it must be a very old one going way back. Ahead, stealing the show, is the old bombed-out tower of the kirk — all the handiwork of the Luftwaffe, though big Hermann's Heinkels didn't quite finish the job. That was par for the course with big Hermann.

The old village inn and the other old standards now either face or rub shoulders with new apartments, as is wont to happen nowadays in most of our small settlements. But Cardross has an ace up its sleeve in that it is reputed to be the resting place of the great Robert the Bruce no less (top that, if you will).

The climb out at the other end, after a near flat mile or so, is a blessing in disguise, because the height it affords gives a glorious long look right down the sea-

The Bridge Street Bridge from the cycle path, as it starts to make its way along the west bank of the Leven. The bridge is as fine a specimen of craftsmanship as you are likely to see. I do, on occasion, use the cycle path through the Vale of Leven, though I realise that most riders will find it just too meandering and time-consuming when they are on such a long trip as the Dunoon run. However, it is so peaceful and enjoyable to ride beside the river in places that I make the detour from time to time to ride along it, just for the pleasure it brings.

fairing firth, with mountains aplenty to add to the stunning seascape. As I mentioned in the return from Kilcreggan, driving down here at night with the lights glowing on the far bank, is a stunning sight in itself. But the daytime view isn't bad either, and the curves of Ardmore headland's bays simply draw your eyes into them and beyond. Wunderbar, you scream, as down again the road takes you back level with the river and rail and into the roughest of overgrown fields which precede Helensburgh's arrival.

Then it's back into Well-to-do-ville. No doubt about the level of wealth contained within this town's boundary, and that's despite the fact we start off rather modestly at this end. Not long, though, till we're under the rail bridge and onto East Clyde Street and the seafront starts to show, but not nearly as much as it does when we get through the busy centre crossroads and onto West Clyde Street. Now you're talking. Wow; I say again, wow! Serenity succulently served here, all along the seafront. The width and its wonders overwhelm me at this point, every time I ride this road, and even the shy Rosneath peninsula shows itself boldly now as you start to draw level with its headland.

Gentle hills overlook the opulent houses that line the shore in both Helensburgh and the soon to be reached Rhu, whose tight turning cove is a delight to tootle around every time. This before the up and over that takes you past its stunning old churchyard and on down into the openness of the Shandon stretch. This will lead along to the barbed one, Faslane itself, where you now rarely see any activity at the rainbow-painted caravans of the peace camp.

The long pull up beside big bad barbed begins, and the recovery time on the descent to the north gate is always appreciated, from whence the older road to Garelochhead is nearly always preferred to the modern road. Both lead to Whistlefield.

Taking the purpose-built modern A-814 does allow the Glen Fruin road to be accessed, should you so wish to use it to take you back on a loop to Loch Lomond. But that's not today's plan. We're going all the road to Dunoon on the big loop, so that entails the short steep climb up to the Whistlefield roundabout, starting at the far end of the solid stone structures that make up white-walled Garelochhead. Much huff and puff perhaps, till the West Highland rail line is crossed, and after 0.8 of a mile and 280 feet of climbing, we arrive at Whistlefield. Now as I stated in our first run together on the road to Girvan, the structure of the runs I describe will include numerous shorter choices from which to pick from, to suit your own specific needs.

I mention this at this point because, if you were doing the Dunoon run clockwise and decided to come down Loch Long, then at the Whistlefield roundabout or even Garelochhead, you could return to Gourock via the Kilcreggan ferry and make a great return trip out of that alone[3]. It would come in around the 57-mile mark.

Whistlefield itself is a rather strange wee place, sitting so high up in the hills all on its own. The former inn, now a house, was a much welcome resting stop for travellers, and some railway houses were built to support the former station. Now it's best known for the famous Green Kettle Inn, with its Bikers Welcome sign outside the door. By all means, stop for a break if you fancy it, though when they say bikers, I don't know if they mean the motor boys or us.

After passing the Kettle and the small cluster of homes, descend down and under the rail line this time on what is, in my opinion, as classic a stretch of West Highland road as you'll get. It's only short but I really enjoy it, especially when coming the other way. There then follows

3 - I give the details for this route at the end of the Kilcreggan run.

a bit of undulating, passing what's left of Whistlefield, then it's into the trees. But during a break in them, look to your left and prepare to be impressed.

That down there is no longer the Gare Loch, because we've flipped over the hillside onto the slopes above the mighty Loch Long. Slender and dramatic best describes the Long one from here, right up to its termination at Arrochar. Incidentally, its name has nothing to do with its length, which is considerable in itself at around 20 miles, but rather means Ship Loch.

Nowhere is it more dramatic than at this point, where it meets the stocky Loch Goil butting in from the northwest. Still, strong, and solid is the scene where both waters meet. Adding to the already considerable

Passing the scenic Ardmore Point, which will always show well on the road between Cardross and Helensburgh. It is a fairly tight and fast road here, but this is a great downhill section (anti) after the initial climb out of Cardross. The views of the Clyde and the steep, rugged Argyll hills to come, are magic from this stretch of road.

seriousness of the show, is the plunging, narrow, conifer-clad headland of Meall Daraich, which splits the two lochs. It pointedly drops down to the water's edge at Carraic nan Ron. The shapely Creachan Mor, that we know so well, guards the left, with the equally rough Clach Bheinn the right. There's plenty more of the same to come and I do mean plenty, as now we meet the trees, which do a very good job of concealing the massive Finnart refuelling dump of the Royal Navy.

It's very difficult to judge the size and scale of this place when you see so little of it from the road, but on occasion you will come across some massive tanker berthed alongside, unloading its cargo into the fuel tanks on the hillside.

The serene purr along Helensburgh's waterfront is always a delight, and good respite on flat tar. That is welcome after so much upping and downing to get here (clock), and knowing there is still a bit more of the same to come. It could not have been quieter or calmer in the photo above.

The road dives, really dives quite dramatically, down to the lochside on a bending 1:6 gradient, passing a couple of old semi-derelict hobbit-looking houses on the way. Gratitude is expressed when the safety and flatness are gained, as the road surface on the drop isn't the best. But behold, in front of you is a bit of serious sea loch riding that is as damp as it is dramatic. It can start off particularly so (dramatic that is), for just ahead of you along the sea wall and through the largest and thickest of rhododendrons lies Glen Mallan jetty.

This very remote pier sits silently isolated a lot of the time, but on occasions there can be seen berthed there the battleship grey lines of the Royal Navy's front line ships and supply vessels. These are here to get rearmed from the arms' dumps sitting high up in Glen Douglas, and can include aircraft carriers which have to be able to turn round in less than half a mile's width, as the Long stays uniformly at that breadth all the way to

the end. This is approximately 6 miles away when it gets to Arrochar, and those 6 miles are of identical character to what surrounds you at Glen Mallan. A continuous ride with a real feeling of isolation is about to begin, on a road that is surprisingly rarely flat for being a lochside one.

You will find it undulates, only slightly but enough to be quite testing, for almost its entire length to the top. All the way, you and the loch will be hemmed in by steep wooded sides on both banks, and the sensation and scale of the ride never diminishes for its entire length. What more could any bike rider ask for? Just a better road surface, is about all, as it isn't that good around Glen Mallan and beyond. But 'Hey Presto!' Suddenly that all changes when you trundle onto newly-laid tar, after which you glide your way up to the junction with the Glen Douglas road. Here the smooth stuff stops abruptly. This will have been laid, I bet, to assist all the white vans that make their way up into Glen Douglas to work on the seemingly constant construction of more defence installations and arms' dumps.

This tarmac laying is nothing compared to the private military road that leaves the lochside at Glen Mallan jetty itself and makes its way up into Douglas, sort of joining the public road at the top. At the start of this

The tip of Rosneath peninsula is seen as the fly round and past Rhu marina is made (anti); this sheltered cove oozes charm and tranquillity aplenty, and is therefore a delight to ride round. It is small and cute, and you're round it in no time before making the climb up and over to Shandon and the Gareloch.

road, a sign says 'Police: road closed', or something of that ilk. However, I once rode up it to see where it went and I assure you I have never seen a road in my life that was built to that spec. The standard far exceeded any public road I've ever been on, what with the quality of the tarmac and numerous numbered passing places. This is the very road they use to bring down the goodies from the glen to the ship. When the boys in Whitehall want something done, they're not long in finding the money.

The public road presents another run within a run, for taking the road over Glen Douglas is a great loop in itself. It means a run of about the 68-mile mark for me, and I thoroughly recommend you do it sometime. From Loch Long, it is a long brutal hairpin bend of a start as you force, and I do mean force, your way up through the conifers. This is very tough, but once up there, a wild rough glen will be all yours to enjoy, again on good tar, once the near-sided MOD area has been passed. Only two hill farms occupy this barren high glen, where the steep and at times ravine-like hillsides make for an enthralling passage between the two massive lochs at either end.

That's for another day. For this run, we're back on the A-814 continuing to follow the crash barrier, much as before, and now that we are going along much the same way, I want to relay a rather macabre story to you about one of our most infamous sons – Ian Brady, the Moors murderer. Brady once holidayed here, staying in Arrochar. He claims that he met and befriended a German tourist, who was on his own and staying at the nearby Tarbet Hotel. Brady claims they went down the secluded Loch Long road and that he murdered the tourist there, and hid his body near the road in a shallow grave. He actually told detectives this when they were interviewing him years after he had been imprisoned.

If you are doing the Dunoon run anticlockwise, then there are three shorter run options available to you and all are great looping runs in their own right. The first is the A-817, which runs from the roundabout that sits on the newer road, the A-814, high above Faslane naval base and runs over to the A-82 at the Loch Lomond Golf Club. This road was built to service the nuclear warheads and so is modern and brutal in appearance, but is still a great road to ride. The photo shows what's ahead when you are heading over to Faslane from the Loch Lomond side.

Was he telling the truth? Detectives could find no trace of any missing German tourist from the time, not from the hotel records or from Germany, but this was a long time after the event. Most likely, he was playing games, bearing in mind he never helped with the location of any of the Moors victims, most noticeably wee Keith Bennett. One thing is possible, however, and that is that anyone who was buried on this rarely touched roadside could still remain undiscovered to this day. I'm convinced of that.

And so, with a shudder down our spine, we roll on towards Arrochar. As we approach it, the crash barrier gives way to brilliantly covered walls of moss and fern that indicate just how wet it gets here most of the time. They are as green as the grass in places, and what a damp delight they are.

Shortly, out of the dampness you emerge and onto the shore road of the village itself. Ahead, the whiteness of the hotels and stores are seen sitting behind the early greyness of the houses. The steep but rounded Cruach Tairbet holds court above the village this side, but the Cobbler and Ben Narnain dominate the far shore. Sitting distinctly below them is the white, striking, massive Ardgarten Hotel, so large that it is easily seen even from the east shore. The black and white traditional-looking village inn is passed, along with several stores and the modern community hall, all the time following the solid and curving grey sea wall up to where the 814 meets the A-83, which is the road you would come in on if you travelled via Loch Lomond.

The stillness of the shoreline at this point is in marked contrast to the busy main artery that we are about to join. It has to be said that the Helensburgh road does have the advantage of being quieter than its counterpart, but that doesn't mean that the A-82, for the most part, isn't an enjoyable ride. Far from it. It is the easier, slightly shorter option, and once into a rhythm on it, you can fairly motor along. To take that way, we have to return to Dumbarton and, as I stated before, going straight up the A-82 from Milton would be the fastest and most direct route of all, but is not recommended.

Even round about Dumbarton, where there is a 40 mph speed limit, it is still too busy and dodgy on the A-82 for my liking, though I see plenty of other guys ride it. Once you get onto the open stretch between the Vale of Leven

Dropping down rather steeply onto the side of Loch Lomond on the A-817 when coming from Faslane, it's only when you are making the final approach to the A-82, that sits just about 5 metres above sea level, that you realise just how high this road sits itself. It is a much steeper and more dramatic fall down than you would imagine. It is also very picturesque at this point, with Loch Lomond's islands providing the pleasant backdrop.

and the bottom of the Loch Lomond road, which starts at the Dunglass roundabout, it gets seriously hairy. I've only done that stretch a couple of times myself, and don't fancy it again, to be honest. My preferred option is to ride into Dumbarton and cut across the Vale of Leven into Renton and Alexandria on the A-812. This is simple, flat, and straightforward. It merely entails following the main A-814 through Dumbarton till it crosses the River Leven and, after passing Dalreoch station, taking the first right.

This will take you, rather rurally and leafy at first, along the west side of the vale, passing the large farm of Dalmoak, which with modern encroachment looks a

little bit out of place nowadays. After this, passing under the A-82 flyover takes you into the streets of 'The Renton', whose place sign proudly tells you it was the birth place of one Tobias Smollet. A highly successful writer, whose poetry was said to be sweet, delicate, and murmurs like a stream, it was his adventure book of Roderick Random, followed by another about Peregrine Pickle that made him famous. He actually influenced Charles Dickens, amongst others, and was very highly regarded by the writing establishment. Satire was another of his fortes and I assume (though I could be wrong) it was this genre which landed him a short jail sentence for libel. I am impressed.

The town was actually named after his daughter-in-law Cecilia Renton, it formerly being known as Dalquhurn. As you ride along its lengthy main road, it has come a long way from the very shabby and neglected appearance which it once possessed. The first time I ever entered the place was in the late 70s, through a gap in a fence, after scrambling down an embankment and running across a field to call the AA, when the old Mark II Cortina I was travelling in chucked it on the A-82 just at Renton. When I emerged from the fence, I immediately thought 'Ruddy Nora', or words to that effect. And this was from a Paisley housing scheme boy who knew bugger-all else at the time. It really was that bad.

But nowadays, thanks to some great work by the local Cordale Housing Association, things have improved markedly and not only on the housing front. Another trait which the village has to its credit is its strong community spirit, inspiring various characters over the years, including James Kelly, the first Celtic FC Captain; John O'Hare, who played under the great Brian Clough

The aircraft carrier HMS Invincible sits berthed at Glen Mallon jetty, Loch Long, most likely awaiting rearmament as we trundle up past on the A-814 (anti). It can be a very misty, atmospheric, and dramatic-looking road to ride up, and one that will carry you in similar vein all the way into Arrochar Village. This way is definitely the quieter option, as opposed to the A-82, but it is 3 miles longer and a fair wee bit tougher.

at Nottingham Forest, and numerous others. It is also known to be fiercely left wing, which is no bad thing.

So, buoyantly and speedily we charge along the Renton Road which has at this point become a B-road. It is still the town's main road, though, and comprises some decent modern housing. Things start to open up a bit as you near Alexandria, and the Kilpatrick Hills show well above the sprawling grey schemes on their lower slopes that make up Bonhill, particularly as you pass the Vale of Leven Academy.

When the time comes, it's better to take the sign that says town centre (left), as this is shorter, flatter, and gets us to where we want to go a lot easier than going straight on. It takes us in among the very bright red houses that seem to adorn a lot of this town. The very centre itself is small, whiter, and of tough appearance. Beyond this is a set of lights at a grand-looking junction, complete with a large ornate fountain which hasn't worked in donkey's years — as any local will be proud to tell you.

When I'm coming the other way on the Dunoon run, I will turn left here and return over the Bonhill Bridge, follow the Stirling Rd (A-813) to the roundabouts on the A-82, and re-enter Dumbarton at the top of the Bonhill Road. This runs you down to the large central roundabout in Dumbarton town centre itself, and of course this route can also be used when heading north, but I prefer the way I've described through Renton, as it's less hilly and therefore easier.

Where was I? Oh yes, the fountain lights in Alexandria. Now here we go again, because we're soon leaving this slightly ramshackle working class town to enter the semis and gardens of Balloch. So again we're swapping working class for middle, only this time there's not a bit of greenbelt to be seen. But not before we pass the rather strange and ornate-looking front of what they call the Loch Lomond Galleries. Now a shopping outlet, it was — believe it or not it — a former car plant. A very grand sandstone structure stands on the right and looks more like the front of a stately home, but was actually built by the Argyll Motor Company in 1905 and was the largest car works in the world. It certainly trumps Chrysler for front.

Continue straight ahead to the next roundabout, where there is a minor choice to be made. You can batter straight through to a second one, which proudly has a McDonald's beside it, to lead you onto the Old Luss Road. A couple of houses that should be sitting in the Home Counties let you know you're on the right road, and what a road it is. For this, if you haven't guessed already, was the original A-82 north and is a damn site more charming than anything else that replaced it. We have actually been on the course of the old main road for quite some time now, starting the minute we dropped of the Erskine Bridge and onto the A-814 in Old Kilpatrick.

Since then, the route we have followed was the course of the original main artery north till about 1935, when they diverted it through Bonhill. The bypass that is used nowadays came into being around '72/'73, and is

Not long after passing Glen Mallon jetty (anti), you come to the start of the Glen Douglas road and this is the second chance you have of making a shorter loop, albeit still a great day out. This road will carry you high and wild over to the Inverbeg Inn, but be warned that it is a very tough start from this side.

The wonderful but wicked start up into Glen Douglas from the Loch Long side, and get ready to dig in real deep once the switchback bends finish and the road then straightens and rises up like an untamed stallion. Once up, you'll find that this side of the glen is very heavily used by the Ministry of Defence; most of it is hidden, I might add, and the rest of the glen has a real rugged and wild look to it.

what we know now. But you don't have to use the Old Luss Road stretch from Balloch, for you can turn left at the first roundabout and climb up to the A-82 at the Stoneymollen roundabout and fire down past the Duck Bay Marina from there. It's just that the Old Luss girl is dead quiet and easier, though it does (being part of the official cycle route) run onto the pavement for a short stretch near the entrance to Cameron House, and this might not suit some die-hard roadies. But its moss-covered stone walls and wooded sides on the way there are much to my liking.

With that in mind, I will briefly mention that it is possible to reach this far and all the way up to Tarbet by using the cycle track alone. I wouldn't use it all the way myself, but some would, though it is especially useful and enjoyable going through the Vale of Leven. We joined it briefly at Bowling, remember, and it is simply a case of

following the sign posts into Dumbarton, where it gets a little bit weavy near the centre — too much for most roadies, I admit — but then it does cross the wonderful Bridge St Bridge, which is so ornate and pretty that it puts its nearby modern counterpart easily in the shade. On the other side, it gets seriously good, because now it actually follows the Leven's west bank all the way to Balloch station, where it's only a short hop onto the Old Luss Road.

As you meander round the river bank, it's common to see the boys in midstream using the double-handed salmon rods; quite a sight, and it takes some mastering. It is by far and away the most pleasant way to ride the vale, and that's why I mentioned it. Not one of the road options comes anywhere near the peace and tranquillity that the river bank affords, as it gracefully follows the bends and meanders of the Leven, which flows broadly

Heading towards Loch Long through Glen Douglas. Coming up from Loch Lomond is the easier start, and only two farmsteads are to be found up here so rough is the terrain. The road's good, though, and recommended.

and softly through the vale. Sometimes field-lined, other times touching the housing scheme's back and front doors, and when the sun is on the water, the warmth and quiet have a very calming effect. The pleasure is added to by the occasional passing of old walls and tunnels from yesteryear, which the tree-lined path meets on its way. A flotilla of small craft is met as you near the departure point at Balloch, where, alas, it's onto the road again.

So if you're still with me at this point, then take it easy, for that's just about all the ducking and diving over. It's a fairly straightforward shout all the way up to Tarbet now, with only two or three sections of the old road left to offer any deviation; none of them compulsory, of course. The first is on you straight away, because you can elect to stay on the main A-road or go round past the Duck Bay Marina, which gives a great view up the loch, before quickly rejoining the main road again. This view includes the mighty Ben Lomond (the Beacon Hill) sitting across the loch. So now we're at the start of the country's largest body of fresh water — an awesome loch by anyone's reckoning, and as stunning as they come.

It's especially so when seen from 'yon bonnie braes' on Ben Lomond itself. 24 miles long and 5 miles wide at its broadest, the brute — containing about 12 sizeable islands of various shapes and sizes — won't disappoint on the scenic or dramatic fronts. It simply packs too much of a punch, to be honest. Even if you decide to stick to the modern roadside all the way up, it will still prove to be a great ride, and one you can really get in the flow with. It does start a bit fast and tight till the far entrance to the

Arrochar is finally reached, and the head of Loch Long, too, which is made very dramatic by the fact that the high Arrochar Alps overlook it from the other bank. Here we are looking back down Loch Long, which is one approach route (anti), but we can also reach here by coming via Loch Lomond. You can, of course, ride up to Arrochar by either of those two routes and then return by the other, which would give you the third and last big looping run, short of doing the whole run itself.

Heading up the A-82 Loch Lomond road (anti), and although it is busier and noisier than its Loch Long rival, it is easier and faster to batter along and allows great views across the mighty Loch Lomond once Luss is passed. There is a cycle lane that runs the length of the road right up to Tarbet, but it's slow and meandering, and most roadies will just sit inside the white line on the edge of the road.

Duck Bay stretch is passed, but then it is possible to sit inside the white line, as it is for most of the way, and it feels a fair bit safer when you do.

So amble up to the big Arden roundabout that allows access to the top end of Helensburgh, and the sheer volume of open leafy greenness is nigh-on overwhelming. By now you'll be getting the feel of it, so it's head down, for a fair old shift is coming your way. It's a long straight of time trial proportions that greets you next, where the soon-to-be-reached long slight downslope start is what the doctor ordered to get you moving. Putting in an appearance ahead is the first of the Luss Hills —

A snow-clad Ben Lomond shows well from the A-82 when heading north (anticlockwise). Although the A-82 doesn't quite match the A-814 for drama, it isn't void of good views, either.

Creachan Hill — which starts to make it feel a wee bit more Highland, as the boundary between Highlands and Lowlands is about to be crossed.

After about a mile ahead, you will notice on the right some massive grey gates, now closed, which were once the front door to Rossdhu House, home to Sir Ivor Colquhoun of Luss. This land you are on now was the old stronghold of the Clan Colquhoun, who I believe actually used Dumbarton Castle for a long time. It was actually down to the influential Sir Ivor that the west bank of

It's time to get in a rhythm now as the pull up to the top of the Rest and Be Thankful begins in earnest. It isn't overly steep, but it is long; very long. Once the old rhythm is found, then simply stick to it and that's the best way to tackle it. The superb mountain views on the way up take your mind off the workload.

Loch Lomond has remained so underdeveloped. This, I was told, extended to the building of the new road which came into being in the early 90s. The upgrade of the A-82 from Arden to Tarbet should have taken place way before then, but was always blocked by Sir Ivor, who didn't want his pretty lochside spoiled.

Had the land been owned by anyone else, it would probably have been a compulsory purchase order and end

Looking back down Glen Croe and the A-83 from the top of the Rest and Be Thankful, and a fine view it makes. Please note the old road running below, which has now been upgraded so that it can be used in the event of a landslide closing the main road. It is possible to ride it, but involves climbing over several locked gates. For that reason alone, I don't recommend it.

of story. But not in the case of Sir Ivor, who was not to be pushed around. He was also instrumental in bringing about the top-drawer Loch Lomond Golf Club to the area, which sits just behind the gates; in fact, Rossdhu itself is now the course's ostentatious clubhouse. The course is a Tom Weiskopf design.

The gate is topped by a striking coat of arms, which I assume belongs to the Colquhouns and is inscribed *Cnoc Clachan*. Just further beyond the gates, about a mile or so on the left, is the start of the A-817 taking you over to Whistlefield and Faslane, which is one tough road if you decide on another day to take it. We continue on our way up, though, bending round and passing the golf course itself now, which hides the loch from our view.

In fact, we have been away from the water's edge right from the word go, unless you skirted round past the Duck Bay. We have actually been quite a distance from the shoreline, which will continue for a bit yet,

unless you decide to take the section of old road that is approaching, as next up appears the cut-off for Luss. Now it's fine if you take it, and it's fine if you don't. It's more direct and faster to stay on the new road, though this does involve a bit of a dip and up, as you cross the Luss Water. You're not off the beaten track for long, if you do take the Luss road, so the amount of time lost isn't crucial for the payback of the scenery and tranquillity that goes along with this stretch.

The woods and moss walls are all to be expected, but shortly the loch plays a trump card in the setting you ride through, when the picturesque houses of Aldochlay are passed. They look like a short row of Victorian railway cottages, whose gardens naturally take pride of place. As sweet as they are, the real star of the show will be the steep-sided striking Inchtavannach Island sitting just offshore, whose wooded slopes yield not an inch to fertility. Its twin-humped silhouette is seemingly almost touchable from the shore, and the small moored craft and buoys sitting still and safe between the two are the icing on the cake.

Just for the record, before reaching Aldochlay, there is a bay that contains a statue, actually in the water, of a small boy. Rumour has it that this was put there to mark the spot where a small boy drowned, but that is untrue. It was put there for no reason by someone who, in my view, had more money than sense.

The Welcome to Luss sign is soon reached, where the combination of more pretty stone cottages, overhanging tree branches, and the backdrop of the Luss Hills, makes a most fitting entrance, but you're not quite there yet. For ahead is a straight walled section of flat road.

Now, the young team, please take note: before the modern road was opened, this was one of the few places on the old road where you had any chance of overtaking. Take it from me, it was a long haul being stuck behind a caravan all the way from Arden to the Drovers Inn 24 miles or so up the loch in the old days. Luss itself was best known for playing host to the soap opera, *High Road*, that ran for quite a few years, unfortunately. You don't actually go through the village itself, merely skirting the edge and passing the magnificent white Loch Lomond Arms Hotel, for years known as the Colquhoun Arms. A great wee snack bar and big modern cludgie are at your disposal here. Use as required.

Out the other end and back onto the modern road, where the lochside is finally reached at last, then it's a head down and charge job. Ahead is a massive straight open section taking you all the way up past the Inverbeg Inn and beyond. And it must be said that if you do decide to stay on it, the modern road isn't that bad to this point, either, especially the way that Beinn Dubh appears when you take the first big left hand sweeper after the Luss cut-off, and then Ben Lomond rears up as you start the drop down to Luss Water. Here also, the white farmsteads in the vicinity of Auchengavin add the old charm. Up ahead, the sheer scale of the loch becomes apparent as its monster proportions make up your entire right flank as you go.

Fast, flat, and friendly is the tarmac here, as cars, trucks, and buses fly close by. But at no time do I ever feel threatened, as the use of the unofficial white line cycle lane provides enough space for a comfort zone. The real lane is situated on the other side of the crash barrier, on the other side of the road; by all means, use it if you want. The steep conifer-clad hillside slopes down to the water's edge on this side, with Ben Lomond still holding court on the far bank, as it will for a while yet.

Ploughing on, I've got exactly 30 miles on the clock as I pass the Inverbeg Inn at the start of the Glen Douglas road, which although it has a short steep start at this end, isn't as sustained or brutal as its Loch Long end. Either way, it's some bloody glen and don't forget to do it sometime soon. You won't be disappointed.

A view of the Rest and Be Thankful from high up on Beinn an Lochain, which is the striking big mountain that overlooks the Rest. I took this photo on one of my hillwalking trips, and include it just to show how the road network approaches the Rest. You can see the main road coming from the south actually approaches higher than the pass, and in fact has to drop down to reach it. You can also see the old road, which was a military road, running below it. Please also note the B-828 coming in from the lower right hand side, which we shall also use when coming from Lochfyneside.

Just about to pass Loch Restil (anti) on the A-83, before dropping down long, fast, and curving into Glen Kinglass. You are just about at the halfway point of the run now, and will find that in your early cycling days — before you build up the strength and stamina — you won't be the same man/woman after the climb up the Rest that you were before it. It does take a fair bit out of you.

After Inverbeg, the road will soon dramatically swing right and up as it contours the bulging headland Rubha Mor, where the northbound traffic have two lanes for a short while. Forcing you out as it does, it brings the bulging Ben Lomond's Ptarmigan ridge much closer to you, which is the finest way to ascend it, in my opinion. The sheer effort to cut a way through the rock face to build the road is at its most evident here on the pull up, as getting round Rubha Mor could not have been easy. You swing north, and the Crainlarich and Arrochar Hills start to show. Down below you at this point is a fairly hidden section of the old road that acts as the official cycle track now, as it's totally closed off to vehicles by the inclusion of two or three gates positioned along its length.

Admittedly, the start of this section is easier to gain when coming the other way, for if you don't join it at Inverbeg on the way up, then you have to jump the crash barrier to get on it afterwards. The reason I mention it is because, for the older crew, it could be a bit of a trip down memory lane, as they wouldn't have driven it now for over 20 years; for the young team, it would be a bit of an eye-opener when they realise that this was the main road north not that long ago. No matter what age you are, you can't help but be amazed at just how quickly nature

A look south (going clockwise) at the A-83 as it passes Loch Restil. Ben Donich is the mountain beyond.

has reclaimed so much of the tar back, now that cars no longer come this way.

Both routes come together again before Stuckgowan, where the final run down into Tarbet begins. Views up the loch are snatched through the birch trees, as flat and long, under steep side, you approach. Enter the village by rising through the rhododendrons and then glide down to the major junction, beside which stands the Tarbet Hotel, grey and grand and castellated to boot.

So far so good, with more good to come, though now we technically leave the 82 for the A-83 to take us up and over the gentle rise towards Arrochar. This starts by not turning right, but going straight ahead and running up beside the hotel, which shows its size and age by the neverending continuation of its outhouses and buildings, before the road takes a dramatic sweep left and starts to climb. Nothing too terrible, I might add, where the classic-looking building of the Tarbet Tea Room looks you right in the eye here.

The rest of the village sits entirely on the right hand side, as the left is a wild glen of sinking fields that soon rear up onto the slopes of Ben Reoch, which magnificently towers above the glen. The distance over to Arrochar is not that great, as Tarbet actually means narrow strip of land between two bodies of water. In fact, both villages share the same rail station, which is also just on the right sitting in amongst Tarbet's collection of dwellings. This includes a line of solid grey stone houses and a kirk, sitting below conifer-clad and steep Cruach Tairbet. Slightly wooded and straight goes the A-83 here,

Climbing up to the top of the Rest and Be Thankful, this time from the Glen Kinglass side (clock). And as this side starts much higher than the Loch Long side, the pull up isn't nearly as long or sustained. It's just a wonderful scenic ascent that can be done at a nice tempo, as you're well warmed up from St Catherine's.

Heading south (clock) past Loch Restil, approaching the Rest and Be Thankful, and all the hard work is done for a while now, which is always good to know. Although the descent on the A-83 from the top of the Rest down to Loch Long isn't technical, it can get frighteningly fast unless you're a fearless descender.

as under the rail bridge and descending you begin, right down fast and flighty, all the way to the heart of Arrochar Village itself.

First, you pass the war memorial on the left, which offers the Church Road as an option if you're returning back down Loch Long; a good day out in itself. Going down Church Road is slightly shorter than doubling back when you get into the village, but it's no hardship to go via the village centre either. The final steep sweep down onto the coast is assisted by the dramatic appearance of the Cobbler rising above the far bank. It's here you will join the A-814 coming in from your left, and once again it's welcome to Arrochar. A busy narrow dash round and out of the place is usually what comes next, if you don't need to stop for a break. The chippy, general store, or even fruit shop will suffice for all and sundry.

Watch out for the numerous coaches supplying cannon fodder to the even more numerous hotels. Then it's a flying flat skirt round the loch head, giving a long dramatic look back down its length, before gaining the west side, where you're still right down beside the broad mudflats. The imposing south-east ridge of Beinn Narnain towers above you now, as ahead the road straightens, forced to do so as it has no choice. The Long Loch and the slopes of Ben Arthur allow no room for manoeuvre, as the road rises then falls long away, taking you back onto sea level, where the old torpedo testing station is now being demolished at the time of writing (March 13).

The boys used to test fire the unarmed torpedoes up the loch, where a boat would collect and return them for analysis. The complex contained everything they needed to run the show. The initial torpedoes they used had been made down on Battery Park, Gourock, in the old munitions factory.

Across the loch, Tullich Hill shows its lines and heights well, as do the other ridges cutting into the loch edges right down as far as the Finart fuel depot. This stretch of road is a flyer for both you and the vehicles, and admittedly it can be a bit intimidating the speed they

Swinging round into Glen Kinglass after firing down from the Rest and Be Thankful. As the road continues to tilt in your favour all the way to the Dunoon cut-off, expect to hit 40mph on this stretch easy.

get up to, but it's not too long till you swing up into Glen Croe and get off that fast lochside.

The downside is you leave behind the classic ridge riven looking Long, but even that is quickly forgotten, because now you enter into the heart of the high Arrochar Alps, and for the first time we are actually riding through Munro country. Not the clan, but the mountains. 3000 feet above, they tower, though not the two either side of us at this point; the Brack to the left and the Cobbler on the right both only make Corbett height. Still, they are craggy, steep, and impressive the pair of them, and they make you feel miniscule, as you trundle below them in awe. They are really sensationally steep and the whole setting now is alpine, especially so if the hills are still holding snow.

It's now where the climbing begins, as we are coming to the start of the pull up to the Rest and Be Thankful, which is the highest the road will get to on the entire run. It starts off with a small testing pull up over the Croe Water, which is delightfully walled and wooded.

Then as it's always been up until now, round the bend and onto the lower slopes of the climb in among the fir trees. Dig in and get into a rhythm for the long slog ahead. You may have noticed that I said 'up until now' there, because for the first time in a long time it appears we have been offered an alternative to the main route.

It just so happens that recently I got my hands on a book by an old cycle tourer called Harold Briercliffe. He did his riding back in the 50s, and it was interesting to hear him describe old roads and railway stations that have long disappeared. Up until I read his book, I'd always thought of the Rest and Be Thankful climb as quite an exciting challenge, but Harold did not. Compared to the old road, he described it as a' monotonous dour pull up'.

Due to recent landslides, which have continually closed the A-83 in Glen Croe and caused a long diversion for motorists, they decided to upgrade the old road that sits lower down on the valley floor and use it as a back-up in time of emergencies. Good idea. This now means that the opportunity presents itself to ride the road of yesteryear, finishing with the more bending and dramatic ending that old Harold so coveted. Or so I thought. I decided to try it out the first chance I got, where you join it on the left just after levelling out after crossing the Croe Water. At its start, there is a green sign saying Croe Forestry Commission or the likes. Now at first, it is great. There is

Heading up Glen Kinglass from the Dunoon road (clock), and mighty Ben Ime looks just so impressive. This is quite an arduous stretch, as it is long and sustained, followed by the final pull up to the top of the Rest itself.

Coming to the main junction on the B-828 (clock), where Gleann Beag meets Gleann Mor. We want to turn left to take us up to the Rest and Be Thankful, but it will involve a fairly tough wee climb on single track road to get there. Although it is a great alternative to using the main road coming this way, it is not only harder but maybe more important for such a long run, as it can knock you off your momentum and rhythm, it's probably best to stick to the main roads the first few times you do the Dunoon run, before trying Hell's Glen

continually climbs from the word go, the old one stays fairly low till near the final rear up.

All I can say is that old Harold must have liked his climbing and must have liked it tough. Very dramatically and Pyrenean-like, the road climbs, but there are no switchback bends at the beginning to take the sting out of the steepness that reaches 17 or 18%, though it's not too sustained at that level. The welcome high switchbacks make life a lot easier when you do reach them. Well, they would do if another locked gate wasn't barring the road. And, being without a style means it's a climb and lift over job. This is followed by another locked gate at the very top, which can be walked round, leading out to the earlier mentioned high perched snack bar, on top of the Rest itself.

What's my verdict? Well, quite simply the gates kill it. If they weren't there, it would be a serious option to the long pull up on the 83. As it is, I won't take it on again unless they are removed; the ones in the middle, that is. So for the time being I'm sticking to the 83 and, as I was saying right at the start, its rhythm and dig in time. It's not too steep the old rest road, going up about 6 to 8%, giving you the chance to purr up it at about 10 mph. But

no traffic on it normally, as it is guarded by a gate that is easy enough to go round, and you're on your own then.

Serenely along the side of the Croe Water it starts, then on up through the trees, looking up ahead at the shapely snow-covered Beinn Luibhean. After a slight rise in the road, a locked gate was met, shortly followed by another locked gate. Now admittedly, both had broad low styles next to them, but that isn't what I'd hoped for or expected. Anyway, being new, the tarmac was first class so I soldiered on. All the time the main road sat busily above, as in my valley solitude I made my way very straight and feeling tiny, to the foot of the climb. I guessed it would be steep as, unlike the modern road that

Approaching the Rest and Be Thankful on the single track coming up Gleann Mor (clock). If you want to use this route when going anticlockwise, bear in mind it will be signposted for Lochgoilhead when you reach the Rest. To be honest, you will be even happier to reach here coming up from Hell's Glen than you would normally, but I still like to take this road from time to time.

it's long, and I do mean long. So you know the drill on the long hills: no going from the gun; leave that till the last third.

The road's hillside position allows you good views down and across the valley floor of Glen Croe, as you make your way below the steep sloping hillside of Beinn Luibhean (Peak of the little plant), which is the one that is always subsiding and causing the problems.

The old crash barrier is reassuring on your left, as the drop is quite considerable. It's the high craggy outline of Beinn an Lochain that dominates the skyline as you finally approach the summit, and you realise

A great view of Loch Fyne from the start of the B-828, which can be gained after clearing the initial long pull up from Saint Catherine's on the A-815 (clock). You can, of course, continue on the A-815 till you reach the A-83 in Glen Kinglass, or by turning right onto the B-828 head down into Gleann Beag (Hell's Glen) and go that way.

that the Rest and Be Thankful was very aptly named. As the road actually goes higher than the bealach, then it is a small dip that comes before you finally pass the carpark at the top, which contains the snack bar. Behind this runs a single track road that will take you down to Lochgoilhead. Now the reason I mention this road is because it can also be used as an alternative to the main route, and is one I have taken many times before.

It involves a screaming deep dive down Gleann Mor (Big Glen, the B-828) into a place that is so sheltered it can provide some cool on a really scorching summer's day. The mountains simply tower above you on all sides as a quaint old railing is followed beside the wooded burnside, then a right turn is required to take you up the Hell's Glen or Gleann Beag road (Small Glen, the B-839). At first, the place is so peaceful and silent, as it holds very old deciduous woods and the pleasure factor goes off the scale here. But not for long. For higher up is where it gets sore, real sore, as the 20% gradient bites hard, though the smooth tarmac helps a bit. You actually climb well above the A-815 near the finish, before dropping down to it, at a point still high above mighty Loch Fyne.

Nearing the bottom of Gleann Beag (clock), and isn't it oh so wooded and pretty? Keep your eye open for flycatchers flying about. You can still find a cool spot down here even on the hottest of days.

A great view up Loch Fyne from Saint Catherine's (clock). If doing the run clockwise, I personally don't start doing any serious climbing till I reach here, with about 40 miles on my computer. However, it's a long hard pull up from here to the top of the Rest and Be Thankful.

The big plus of going that way is its quietness, and although it is slightly shorter, it's harder and you can lose your rhythm and momentum — something you have a lot of when sticking to the main route, to which I now return. From Loch Restil (at the Rest and Be Thankful), sitting right below the imposing face of Beinn an Lochain, you are now high in both height terms and feelings, having conquered the major climb of the day. To continue on the 83 is not a problem; anything but. Run along beside the stunning little lochan, taking in the surroundings all coming at you so quickly, as pumped up ye be. You're actually riding the Bealach an easain duibh. You know that you've got a great height advantage, some of which is just about to be cashed in pronto, as the road starts to dip down into Glen Kinglas. Ridges are running in from all directions as you negotiate this high mountain pass.

Beinn an Lochain's northeast and the semi-distant Binnein an Fhidhleir's northeast ridges, are the two majors facing you. You hurtle down past the first one, heading for the foot of the second, in no uncertain terms. *Magnifico* is the only word in Spanish I know to describe it (but that's only because I don't speak any Spanish). What a charge down it is, plummeting fearlessly down and round the long sweeping left hander that opens up the west to your gaze, right down the full length of the long, bolt-straight Glen Kinglas. Almost V in shape the Kinglas and as classic as they come, as the north and south facing slopes run up toward the summits of the two previously named mountains, and the old military road with its aged bridge runs parallel with you on the left.

Although it's flat at first, it soon starts to drop, and if a breeze is behind, expect to reach speeds of 40 mph, even if you are on your Jack Jones[4]. In fact, it might take a bit

4 - Jack Jones is rhyming slang for being on your own. It usually requires more than one rider to hit speeds of 40

of stopping when you do finally reach the cut-off to take you south to Dunoon.

You're back on the old A-815 again, and who's complaining? The black and white bending crash barrier welcomes you in, and a downhill straight gets you off to a flyer; just as well, for there soon begins a long lengthy haul up through the trees to take you high above the Fyne, where you emerge at the Tinker's Heart, after about a mile or so of pulling up. This is a spot in a field where the gypsies and others would come from time in memorial to get wed. It doesn't look much, I must say, despite the fact that it has just been restored a bit.

Across from the Tinker's is the B-road that will take you up, then down, then up again to above the Rest and Be Thankful. In fact, it is a much more useful alternative from this end, though just as tough. It's good to try it after a while, but probably best to stick to the main road at first, just till the old stamina gets up to scratch.

The white walls of the Inveraray buildings can be seen

mph, but it can be done solo on this stretch.

A fantastic view right down Loch Fyne from Strachur (anti). It is a mighty mesmerising big sea loch at times (the country's largest), but now we're just about to swap it for the freshwater of Loch Eck.

Coming down the side of Loch Eck on the great A-815, and you won't find a better bit of road to ride on just about anywhere. I said it many times in the text and I meant it: you will never tire of riding the Loch Eck road. The slender, elegant lines of both loch and road will keep you flowing and flying all the way down, and it's over all too soon.

even from this far away, sitting on the far bank of the broad Fyne, whose gentler hills lack the drama of the Long. Still, she is a magnificent sight, with Strone Point jutting into the loch hiding little Loch Shira behind it.

I've got round about 50 miles on the old clock at this point, and the road sign ahead says its 25 miles to Dunoon. Now, if this is a hot summer's day, then you will be sitting high in the full blaze of the old currant bun[5] and might feel in need of a cool down. Well, don't let that worry you, for you are about to get some assistance in that department from a descent of exceptional quality and length. From here you will follow the road down, being entertained as you go, swooping like a hawk to the shore of the Fyne, and not levelling out till the Saint Catherine's sign is met. Phew! 'That was the business', no doubt you'll be saying.

Then it's back beside the big boy once again, only this time we are much further up the loch than Otter Ferry and won't be taking that road today. There's not a lot to St Kate's itself, especially now that the hotel sits semi-derelict. And as it kind of fronts the place, then it gives it a bit of a shabby look, sitting right across from the jetty as it does, where you often see guys fishing. The jetty may have been the spot that serviced the old ferry which ran from here to Inveraray, and which was the preferred option of the Campbell high heid yins, the Dukes of Argyll, to get to the Lowlands. In fact, a traveller's inn was here from as early as 1460, though I don't know if the

5 - Currant bun is rhyming slang for the sun.

Another look down the dramatic Eck, when heading south. When it's misty and damp, I think it's probably at its best.

present day hotel is on the same spot. It didn't seem that long ago that the hotel was doing well and looking good. It's a bonnie, solid, traditional-looking building, and I hope it will get restored to good working order soon.

When you leave, you are entering a great stretch of road from here down to Strachur that sits on the loch all the way, curving, rising and falling gently, or on occasion gliding straight. If you're fit enough and still have a lot left in the tank, then this is one of those bits of road that you don't want to end, no matter how far from home you are.

You know you are nearing the village when the shapely rounded top of An Carr is seen beyond the Scots pines that stand by the roadside; this comes after several similar miles of being guided along by the birch trees that hide the broad Fyne from your view.

The rises make your heart start jumpin',
The downs they find your pedals pumpin',
The straights they find you flying past,
These few short miles have gone too fast.

It's swerve and then straighten up beside the loch. Right down on the shingle shoreline now, and the view down the broad one, with the marker buoys in waiting, further reinforces its bulk. The view is so mesmerising that it's rare you ever notice the massive big stately home that sits through the trees on your left. The bay curves right, running away from you south westward, completely in concert with An Carr's southwest ridge running above. Find yourself slowing down to take it all in? Join the club. It's a common pastime of mine.

Now comes a small fly in the ointment, which starts as the road bends left to take you off the Fyne and over to Glen Branter. This short steep climb was enough in the old days to force men who were participating in the 'World Famous Tour' to get out of the carriage and walk up the brae, before reboarding to continue on their way to Loch Eck.

Don't forget that the filling station standing on the left does have a good coffee machine, should you fancy one at this fairly late stage in the run. If not, continue over the rise, which will peck you out a bit, and then glide into the Branter. From the word go, the wild high craggy peaks above the Eck catch your eye, even though they are still a few miles down the glen yet.

You start to make headway through the sheep fields and firs, and the anticipation is mounting as you know the start of the slender and sensational Loch Eck is nearing. It's one of my favourite stretches of road, as I've told you before. And with that knowledge, I'd like to quote Glen Branter's former famous Laird, Sir Harry Lauder, who would sum the place up in three words, 'Ter-rif-ic'. Terrific indeed, for soon we're into the ferns and woods that shortly lead us onto the waters of the Eck. You know you're there when you pass an old tin roof rusty shack, and then the 7 miles of pleasure begins. For the last time, let me just say, 'You'll never tire of riding the Eck.'

This is the first time we have ridden its full length southwards, and it's as stunning as it is rugged. The crags of Beinn Bheag and then Clach Bheinn give the far bank a wild and Highland look, one most fitting, as round the early bends you guide your machine. You're going to roll and joust with all the wondrous wild that the water's edge can throw at you for the next few miles. So settle in and enjoy the ridges and ravines that accompany you on the way down. When heading in a southerly direction, it's the imposing bulk of Clach Bheinn that dominates the scene. And I think it's an even more picturesque loch when going this way.

Passing those big impressive Yankee fir trees at the start of Ben More Gardens. I usually stop just to admire them, regardless of which way I am going. Contrary to popular belief, they aren't giant redwoods but rather Douglas firs and giant sequoias.

Coming round the Holy Loch, and all is bright and breezy after just leaving the Western ferry (clock). From here, it's obvious a good day is in progress, and we're off with a lot of optimism, knowing the beauty that lies ahead and that a warm dry day awaits us.

Looking back at Dunoon pier after boarding the great wee Argyll ferry (anti), and — despite its age — it still looks resplendent in the afternoon sun. Time now to settle down with a coffee and get a well-earned breather.

The short departure from the lochside soon comes when we pass the old Whistlefield Inn, and then glide back onto the water. I've described the Eck in detail on some of our previous runs, so I won't go overboard on this one. Suffice to say, the tree-lined bends will always be to your liking and will never disappoint at any time of year or weather conditions. In my opinion, only when you've ridden the Eck in damp conditions will you really get the feel of this misty magical place.

So down we go, through more rocks, bends, ridges and the like, passing the Coylet Inn, chicken coop and all, then finally clearing the loch. The rise and dip are taken before the big firs in the Ben More Gardens are passed, and then it's into Glen Eachaig and on towards Dunoon. Still in the trees at first, then the glen opens up into the sheep fields as it crosses the River Eachaig, before swinging left

Passing a bright-looking Cloch Lighthouse, heading for Gourock, and all's well with the world as there is still a wee bit more rest time up our sleeve till docking. You really appreciate the ferry crossing more when going anticlockwise, as you are still quite fresh when going the other way.

and passing the entrance to Glen Masson, and then the outlying houses of Sandbank are entered.

The Holy Loch's flat width always makes a welcome sight, and shortly is reached the sanctuary of a break on the old ferry, which is most welcome with 75 miles on the ticker. To get to it, though, we've still got a little bit to go, and across the Clyde now, Gourock and Greenock can be seen.

A store is passed on the right, just before the left turn to Hunter's Quay is reached, and don't forget that cheap ferry tickets can be purchased here to save you a few quid in the short and especially long term. As I've stated before, if you plan to ride a lot on this side of the water, then get a 10 ticket job for either the Argyll or Western Ferries, or better still both. There's no time limit on either one, so they will both do for many a long year. You can batter straight in on the A-885 and go for the Argyll girl direct, or turn left and take your chances with the Western first on the old A-815. I always hug the lochside, as it's the prettier option and gives me two bites at the cherry.

If there is no red devil sitting handy at Hunter's to take me across, then I'll soldier on to Dunoon pier for the bluebell. Remember, it leaves this side every 30 minutes, except in the quiet afternoon period.

Going round the curves of the Holy Loch always gets you fired up, as you put on a little spurt not wanting to be beaten by seconds for a boat. Swerve and curve, swerve

Passing the Western ferry on a mist-covered lower Clyde.

Approaching MacInroy's Point, having crossed over on the Western ferry this time, and it looks great in the mist. It means, of course, it's time to mount the old trusted steed again and to make the long way back home, wherever that may be for you.

and curve, round this point and that bay, one of them being the curiously named Lazaretto Point. I thought that this had to have an Italian connection, but apparently not directly.

It seems there was a quarantine station built on this site in 1807 to prevent any disease arriving along with the imported bales of hay. The name stems from this place, as *lazaretto* is of Italian origin and indicates a hospital, catering mostly for lepers, with the name *lazaretto* most likely coming from Lazarus, the patron saint of lepers.

Armed with that useless bit of information, you will hopefully be boarding the old Western, where it might be possible to grab a coffee in the wee Coffee Ahoy shop across the road. If you get the chance, it's always good to do it as this tub has no refreshments on board, remember, unlike its Dunoon-based counterpart which does. It can be a real bonus to get some grub and caffeine into you for the last leg of the journey, which will be 23 miles for me, with the big pull up out of Inverclyde still to come.

You really appreciate the rest when coming this way as, for me at least, it's been a non-stop 75-mile ride so far, in sometimes tough conditions, and that makes the warm saloon of the ferry even more appreciated. That, of course, can make getting off it even more daunting, but sure as hell that time will come, and when it does it's chucking out time again.

Not to worry, you're quickly purring along the pretty old front of Gourock, which gets you back in the swing of things. Now if the worst comes to the worst, you have the option of jumping on the train here, should you need it. You may be canned, or the weather's turned real nasty, or mechanical problems arise, or some bloody thing. In fact, it is one of the advantages when doing the Dunoon run anticlockwise that a bit of support appears at this point, and it's no disgrace to use it. Most guys have had to jump on it at one time or another, so feel free if you need to.

However, all being well, you should still be able to motor on into Greenock on the old A-770. In previous runs I've covered my return home from Gourock in a fair amount of detail, so don't want to bore the drawers of anyone who has read each run from the start in sequence. However, if you've jumped to the Dunoon run because you want to have a go right away at this old classic, then briefly your main options to return to the Paisley area are either via the A-8 right along to the bottom of the Clune Brae, which is climbed, before returning through Kilmacolm and Bridge of Weir by either road (the A-761) or cycle track. Or you can climb out of Greenock by cutting off the A-8 at the fire station and ascending out of the town on the Kilmacolm/ Auchmountain Rd (the B-788) and taking one of a number of options to reach the same destination[6].

Bear in mind that before attempting such long runs, most local riders will have become familiar with the quieter back roads in their area. Then when the time comes to tackle a long job, most will have a preferred route of hopefully quiet return. As I have outlined in the last few runs, and also generally speaking, main road riding is usually faster and easier than using the unclassified or B-roads, and this is the case when returning from Inverclyde. So you will find that coming back via the Clune Brae isn't as taxing, say, as returning via the Auchmountain and then Quarriers, especially if you finish by the tough Kilbarchan, Elderslie route.

However, coming home the hard way gives a real sense of satisfaction, and especially so for me when purring along Foxbar Rd with all the climbing over. Now, if that doesn't boost your morale...

Till the next time.

Liam Boy

---

6 - Bridge of Weir, that is.

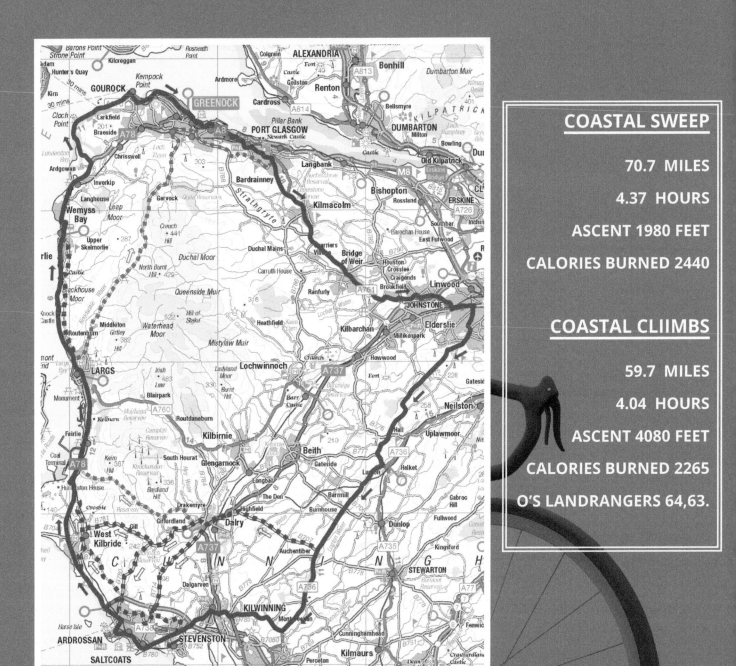

COASTAL SWEEP

70.7 MILES

4.37 HOURS

ASCENT 1980 FEET

CALORIES BURNED 2440

COASTAL CLIIMBS

59.7 MILES

4.04 HOURS

ASCENT 4080 FEET

CALORIES BURNED 2265

O'S LANDRANGERS 64,63.

ROUTE SUMMARY

COASTAL SWEEP & HIGHER RD ROUTE

Gleniffer Rd B-775
Lugton
Auchentiber A-736
Torranyard A-736
Benslie
Kilwinning

Stevenston
Saltcoats
Ardrossan
Seamill
Fairlie
Largs
Skelmorlie

Wemyss Bay
Gourock
Greenock

Port Glasgow
Dubbs Rd

Whitehurst Park Rd &
Meadow Park Rd
Kerelaw Rd & Middlepart
Burns Ave
Stanley Rd
Ardrossan High Rd

Routenburn Rd
Skelmorlie Castle Rd
& Long Hill

COASTAL CLIMBS ROUTE

Gleniffer Rd
Lugton
Auchentiber
Dalry Via B-707
Fairlie Moor Rd
A-78

Fairlie
Largs
Douglas St &
Brisbane Glen Rd
& Old Largs Rd

Greenock
Auchmountain Rd

Port Glasgow
Dougliehill Rd

ALL ROUTES RETURN

Port Glasgow
Auchenbothie Rd

Kilmacolm/Cycle Track
Bridge Of Weir
Paisley

All roads named in the higher road route are adjacent to their relevant town names in the left hand column

THE CLYDE COAST

DOON THE WATTER

We've covered a fair bit of ground on the old bike so far, from as far south as Girvan to the Erskine Bridge, which has all been held together by the solid broad thread of the magnificent River Clyde. Covering all these runs, in part at least, is the Clyde coast run itself. This comes in for me about the 50 to 70 miles mark, and therefore is short enough to be done on a short winter's day or long enough on a long summer's one. Numerous permutations are available for this outing and especially the amount of climbing that is involved. It can be adjusted to include three or four big climbs, should you be in the mood for some serious ascending. Alternatively, a long flat coastal jaunt is at your disposal to afford you views of the Clyde and its islands that you won't get on any other run.

For a lot of riders who are based around the Paisley area or beyond, this is a particularly personal bit of ground being covered, as it will most likely be the turf they cut their teeth on. Like most things in life, the first ones always hold a special place in your heart, and the cycling I do down and around the sea and moorlands of North Ayrshire and Inverclyde certainly have that aspect for me at least. Even after all these years of riding, I still enjoy my jaunts down among the villages and beaches of my home resort, as much as I did when I first started out.

A great sweeping arc can be made, starting with the Gleniffer Braes normally, and then continuing through Kilwinning and Ardrossan, all the way along to Port Glasgow, taking in the Cloch Road at Gourock, to make a most pleasant tour of the coast. I tend not to include Irvine in this run, as the A-78 is busy dual carriageway around the town, which must be ridden at some point and therefore I avoid it for that reason. Certainly, it is possible to ride down among the towns of Ayr, Troon, Loans, Barassie, and the like, but I tend to keep that a separate run, and I included the roads to and from them in the first run we covered down to Turnberry. If those

Starting out on the Clyde coast run (going clockwise) and climbing up the steepest part of the Gleniffer Braes on the B-775, which is just as it passes the start of the great Sergeantlaw Road. As it's a fairly long climb, it's best to sit for most of it if you can. Easier said than done on occasion, of course.

COASTAL SWEEP

So, for the first time in a long time, we're heading off up them thar braes, which means a puffin-stuff start. Never mind that, it's just good to be back on the old girl again, starting to feel the effort as the early tough bends are climbed, before the little bit of respite you get when the road briefly levels. With the warm up over, it's knuckle down time when onto the short steep section the wheels take you, between rock and wall, passing the Sergeantlaw Road and shortly the yellow/brown garish, never-finished hotel. This three-storey high, square block monstrosity should never have been built here, but somehow it was. Where

> Paisley high flats catch your eye
> Mist and birds above you fly
> Macdonald's well has now run dry
> Round higher bends you must still try

> At last the barren top is reached
> With fifteen minutes of digging deep
> The suffering was enough to weep
> But keep your counsel, don't you speak

Instead, smile warmly and be grateful that you have cleared the climb, and be even more grateful that you can actually do it. Many can't; don't forget that. It doesn't matter how fast you were, or how strong you felt, or how much extra weight you are carrying. Your health is your

more southerly towns are your destination, then the unclassified road over to them from Dundonald is a most spectacular approach, but only one of many.

Sitting above the coast road, in between Kilwinning and the Port, are two high moor roads that can be as tough to ride as they are atmospheric and barren. To add to the pleasure, there are some less well known roads which sit just slightly higher than the main A-78, and also provide great views along with the coveted quieter riding. Several roads cutting inland all along the coast make it possible to cut short or change the run as required, so you can make this one up as you go along.

As it happens, I will guide you round the coastal sweep in a clockwise direction, as that is the way I usually do it. I do, however, like to tackle the high moor road that passes Loch Thom in the opposite direction, as it gives a great long classic descent down into Largs. It's all good stuff, as usual, so read on for more high calibre road riding. You won't be disappointed.

The view you get descending the Gleniffer Braes when doing the Clyde coast run anticlockwise, and for me it makes for a fantastic fast finish. Ahead is the broad expanse of the Clyde Valley and the sensational spread of Glasgow, which makes for a most awesome sight after all the hours of greenery and numerous small settlements that have just been ridden through.

Firing on down through the Hall Farm crossroads heading for Lugton and the A-736 on the B-775 (clock). I urge you to exercise caution here, as cars emerging from the side roads may misjudge your speed. It's all part of the great fall down from the high point of the braes, however, and makes for a great start as you head out west.

wealth. Don't sweat the small stuff, as all that can be improved and adjusted later.

The slight dip passing the electric sub-station is a godsend, so make the most of it, then start the long straight purring section that takes you along in moorish garb towards the big left hand bend that signals the fairly gradual pull up to the far end of the Sergeantlaw Road. More fields of tussock line the way, as behind are left the evergreen sitkas.

After swinging equally hard right, it's 'Away the lads!', for soon the flying descent down through the aged buildings of Hall Farm will begin. To my surprise, they have tiled the roof of the old barn on the right, which has stood at the junction of the road to Howwood since God knows when. In fact, the Hall Farm crossroads is just steeped in old; simple as that. Again, as I've said before, how the edge of the house – that literally juts into the road – is still there, is absolutely beyond me. Perhaps the red paint trim round the windows' edge acts as a warning, on this now derelict whitewashed old relic.

A split second takes you through the place and then on, going strong, to the T-junction with the B-777. Turn left to Lugton. A swooping minute or two is all that is required to take you to the Canny Man public house. It's a bit of a pity they changed the name of this pub only fairly recently, because even maps as far back as 1895 called it by its old name, The Paraffin Lamp. This is one of several pubs that would need to be passed in bygone days by merchants, drovers, and travellers, as they returned on their way to Irvine from Glasgow along the A-736.

Each one of these pubs had a local name; the Paraffin's was the 'Lug Em Inn'. And at the Lug Em, turn right onto the Irvine Road, still known in places by its old name of the Lochlibo Road. It was constructed about 1827 to replace the older, more meandering, main road and was a tolled or turnpike road. This was one of two that ran out of Lugton, the other was the now A-735, which takes you to Dunlop. And the turnpikes were so called because of the way they looked and operated.

A very simple wooden barrier that looked like a pike (the weapon, not the fish), would swing or turn open after a toll had been paid, and that's how these roads got their name. Although a charge had to be paid to use them, they were a great improvement on what had gone before, and were also responsible for setting the actual length of the mile as we know it today. Previous to that, there had been quite a lot of deviation in the distance, with Scots miles, Irish miles, long miles, and short miles, all in existence. The tolls were finally scrapped in 1878.

And so off we go along the now fast A-road, one of my favourites in the whole area, I must admit. You don't see many old milestones in this neck of the woods, because they were removed during the Second World War so as not to aid Jerry, should he so happen to invade.

It's a fair old tootle along this western artery, which gives you access to the Clyde and its dwellings. You go flatly at first, getting into the groove for the several long gradual draw ups ahead. They're not slow in coming, with the first one appearing as you pass the duck egg-selling farm at Gree. Behind this sits the raised embankment and beautifully built bridges of the former Lugton to Ardrossan rail line. Though, unfortunately, the magnificent Gree Viaduct has now gone. It didn't have much of an innings, this one; it closed in 1934 after opening in only 1903, though it has to be said it was an impressive construction by the Lanarkshire and Ayrshire Railway Company.

The rise now being taken is very gradual, but does go on a fair wee bit. There's always another rise ahead, after the one you've just cleared, but eventually the road does reverse its angle and it's a nice long easy gradual glide

Now a tandoori restaurant, but at one time the famous Torranyard Inn, it's here that we take a right turn after coming down the hill ahead to take us to Benslie and then into Kilwinning on the Fergushill Road. We're off the fast A-roads at last, thank heaven.

Heading out on the A-736 Irvine Road just before Torranyard (clock), and the road is at its highest here. It means we haven't turned right at the Blair Inn and taken the B-778 down to Kilwinning, but instead have stayed on the 736 a little bit longer and will approach Kilwinning via Benslie by turning right at the old Torranyard Inn.

through the crossroads and buildings of Burnhouse. The road you actually cross here is the B-706, which is much older than the one you're on, and was the traditional route from Beith to Kilmarnock.

The village was locally known as the Trap, principally by farmers' wives. The place did indeed trap many a thirsty farmer on his way home from market, and had not one but two inns in which to snare them. They were the Waggoners and the Burnhouse Inn. The latter became known as the 'Trap Em Inn', from whence came the village nickname of the Trap. The flags on the modern day caravan sales site are a great help in determining exact wind strength and direction, which is always good to know. You pass it just as you leave.

Now you find yourself once more gliding the blanket green, as through the rough pastures you go, still gaining height very gradually. The fields gently roll away up to rounded soft ridges quite a distance away. Now, when I say the blanket green, that will depend on the day and time of year, of course. For if it is a cloud-covered, grey, cold, spring one, for example, the landscape here resembles the Somme Battlefield in places. In particular, the way that sparse barren trees and building silhouettes appear through the grey, as they stand out on the ridges themselves. All very eerie and atmospheric, I must say. My thoughts always turn to those poor lads who had to endure the barbed wire back then. And this is another of those moments in life when you feel glad for what you've got.

Long and straight goes the 736, before becoming a bit more interesting as it curves and climbs up to the houses and side roads at Auchentiber. Now, here today stands the Blair Tavern, but in the past this was the domain of the Cleikum Inn, known as the 'Cleek Em Inn'. I don't think it actually stood on the site of the Blair, as it is known nowadays, which itself was a former garage.

At Auchentiber, two roads run off to the right, the first being the rare B-707, taking you down to Dalry. This is a great approach route to that town, and is ideal for gaining the coast via the high Fairlie Moor Road and also three other important routes, which give access to Saltcoats, Ardrossan, and West Kilbride. It is not only a great cross country route, but also very quiet into the bargain, and one I really enjoy every time I take it.

DALRY VIA B-707: ALTERNATIVE ROUTE (COASTAL CLIMB START)

It begins with a long straight between the hedgerows; the silent contrast from the speeding A-road is very noticeable, before a pleasant curving rise takes you up past the solid-looking, red and white outbuilding at Sunnyside Farm. After this, it's into the forgotten lanes of yesteryear. I say that because, after making your way in a short distance, you hit the crossroads at Auchenmade, where you find a large white former farmhouse now used as a base by a vintage wedding car hire company. I'm no great motor man myself, but even I must say they have one or two most splendid antique vehicles in their line-up. Not that I will be requiring their services any day soon, I hope (with a bit of luck).

But despite this rural scene at present, that wasn't always the case here. There once stood a brickworks, be jabbers! Christ knows whereabouts, as there seems no sign of it now. It was served by the Lugton to Ardrossan rail line, which had a station here, and some old railway cottages seem to have survived. But today the hustle and bustle has long gone.

A left turn means a long quiet straight all the way to Kilwinning, and the road sign says right for Beith, but this whole area is a labyrinth of back roads which I often use to get home. A good O/S map helps with getting to know them all in the long run.

Dalry's our gal, however, so batter straight through and more of the same follows, with the slender tar finding more rough ground and rows of hawthorn, dipping down

Entering Kilwinning on the Fergushill Road (clock), and it is a great way to approach the town. It's a pleasant meander through the hedgerows from Benslie on the B-785, with the tower of Kilwinning Abbey acting as a beacon to guide you in.

as it goes over the Dusk Water, before pulling strongly up to the crest of the hill by Knollhead Farm. Well pumped up at this point, you fly down through the next wee crossroads that contains two isolated houses which appear to constitute Auchenmade Terrace (former farm workers' houses). Then more downhill riding shortly brings up the smattering of houses at Kerlochsmuir – nothing more than a row of white homes – which sits above and just outside Dalry. The next country road junction means you have joined up with the back road which we used when heading to and from Ardrossan for the Arran run.

Dalry rooftops show the way down, out of the semi-roughness and back roads, letting the now joined A-737 take you once again over the Garnock and into the town. It runs you up to the lights in the centre, with its brilliant battered old buildings, where you must turn left, still on the 737, and onto the Kilwinning Road. At the next set of lights, about 100 metres away, you are in pole position to choose between four great ways to the coast. All of that is still to come, and I will return to these routes all in good time. In the meantime, we are still on the main sweep of the Clyde run, so we shall return back up to Auchentiber.

This is a small hamlet that also contains the B-778, which runs you into Kilwinning, and was the one we took to reach Ardrossan on the Five Ferries run. This road I often take when doing the Clyde coast run, but as we have already covered it, I will on this occasion continue on down the Lochlibo Road as far as Torranyard. It's just under 2 miles up the road. It's here you will find the last of the inns on the old turnpike, and as it was the last the Torranyard Inn was known as the 'Turn Em Out'. I like the stretch of road that takes you to it, because of the way it climbs slightly through the rough and conifers before opening out broadly at the road's highest point. Then, after a couple of long bends, it drops delightfully down to the hamlet of Torranyard.

Irvine Bay and Arran show themselves well on the descent, and it puts you in the mood for what's to come. The large caravan park behind the inn, which is now a Tandoori restaurant, is booming again. Some charm is still attached to the small, white, slate-roofed former pub, which even today retains a feeling of isolation. Turn right across from the inn to take you down the bends to Benslie. Now, my parting shot about the old Lochlibo and its inns relates way back to the time of the body snatchers, who were meant to supply the medical

Kilwinning Abbey and its tower makes for a fine sight from quite a distance away. It only takes a short detour to visit it, and is well worth the effort. You will have seen it from afar as you approached on the Fergushill Road down from the Torranyard Inn.

profession with only corpses. This was before the Anatomy Act of 1832 put a stop to all that nonsense.

Rumour has it that numerous tramps went missing in this area, and it was strongly suspected that they had been murdered in and around the Torranyard and Cleikum Inns, and were sold on to the medics to save the body snatchers the trouble of digging up graves. When the Cleikum was finally knocked down, a number of old walking sticks were found among the ruins. So, could it be true? We'll never know for sure.

COASTAL SWEEP: KILWINNING VIA BENSLIE AND FERGUSHILL

Anyway, by now we're haring through the hedgerows and enjoying every minute of the twists and turns on this very quiet back road. It's a proper delightful ride, I must say, especially the way that it leads through the trees on its approach to the hamlet of Benslie itself.

Fergushill Kirk and spire is very prominent from afar, as Arran again shows it lofty peaks across the fields. Not much to the place, but a quaint wee junction shows the signpost saying right for Kilwinning. This is you running onto the Fergushill Road itself now (the B-785), and it's another pleasure to ride. It's flat going through the fields and near woodlands of this forgotten corner, coming along quietly between the hedgerows, skirting the edge of this old mining area as you do. The road bends brilliantly early doors, and then straightens as it brings you into Kilwinning. The prominent square-shaped tower of the old Kilwinning Abbey is a most fitting landmark, and would do any town proud.

Arran's peaks sit right behind it, so it guides you in a most stunningly splendid fashion, drawing you down the Fergushill, passing the shops and houses of this solid old scheme, as you make the long gentle descent to the busy junction with the A-737. Turn right, when you get a chance to, and this takes you over the River Garnock and into the town centre. But even before the river is reached, you almost immediately pass the B-778 coming in from the right. This is the way you would have come in had you turned right at Auchentiber.

KILWINNING VIA THE B-778: ALTERNATIVE ROUTE

We approached Kilwinning on this road when doing the Five Ferries and, as I stated earlier, it has been used by me on numerous occasions when doing the Clyde coast

and is in itself an excellent approach route. So just to refresh your memory, after turning right before the Blair Tavern, the road soon swings left as it brings you highly through the Auchentiber Moss. This type of habitat is mostly missing in the lowlands now, due to drainage and modern farming practices. So make the most of its rarity as you go, filled as it is with its Blaeberry, Bog Rosemary, and the like. The land here holds a high flat stillness, sometimes suppressed even further by low blanketing clouds.

Follow the road very long and very straight, with great anticipation. The descent to the town, when it comes, diving through the trees and curving into the streets, is one to be enjoyed and savoured. Both this and the Fergushill Road approach come out literally side by side, and when they do, you cross the Garnock and climb up and round to the traffic lights in the town centre. The grand tower of the abbey is still visible above the houses, and although it would take a slight detour to see the remains of this fine old relic, it's worth it to admire what's left of the place. Although it goes back to the late 1100's, the bell tower wasn't built till 1810, to replace the previous one which was struck by lightning.

As for the town itself, it's busy and tight with buildings and traffic, as you turn right at the lights and then cross over the railway at the main junction Kilwinning station, before bending left onto the Stevenston Road that runs through older and finer houses on its way out of town. Then the A-738, as it's officially known, becomes a little

Expect some great rollercoaster fun-filled riding on the back roads between Kilwinning and the Dalry to Saltcoats road (the B-714) if you decide to stay high, as opposed to sticking to the coast road. It is all single track road riding, meandering delightfully between farms and allowing great views of the Clyde as you go. Here we are just to the east of Diddup Farm, heading towards it, going anticlockwise on this occasion.

If you decide to do a coastal sweep and hug the coast road as much as possible, then you will get great seaside riding such as this round the South Beach Ardrossan (clock). No matter which route you choose, there will be delights in every single one.

scatty around here, as it runs past dense wooded copses and the like. This is followed by the fire station, before the ubiquitous supermarket – in this case a Morrison's – rears its ugly head at the mega-busy roundabout signalling your arrival at the A-78. Now, it can be a bit of a mission impossible job to get across this one, as the constant traffic flows up and down towards Irvine.

The Three Town's bypass feeds in from the other side, so it's a busy old place at the best of times. Nothing else for it: wait your chance, then dive across into the safety of a bus lane, be God, and I'm always glad of its sanctuary. The next half mile or so isn't the prettiest, as it's a busy straight burl along past the cemetery, where even the coast is hidden well behind the distant factories and works of the Ardeer Industrial Estate. But fret not, for soon it will improve. Up ahead comes a roundabout at a Jet filling station, where you have a choice as to which

way to proceed. It is fine to go to the right of the Jet and stay on the former main road, now surpassed by the bypass, but I do recommend the left.

If you decide to go right, this means you stay on the A-738, as you climb steadily up Glencairn Street, past solid old council houses then the bungalows, onto the aptly-named High Road. The extra bit of height you've gained allows the peaks of Arran to appear above the rooftops, once you swing right at the top. The higher road continues straight, fast, and quaintless, as it slowly descends, running long into the distance, running long through the urban, before it meets the wonderful Dalry Road (the B-714) coming in from the right off the Sharphill. This is an escape route back into the hinterland, if you so need one, but it is much better to ride this favourite of mine towards the coast.

DALRY TO SALTCOATS VIA THE B-714: ALTERNATIVE ROUTE

This one starts off from the Kilwinning Road (the A-737), just as you're leaving Dalry, beginning at a white house that looks more like a church. The road sign says 6 miles to Saltcoats, and begins with a short brutal ascent, which starts the moment you cross a hump bridge controlled by a traffic light. As tough a start as it is, once up it soon becomes a wonderful rolling glide through rich fields and fair farms. It won't take you long to find out why it's one of my favourites. This road will slowly and stealthily climb continually from the word go for a couple of miles, and this adds a great feeling of expectation, as impatiently you draw near the crest of the road that will open up the view of the Clyde coast in a most fantastic fashion.

Even the softness of the daisy-filled dairy meadows, full of Ermintrudes (moo cows) and buttercups, can't distract you too long from the thought of the vista awaiting. The fields that roll up on your right into the higher ground still retain their richness. Those bloody ugly wind turbines sit atop the hills now. and hopefully the powers that be will come to their senses and get shot of them sooner rather than later. I'm not holding my breath. of course. After approximately 4 miles of this fairly quiet, most pleasant riding, which has delightfully levelled out on the approach to Meikle Laught Farm, the top of the Sharpshill roundabout sign starts to appear.

Then behold, the long gradual sweep of Ayr Bay running away from your left comes into full view. It has been showing partially for a short time before, but it's nothing to match the full show. Never will the broad blue firth disappoint when you see it from this excellent vantage point, over the low-lying red rooftops of Stevenston. Knowing that now there comes a great straight descent right down to the coast on an effortless dive, enhances the situation even further. The carpet of patchwork green suddenly gives way to the blazing blanket of blue marine and, as this road isn't too busy, it will all go quiet sooner or later. And when it does, well… What can I say?

I usually stop for at least a moment at least to take it all in, before the gentle curving roll forward starts towards the large by-pass roundabout. It steadily gets better as you near it, then once through, the descent down begins, rod straight and rod great. It's fantastic flying into the Saltcoats streets, where Arran appears with the clearing

of the industrial estate's iron railings on the right. Like Ayr Bay, it's another never-tire-of view, where the fun continues till the white church that sits at the junction with the main A-737 is met. And now we're back where we were before I diversified.

Continuing along the A-738, it's much the same to follow on the High Road, soon becoming the Parkhouse Road, which will carry you on through Saltcoats and then in and out of Ardrossan. Seaside bungalow rows appear on the right, just before you enter Ardrossan, where shortly Glasgow Street is passed on the left leading down to the Arran ferry. Then almost immediately on the right follows another escape road back in – our old mate (the B-780), the Dalry Road. And, just like the previous road coming down off the Sharphill, I much prefer to approach on this road rather than depart on it, unless I'm coming from Arran and returning home.

DALRY TO ARDROSSAN VIA THE B-708: ALTERNATIVE ROUTE

We covered it on the Arran run in Book 1, of course, but just as a quick recap, you gain it from Dalry centre by turning right at the early lights on the Kilwinning Road (signposted Roches Way) and then turn first left onto Sharon Street, following the ferry signs. That's you on the B-780, where its dipping, climbing, and curving gait takes you all the way out to Munnoch Reservoir. There, the left turn keeps you on the same road and runs you up past Busbie Muir Reservoir and then wonderfully down to meet the 738 in Ardrossan. So, again we meet up with our initial route, and proceed along much as before. Just as you leave Ardrossan and its great old shacks, a road coming in from your left is met, this being North Corsebar Road.

COASTAL SWEEP: ARDROSSAN SOUTH BEACH ROAD

This is where you would have come out had you turned left, instead of right, back at the Stevenson Jet filling station. It is the more scenic and interesting route to go left, and that is the reason I recommend it. Not that you would notice at first, for it takes you down the tough-looking Boglemart Street (the B-780), passing tightly-packed houses and stores, before emerging out past the open grounds of Auchenharvie Academy. The whole area has never recovered from ICI pulling its plant out from the nearby Ardeer Estate. As it was such a big factory and main employer, its departure had a major economic impact on the area.

The area itself was once a heavy industry stronghold, with pig iron and coal mining dominating the landscape and economy, with over 30 mines situated just south of the town at Ardeer. The whole persona of the Three Towns area[1] is one of much needed regeneration. At this point, you're close to the coast, but it's hidden by the railway and its walls, and the road here is always busy and bustling with traffic. Not too pleasant at the moment, but the Saltcoats sign is just ahead and, after another short burst of buildings, you rise up to cross the rail line just before it reaches Saltcoats station. Ah! The memories.

Kilwinning isn't the only town that provides an approach to the coast from the A-736, because by taking the B-707 just before the Blair Inn you will shortly arrive in Dalry, and this provides no fewer than four great approach routes to the Firth of Clyde. The above picture shows you pulling up to the traffic lights in the town centre (clock), and I have to admit that Dalry itself does have a pretty run-down look to it.

Go hard left for the coast road, and soon will follow Ardrossan South Beach, where it just feels so nice to skirt round the long curve of this holiday hotspot. Not much has changed here from the 1960s, as my old photographs show, and I'm not complaining. I don't want it to change. The same houses can be seen in the background of

some 1966 snaps taken by my family, and of course the stunning Arran hasn't changed and neither has the salt air. Just for the record as we leave Saltcoats, the place name comes from the time when they used to extract salt from the water, which was done in cottages along the beach. These were known as cotts, and the modern day name derives from the salt cotts.

Now we're in Ardrossan. It's a place we know well from our earlier runs, heading for that magical boat to take us across to magical places. But we haven't contoured round the South Beach yet, and as we go round, the spire of John's Church at the end of Arran Place is very prominent. So, too, is the jutting headland to its left that gives Ardrossan its name. The rest of the curve is made up of shoulder-to-shoulder, two-storey stalwarts (houses) for the most part. This presents a most impressive facade, which would do any seaside front proud.

There is always some activity around the South Beach, even on the coldest of days. But on a warm summer's one, there's plenty. Hardly surprising, as it's a great setting, looking out across the weighted water. The sands and shoreline do make a most curvey line to enjoy and follow, as does the whole scene; always pleasant, always uplifting. This is especially so as it will be the first time that day that you will taste the salt air, and that is always a very special moment on any coastal run. What a joy it is to belt round the bay, sun glinting on the water. And if Arran is holding a blue hue, then the next few miles down the coast is nought short of unforgettable.

Soon the white buildings at the far end of Arran Place are reached, then you bank right off the bay and into the busy Princes Street. The level crossing with its bright signs and lights hits you first, and then you meet with

1 - The Three Towns is the collective name given to Stevenston, Saltcoats, and Ardrossan.

The B-714 Dalry to Saltcoats road is one of my favourite roads to reach the Clyde coast with (clock), and that's not only because of the way it runs. It's also because of the views you get at Sharphill just before it descends long and straight into Saltcoats. Here we're looking over the rooftops of Stevenston out into Irvine Bay.

the traffic toing and froing from the ferry terminal, along with the rest coming from Jewsons and Asda. They all sit to the left of the busy crossroads with Harbour Street. This all makes for a bustling wee quarter, which is tightly packed between the old paint-flaking buildings. One of which was the former Lord Carson pub; how Rangers could do with his leadership at the moment.[2]

Get over the crossroads and head out of the mayhem, as you swing by the rest of the harbour with its new flats and small marina. This leads onto North Corsebar Road, which soon joins the main drag the A-738, meaning that you come together with the higher road at this point. There's nothing else for it but to run out of town, meeting the new bypass at the Montfode roundabout as you do.

---

2 - Lord Edward Carson was the loyalist leader who opposed home rule in Ireland in 1912. He was the man who created the Ulster Volunteers who were the forerunner to today's UVF, and he was Ian Paisley's hero.

As for the bypass itself, it does run high and is able to give good views of the firth and Arran as it heads north, but I don't ride it because it's too busy and I think it's best left to the cars. So I never get to this point with its assistance.

We're now going to purr, and I do mean purr, along the seafront and be entertained by the delights of the beach and the views beyond. This will include both the firth and the shore, for there are green and pleasant views all the way along inland now, and they even give the mighty Arran a run for its money. The road will take us finely and flatly all the way along towards Seamill, now that we're sailing along on the coast hugging A-78. The one and only slight drawback with being on the trunk road 78, is its busyness. A cycle lane does run parallel with the road, which is great – or it would be if they hadn't put stupid barriers along it at regular intervals. For that reason, I always stick to the road.

It's flat open fresh air fortnight riding between Ardrossan and Seamill (clock), and as you're right down next to the shoreline the beach itself will provide the foreground to some stunning seascapes as you batter along.

And what a great road it is. The long line of the beach's curve and the equally impressive bluff of Boydston Braes sitting just inland, with all its old high wind-slanted deformed trees, pulls you along further. The red-roofed bungalows of West Kilbride sit smartly on the steep green rises that overlook the lower set of bungalows of Seamill. In a word, airy; I repeat airy. That's how it is here. You're wide open to the full blast of the elements, and it's no wonder the trees are bent double the way they are. But, boy, what a stretch! The rocks will show if the tide is out, as the sandy beach's reach is very limited here. But that is about all that is limited, as it's full on for the rest – the sea, the sun, the wind, and the waves, all giving you the oomph to go flying into a village that seems to have an identity crisis.

Is it a village in its own right, or is it a suburb of West Kilbride? The welcome sign put up by the council is a bit of a good old-fashioned British fudge, stating 'Welcome to West Kilbride incorporating Seamill', so make up your own mind.

Before you even get into Seamill, the first of several roads leading in and out of West Kilbride is passed, running very eloquently uphill to your right. The upward course is a must in this neck of the woods, as a number of rather short steep rises abound in this area, giving a great backdrop to an already very pretty setting. West Kilbride is not a village in need of a soup kitchen, neither is Seamill. Its houses and its well-known hotel, the Hydro, conceal the dramatic flank of Arran when you first enter its long flat main road. But that all changes when the road rises quite abruptly, and a great look over the rooftops onto the Clyde can be had again.

Pump, pump, pump on the pedals till the rise is cleared, passing another road on the right taking you into the centre of West Kilbride by a short steep climb. Not surprisingly, the view of the jagged island from this road, the Yerton Brae, is good, though not so good as the next road, Jacks Brae, where the view should add a couple of grand at least to the house prices. Not my concern, to be honest, as they're all just a tad outside my price range. But not to worry; if I bought a house on the coast, where would I cycle to?

So, out the other side it is, after clearing the last of the Kilbride stoatirs (large houses), and away we go, firing long and straight between the flat belt of fields that form the base between the Kilbride Moor and the coast, which has been taken from view by lump and distance. The lump being that of Goldenberry Hill, whose height allows no scene except green, forming as it does an impenetrable barrier between you and the blueness. But as way of compensation, ever closer draws the rough high Fairlie Moors face on your right, which adds a touch of rough drama to this tame tranquil scene.

We pass the pretty B-782 (Hunterston Road) doubling back hard over your right shoulder — another West Kilbride escape route, but not the last. This will come up shortly and invitingly, once we drop down, long and straight, on our way towards the first large Hunterston roundabout. It's the one that sits below the two blue corrugated iron monsters that dominate the skyline, as they sit on the hillside above at the railhead. Their job is to accept the coal that is transported up to them by the enclosed conveyor belt from the ore terminal, then it is loaded onto the goods wagons.

Now, just before you reach them, a road will appear on your right at Kilruskin and this is the one that feeds from the back end of West Kilbride. It starts right at the junction with the B-781, the main approach route from Dalry.

DALRY TO WEST KILBRIDE VIA THE B-781: ALTERNATIVE ROUTE

To come in from Dalry on the 781 is a true pleasure and joy, and the road itself is simply a break-off of the main route we used to access Ardrossan and Arran. If, on occasion, you wish to approach on it (thoroughly recommended), all you have to do is follow the Ardrossan Road (the B-780) out of Dalry as far as Munnoch Reservoir, but don't turn left this time. Instead, go straight ahead and onto the B-781.

The show-stealer as always will be the Isle of Arran, and this is one of its many guises seen here as the ride along the busy A-78 is done in glorious sunshine.

The fun begins with a long climb on a road showing double white centre lines, which pulls you up into slightly rougher ground than you've just ridden through. It takes you on towards the rises and fields that border the back door of a village that has a most pleasant demeanour.

The road is superb, drawing you long and invitingly ever westward, through open soft fields at first. Above, on the right, sit the high moors containing the Fairlie Moor Road, which we'll ride shortly. In the meantime, we continue on the B-781, where the road starts to bend gracefully and elegantly as it approaches Blackshaw Farm, and for the first time both the Clyde and Arran's jagged flank put in an appearance. The scene reaches its climax just after passing Balles Farm, as you bank right and fly towards the bends below.

Across the fields, looking west, the view is one of the best that the Clyde coast has to offer. It won't be much more than a fleeting glimpse, bearing in mind the speed at which you will be taking the bend, but it's still that good you will be thrilled by it nonetheless. And that's because it has it all – the serenity of the green fields in front, stretching right up to the roof tops of Kilbride; beyond them, the thin slither of blue Clyde, where on top sits the jagged isle of Arran herself, using her peaks to pierce the cumulus clouds that get snagged on her horns. What a sight it is. And had your riding partner in days gone past been old Dan Maskell (he of Wimbledon fame), you're sure to have heard him mutter, 'Oh, I say!'

Once you straighten out of the Balles Farm bend, you will quickly go through a great series of wooded curves,

Another alternative to the coast road is the great Ardrossan to West Kilbride high road, which runs off our old mate the B-780, which is the one we use to gain the Arran ferry from Dalry. Turn right onto it just before you reach the new bypass, and get ready to be entertained, not only by the views but also by just how much the wind has shaped the few trees there are along the way. Here we are on the early part of it, heading for West Kilbride (clock).

direction of your choice; all depending on your plans, of course.

For us at the moment, don't forget we are still on the A-78 at Kilruskin, about halfway through our great sweeping run of the coast, and so far so good. Up to this point, it has been good-to-great riding in places, where the only drawback since hitting Kilwinning has been the volume of traffic. This has been especially so since we met the A-78 north of Ardrossan. It is also possible to get to this point of the run at Kilruskin by using a more scenic and quieter higher level route, which is recommended for its views and its safety. This one starts way back, just as you pass the rail station at the start of the Stevenston Road in Kilwinning, and requires you to gain access to the quiet country roads between there and the Dalry Road at Sharphill (the B-714) above Saltcoats.

flowing down them and arriving into the back end of the village, guided in by a row of houses which begin with an impressive old farmhouse. Now, there are options aplenty here, for you can turn immediately right to run you right down to our present position on the A-78 at Kilruskin, or you can bear left and enter West Kilbride. If you do, then enjoy – and I do mean enjoy – its charm, before you leave on any number of great ride out roads, to take you in the

KILWINNING TO WEST KILBRIDE: HIGHER ROUTE

To gain the beginning of the route can be not difficult per se, just a little less straightforward than it might have been at one time. For the country road itself starts at a new roundabout which lies at the end of Ashgrove Road, which at one time could be accessed directly from the Stevenston Road right at Kilwinning rail station. This has now been barricaded off to cars and would require the use of the pavement to get onto it. The next turn right onto McLuckie Road (signposted Park and Ride) can also be used, but it would also require a pavement to be mounted further up the Ashgrove Road. So, despite the fact that it is shorter and perfectly feasible to reach the roundabout this way, and is used by myself, if you want to stick purely to the roads then you must ride on till you come to the first set of traffic lights further down the Stevenston Road, and turn right.

A great view of Arran from the Ardrossan high road, which is a real quiet and somewhat hidden and forgotten road. This makes it ideal for cycling on, especially on a long hot summer's day, when you might be able to catch a cooling breeze, with a little bit of luck.

Looking down on Munnoch Reservoir from the B-781, which is the Dalry to West Kilbride road; it only becomes the 781 after the B-780 turns left for Ardrossan at the reservoir. This is a fine route to West Kilbride that offers great views of Arran's peaks, especially on the descent of the great bends that run past Ballees Farm.

This brings you through a large grey housing estate to the start of the country road, which you gain by turning left at the new roundabout. Voila, into the very narrow lanes you go and up, up slightly to a T-junction, where the right turn takes you round and past a few farms – with funny names at times – with fields whose edges have grand old trees guarding their borders. Auchenkist Farm has two wonderful ancient old trees guarding its entrance; I think they are beeches.

Pass there, and continue down and straight before climbing up to Lochwood Farm by a short set of steep turns, where the climb gives great views of the coast as

Once West Kilbride is reached, there are numerous options open to you about which direction to go in next, because several great roads fan out in all directions as they leave the village. They are all of equal good character and won't disappoint, no matter which one is chosen. This one is the B-7047 (Chapelton Road) heading south (anti) back towards Ardrossan, which provides wonderful high views of the coast and the harbour enroute.

you swing by the splendid farm building itself. Just watch out for their dogs sunbathing in the road.

It is a most pleasant curving jaunt round the hedgerows here, and if it's spring and the daffodils are out, it really does feel like you are following the yellow brick road. From the height gained at Lochwood, there is another up and down before the delightfully-named Diddup Farm is reached, and then the final up and down sees us on the Dalry chappy itself. That was magic.

We then gain the great crest of the road and fire down into Saltcoats. On the way down, we pass another road on the left which can also be used to gain the Dalry Road from Kilwinning, and this is as pleasant as its higher counterpart, though less scenic and less taxing.

To gain it, turn right further down the Stevenston Road (Kilwinning) at the fire station, and when you hit

The fourth and final coastal road from Dalry is the finest of them all; the mighty Moor Road. Don't forget to turn right at the cemetery as you leave town on the B-780 heading for Ardrossan. This picture is taken very high up right on the moors themselves, and shows how narrow the road is and how bleak is the going. Beware of wandering sheep on the road, as they do seem to be very reluctant to give way to cyclists.

the end of the straight at another T-junction, turn left. Turning right will take you onto the higher route we've come round. Go over the bypass, turn right and follow the signs for Ardeer Golf Club. Don't go into the golf club, but continue straight ahead and you're now on the Kerelaw Road. Follow it round delightfully over the Stevenston Burn and through the fields just above the town, meandering in a general westerly direction. At one point, you do go close to the infamous Kerelaw School, which has now closed, I'm glad to say. The back road then steers you through the Middlepart, as it's called, up to join the Dalry Road, just below the bypass this time.

Whichever road is taken to get to the B-714, head downhill when you reach it, but not as far as the bottom this time. Instead, take a right turn halfway down into Burns Avenue. You'll know which one to take when you see the McConechy's tyre place on the right just after it.

I assume it's called Burns Avenue, as the street map tells me it is, but for all the times I've ridden it, I've not once seen a street name on the road itself. Anyway, let's safely assume that it is, and soldier on regardless. We are now into a total change of scenery on this stretch, with our surroundings no longer green but the light coloured walls and darker shaded roof tiles of this solid old looking council estate.

That's the script till the road rises a bit and you find yourself into one of the newer, sprawling housing developments that now abound in the area. This one's a biggy. The Burns baby then curves and dives down,

All four of the Clyde's biggest islands open up and show well on the often breathtaking, often screaming-straight-down hairy descent on the Moor Road. Climbing up from Dalry is the easier option of tackling the Moor girl, as brutal is the only word to describe the ascent from the A-78 side. The scene as you descend to the coast is absolutely stunning, and it makes all the toil to get up and over this great old road more than worth it.

Just about to pass through the cattle grid that signals the highest point on the Moor Road, and it's one of about four of these bloody things that must be ridden over, which does spoil the descent down to the coast somewhat. It's shake rattle and roll over every one.

through all the new stuff, to the mini roundabout on the Sorbie Road, where a more or less straight through tack finds you running along Stanley Road, Ardrossan. You're right back into old council stock again, which is much more to my liking, and why not? These old stalwarts have stood the test of time; bearing up to the best battering that the Clyde coast could throw at them over the years.

The old Stanley goes long and straight, and finishes when it abuts the vaunted Ardrossan to Dalry Road. You know this one only too well by now, as it's the very one we fired down for that fantastic ferry. Turn right up it this time, though, and climb through the Chapelhill roundabout, taking us through the new bypass, then shortly take the narrow road on the left, which sees us on the Ardrossan High Road. Prepare to be entertained and then some by this one, as you're in for a bit of a treat here all the way along to West Kilbride.

Despite the fact you've just gained a fair wee bit of height, you're just about to gain some more. Not big time, I hasten to add, but enough to give you quite a commanding panorama of the seaboard, and when you do get over the rise in front of you, the narrow grey band of tarmac you're on runs through rich fields for the most part. Now, a few – and by that I do mean a handful – trees line this road, mostly in the vicinity of High Boydstone. Some of these poor buggers are so badly battered by the wind that they look like they should be in a care home, while the rest have had their trunks twisted by the blow, and look like contorted works of art.

But that is just an indication of the forces of nature here, which never fails to impress as you spur along the straight top of the road, ever eager to get the best view of the seaboard. You'll find yourself constantly on the lookout for the next jaw-dropping scene. This won't be long in coming, of course, not with Arran holding court just offshore. At times, it's the sheep and lambs that occupy the green squares to your right, which are all

Nearing the bottom of the Moor Road on a hot summer's day, and the massive coal heaps inside Hunterston are unmissable. Beyond, Millport Town can just about be seen. By now your wrists will be screaming at you, due to all the hard braking you have been doing, and they will be glad to bottom out and have the pressure finally taken off them.

looked over by the white wind turbines on top of Busbie Muir. From fairly close up, they do possess a certain slender elegance, I must say, but that doesn't mean I'd like to see any more of them planted.

From above Kirkland Farm access road, you look directly over its head and fields to the semi-distant Glenhead Farm. This sits right at the bottom of the long, gentle, angled south ridge of Tarbert Hill, with its long lush green line graduating up to the right. Over your left shoulder, Ardrossan Harbour hasn't given up the ghost and is still visible. But the golden girl herself – Arran – as always, steals the show; no complaints about that, of course.

The fields in front of you gently roll down toward the coast, and the buffer zone that they provide from the

Largs church steeples always make such striking landmarks, especially on the descent of the Old Largs Road from Greenock when coming down the Brisbane Glen Road (anti). It is a fantastic long slender beautiful descent coming off the Muirshiel hills as it does, and is without doubt a stretch of road to really look forward to. The seascape opens up little by little on the way down, and enticingly shows just a little bit more with every bend taken.

A-78 means the road you're on couldn't be any more different from the busy trunk road.

The high road drops away gradual and long towards West Kilbride now, so follow it down with speed and pleasure among the pastoral. For pastoral it is, leading down eventually in a twist and a turn to Meadowhead Farm, with its rich arable and dairy fields. Even the slopes of Tarbert Hill are criss-crossed pleasantly with hedgerows and fences, still able to provide grazing, so fertile is the soil on the lower sides. Tarbert is a most pleasant height, particularly the way it rolls up and over its own top to provide such a soft gentle finish. Like a lot of the hills round about Kilbride, it is coated in places with yellow gorse bushes, which make for a most colourful splash against the green background they sit on.

Next, the steep drop down into the village itself, and its anchors on for the wee mini roundabout at the bottom. When you've dropped into the well looking houses, continue straight ahead to run along the top of the village; this is the best route to keep you on the higher road for as long as possible. However, if you want to join the 78 a bit earlier, for any reason, then turn into the centre just at the railway station and take your pick of routes. As for the station building itself, you will have to look long and hard for a more quintessential and delightful looking Victorian specimen; West Kilbride, in its cream and red colours, takes some beating.

And the village? Well, it's one you would never tire of looking at, let alone ride through. It has the look of an

Taking the bends on the descent of the Brisbane Glen Road, all done without a care in the world, just the way I like it.

it seems to be bowing politely as you pass. Next comes a quick one-two, as you double dive under the railway and back, which is a magical wee move. And just before you return to the main road side, you pass the most rustic-looking of farm houses imaginable, the grey and red-trimmed North Kilruskin.

COASTAL SWEEP CONTINUED.

After this, you pass under a most splendid arched rail bridge to return to the A-78, and when you do, it means that once again both the high and low routes have come back together. As you continue on towards Fairlie, the big roundabout accessing Hunterston power station is shortly reached, and the true scale of those big blue corrugated iron-sided monsters can be truly appreciated. For monsters I've described them, and monster-sized they are. The conveyor belt from the coal terminal feeds right up to the two massive sheds containing cranes that load the coal to the trains, and what an amount of coal they load – around 2800 tons an hour. Now, if I were a master of understatement, I would say, 'That's quite a lot.'

But I'm not that corny, I hope, so I will carry on in a similar vein, crammed in between the trees and sandwiched between the two big Hunterston roundabouts. Roughly halfway between them, comes a sign saying Moor Road, Dalry 6. Now there's an intro.

If you like your climbing direct, dramatic, and brutal, then turn right for a treat. For 2 miles it will climb, narrow, and straight, the old moor girl. And not once but twice in its early stages does it hit a 1:7 gradient. 'Ouch!' or words to that effect, because it's a sustained little critter and will do exactly as it says on the tin and take you very dramatically over the moors to the North Ayrshire town.

COASTAL CLIMB: DALRY TO THE A-78 VIA THE FAIRLIE MOOR RD.

So yes, it is a return route, and what a return route at that. Not the easiest, but one of the best, just in the way that it takes you in from its high moor stance, diving, twisting and turning, through the farms in its lower reaches, then into the town in quite some style. It's quite a different story with the Moor Road when coming the other way, though. For it's a long meandering gradual job of an ascent if you're heading west. The start from Dalry is not signposted, and therefore if you don't know where it begins, you won't know where it begins. However, it's

old weaving place and the reason for that is it was an old weaving place. That wasn't yesterday, of course, but back when that sort of thing was in vogue, in the 18th century. Nowadays, the local area is still known for the quality of its potatoes, earning the place the nickname of 'Tattie Toon'. There has been a hamlet here for centuries, and it is also chronicled that Roman General Agricola stationed 30,000 men here in 82 AD. Perhaps he was angling for a block booking discount at the Seamill Hydro.

By all means, if the notion takes you, nip into the old narrow streets of the village and depart over the dramatic Jacks Brae, or head out the soft fieldy Hunterston Road (the B-782). Both these routes are a pleasure to ride.

But the most direct way, when you pass the station, is to carry on the top road, which is gained by a wee shimmy round the short one way street system, before continuing on down Gateside Street. You will, of course, pass the road to Dalry coming in from the right, before firing long and fast down through the fields that edge the railway. Great riding here, there's no doubt about it, and in a while you meet an old tree that's bent so hard by the wind

Approaching the Outerwards Reservoir on the long road into Largs when coming down Brisbane Glen, and look out for the nasty wee twist in the road just before the reservoir is reached. Arran's peaks can just be seen way in the distance, and it's these glimpses of what is to come that will continue to draw you in all the way right down to the coast road.

not a lost cause to find it, as it heads off to the right, just after you pass the cemetery gates when coming out of town on the Ardrossan Road, that old stalwart and china[3] of ours the B-780. The wooden houses of Wingfaulds Avenue, in their dark tarry garb, line the left, with the cemetery wall guarding the right flank as you head out into the hinterland.

This starts off very enclosed from the word go, as the road tightens into single track straight away, and trees, stone walls, and hedgerows hem you in. But not for long, as a swing in the road sees all open up before you, and then you are meandering through a wee green paradise. No problem here, with no steep rises to tax us,

it's gentle rise after gentle rise, after bend and hedge. A hand-painted road sign quaintly shows the way as you approach the house at Baidland Mill. Continue enjoying the rises, and the houses – one of which seems to have its roof run into the rise it sits on. All the time, there is a gradual movement out of the lushness of the farmland, towards a more rough type of pasture, and this becomes most noticeable when you pass the big red painted sheds of Auldmuir Farm and shortly gain the side of the Caff Reservoir.

It's a typical upland dam, the Caff, with a look of forgotten character about it. This look is aided by its surrounding, aged, iron railing, bent, broken, missing in places. The sort of fence that is so dilapidated it couldn't keep 'weans oot a close'. But I've always been drawn to places like this, and this small water is no exception.

3 - China is short for china plate, Glasgow rhyming slang for mate.

Up on top of the old scenic route, as they call it. Once over the Rottenburn Bridge, which is centre of the picture, you flip from North Ayrshire into Inverclyde when going clockwise. There is still plenty more really enjoyable riding to come, and no matter which way you ride this wonderful old high road you will get a fantastic view-filled descent to remember.

old Moor frog,[4] though for the most part not too busy or potholed. Though it does in places have more than its fair share of small stones littering the surface.

All around is tussocky light brown grass, more or less wall-to-wall, but in amongst it you've got darker heather just to add to the bleakness. Up ahead is a dip in a ridge that you rise toward, and as you reach it you cross a cattle grid. Once you get through with the usual teeth chattering, then it's glide and dive time for the next 2 miles. This starts off by swinging gradually away in an arc to the right, before plummeting down onto the A-78 like a banshee on heat. In doing so, what will open up in front of you will be all four of the Clyde's major islands – well, in part at least – including Millport Town itself.

The rightward arc is done on only a gradual gradient, though a fair bit of speed is picked up on that alone. And what is a pity is that the road surface is probably at its worst here, just when you're requiring a bit of smooth.

Then the steep drop is upon you. You can actually see it coming, but you can't do a bloody thing about it, other than get onto those brake hoods and keep it all under control as best you can. Firing down close to the small Glenburn Reservoir, you hit another teeth-chattering cattle grid as you're about level with it. 'Bugger!' you cry, or perhaps something a bit more colourful. It's real wildfire stuff all this, and soon you're beside and running down the edge of the Glenside Wood conifers, where another wonder of the world appears ahead; this one man-made. Old king coal, and plenty of it. Piled high

Slightly narrower at its eastern dam wall end, it fans out to greater width at its western side, where the slopes run into it gently on either side. Fly fishers' rods swish the air as you cruise by, while all the time you're looking ahead up into the higher ground beyond. There, the white walls of Knockendon Farm house stand out from the barren browns and greens of the moor hills. The farm is reached after you clear the dam, then climb up and round onto a bolt-straight long section of road that rises between lines of overhanging trees.

These make an inviting archway to draw you up higher. A twist in the road is taken at the farm's entrance, followed by another bolt-straight rise, this one having only two or three trees sitting on the right and they are clinging on for dear life. Wind-blown wouldn't describe them. When you clear this rise, you're onto the moors proper and, as barren and windswept as they are, on a hot summer's day they are tranquillity in a bottle. Now, the old sheep up here do like to roam free and they, along with their little ones at lambing time, can prove a bit of a highway hazard as they tend to graze the side of the road a fair bit. As for the highway itself, it's very narrow the

---

4 - Frog is short for frog and toad, cockney rhyming slang for road.

144

and piled wide, every pile waiting its turn to be conveyer-belted up to the railhead and transported away.

Enormously long, incredibly neat rectangular piles, formed and created by humongous machinery, makes for a united front of impressive scale, as does the bending arm of Hunterston terminal's mile-long pier, jutting out into the Fairlie Road's section of the firth. The terminal itself was built in '79 as an ore terminal for the massive steelworks at Ravenscraig in Motherwell, and replaced the General Terminus Quay in Glasgow, now known as Springfield Quay. The larger boats could not negotiate the narrow upper reaches of the Clyde, and so Hunterston was constructed. Sitting behind the coal piles is the man-made-looking island of Hunterston construction yard, which doesn't appear to be doing much constructing nowadays.

The Moor Road is on its final steep section now, you'll be glad to hear, and so will your wrists, as you descend round the last right hand bend. After passing the beech hedge of Glenside Cottage, it's delightfully under the railway to emerge onto the flat of the 78 yet again. Merci!

COASTAL SWEEP CONTINUED.

Now, as you proceed in a Largs-like direction, you enter the second large Hunterston roundabout – this one leads to the ore terminal itself – before emerging out the other side to be pleasantly met by the firth again. You're only a stone's throw from Fairlie now, as you emerge out the hinterland at a sheltered bay, where one of the long pier's cranes just shows itself round the wooded headland. A dozen turns of the cranks sees you pass the green background of the Fairlie sign, then you're into palatial pads and palm trees.

My, my, how the west coast gardeners like to take advantage of the warm waters of the Gulf Stream, with a showing of palms in numerous places. They always add an exotic touch to any village. The initial grand residences hide behind walls for the most part, before the centre of the village is reached and this holds ye olde dwellings of this aged fishing port.

It's a pity that the road doesn't allow an option of riding right on the shore here, for it would allow you to see the fine cottages that line it. Never mind, as the buildings that do line the main road look as old as the hills themselves. And to further emphasise the centre's age, the road narrows and tightens as you make progress

Descending to Loch Thom (clock) and skirting round the side of the biggest dam up here, is always a high wild wonder. The curlew's call often adds to the atmosphere, and if it's not too breezy then it's an absolute pleasure to ride this stretch of road.

through it, with a rise and a dip to follow. On emerging from the tightness, you're on the home straight for Largs.

That old seaside stalwart we know so well is shortly coming up, and to reach it you soon run alongside the stone wall hiding the Kelburn Estate on the right, with the masts from Fairlie Marina's yachts showing left side. Now, it has to be said, fair play to one of the former Earls[5] who resided in Kelburn Castle, for he only commissioned the wall to be built to provide employment for the poor. I've also had the current Viscount Kelburn, David Boyle, in my cab, and likewise can confirm he is a gem of a boy. He has built a mountain bike route in the estate grounds, which you might want to try if you like the offroad stuff.

There now follows a short, twisting, steep and taxing wee rise which will bring you to the lights at the foot of the Haylie Brae, just after you pass the impressive Largs Golf Club clubhouse. The modern, glassy, square building has a porch on its upper floor that must be an idyllic perch on a summer's eve to sit, with drink in hand, and watch players approach the 18th green.

On reaching the Haylie this time, there is no need for another big effort as we're not climbing it today, but firing right down into the mobbed Main Street of Largs. You know the drill in this town by now; we've been through it before, you will do so yourself many times, I assure you. Only on a very poor winter's day will you be able

5 - I was told by the present Viscount's partner, who I had in the cab, that this was the 3rd Earl of Glasgow. Another relation, David Kelburn, also gets a mention in David Niven's autobiography *The Moon's a Balloon*.

Looking across the reed beds to a calm Loch Thom from nearer the Greenock side, so you are more or less on the Old Largs Road stretch of the road. Not even a few well spaced-out cattle grids can spoil the enjoyment of riding this slightly crumbling old gem, which is a firm favourite with us roadies. Expect to see as many bike riders as car drivers if it's a weekend run you're doing.

to charge through unchecked, because the traffic at all other times will slow you down as you approach the mini roundabouts, pedestrian lights, and the like. Use the slow time to admire the curves of some of the town's quite unique architecture; the rounded tenement front at the corner of Gogo Street is superb.

Nice and easy does it, till you get onto the shore front and, with the passing of the white iconic Nardini's Café, then you're away. Flags that adorn the front's buildings flutter frantically at times, or just this way and that at others, but inform you of the wind's ways and allow you to gauge how much effort must be expended on the remainder of the run. Always good to know, of course, for there is still a fair bit to go.

At the moment, though, we don't care as we find ourselves enjoying the seafront and those striking hills behind. They will certainly come into their own if we decide to return home over the old scenic route to

Greenock via the Brisbane Glen Road. And what a road it is, up there with the Fairlie Moor Road for height and remoteness. The two can be strung together to make a great high day, if you're in the mood for it.

COASTAL CLIMB: LARGS TO GREENOCK VIA BRISBANE GLEN/OLD LARGS RD.

This one starts just after you pass Vikingar, with its long ship on the lawn, and it has to be said it's a rather insignificant looking start for such a striking jaunt. Douglas Street is the one you turn up to begin it.

That isn't too much help on its own, because there is only one street nameplate at the start and it is on the wall facing away from you. However, Douglas Street begins right across from Saint Columba's Church, at a red postbox conveniently placed there for our benefit, I dare say. When you turn up into Douglas, the first thing to hit you is the view of the hills beyond, lying slap bang dead ahead. They have a beautiful, serene, green softness about them, with high grey crags to add some drama.

Quite a mesmerising sight, I think you'll find, as you ride past real seaside bungalows in this quieter part of town. The road will swing left onto Brisbane Glen Road itself, and run out past the last of the homes into the start of the long gradual climb, leading you rather magnificently onto the Muirshiel moors themselves. Enjoy! Soft and fieldy is the early going, passing isolated houses and through guiding hedgerows that bring you into the most pleasant dale-like terrain you could wish for. This continues for a couple of miles, before the white of Whittlieburn Farmstead is reached, where the old water bottle can be filled from the standpipe round the back, on asking.

On the final climb up of the Old Largs Road from the Greenock side (anti), just after Murdieston Farm. The double bends before the farm are very steep and brutal, but the rise ahead not so, which makes recovery possible on it.

Thereafter follows a short wooded section, which is very enjoyable and shaded, before the inevitable change of scenery appears and a more moorish look soon takes hold. Though this is not done in any slap-in-the-face way, as can often happen, but comes on gradually and picturesquely, with a gentle long rise up to the nestling Outerwards Reservoir. From here flows the Noddsdale Water, and just for the record, there are two names attached to this glen for some reason – Noddsdale or Brisbane. Take your pick. The dam again has an isolated upland feel, where the road skirts its edge beside another old iron railing, whose rusty brown coat adds the expected quaintness we associate with waters of this ilk.

The hills that flank the right of the Brisbane just begin to lose their drama and steepness, though not totally. But at all times they outshine their left sided counterparts, which look rougher, lower, and lack the grandeur of their opposite number. Up till now the road has risen gently and enjoyably into the ever-narrowing glen, but beyond the dam all that changes when a steeper straight section means that you're on the final pull up onto the top of the road.

Once through the cattle grid and clear of the conifers, you're up. It's nice when you can relax and reap the rewards of your labours, and as the road starts to lie back then that's the time to do it. You're back up amongst the barrenness, and now the pylons are your companions.

Despite the bleakness, it's a great ride up here and on the right day you will see almost as many bike riders as car drivers. Creuch Hill dominates ahead, rounded and uniformed brown, as is the sweep of the whole landscape, which this great wee strip of tarmac allows you to see from fairly close up. There follows a long trending right swing by the road, before it drops down and over the Rotten Burn, crossed by the stone Rottenburn Bridge itself. And just so as you know, you've gone from North Ayrshire into Inverclyde. The road also gives the game away that there has been a change; by the now noticeable white lines either side of it, and the surface improves considerably. Wunderbar!

You climb up, passing what's left of a conifer plantation on the left. There are only some green spruce left, with the rest cut down or looking like grey skeletons, but ahead and below lies Loch Thom. Towards it we speed, curving and diving with glee onto its south eastern bank. That great man himself, Robert Thom, built the reservoir in 1827 along with 13 other smaller dams, to feed the town of Greenock below with all the water it needed for domestic use and industry.

It's a great ride round the side of the Thom and, if you're like me, you'll never tire of contouring round it, lying low as it does in the land and surrounded on all sides by the same brown, barren moor tops that we've just ridden through. The road continues along the south bank till it turns hard left by the dam's dilapidated wall, taking you down and over another cattle grid and on towards Greenock Town.

Once more you run over the moors in a similar vein, though now the distant Lomond and Arrochar Hills put in an appearance. But finally, the road takes a turn to the right and suddenly the blue of the mid Clyde opens up a colourful book for you to savour and enjoy. This is the beginning of the descent from the moors, as you start to drop down straight and speedily past Whinhill Golf Club and the bright green painted sheds of Murdieston Farm. It's quite an exhilarating descent you find yourself in now, and it's about to get even more so. The old shipyard town blows blue from below, what with its cranes and coast, while at the same time the land above the Larkfied vies for your attention in its green coat.

If you want to take the coast road to Greenock and Gourock from Largs, as opposed to a higher route, then by all means do so. It can be a bit tight and busy at times on the old A-78, but it has its compensations as well, with some great curving bends right along the shoreline allowing you to fully get the benefit of all that great salt air coming right off the Clyde. Here we've just left Largs, going clockwise.

At this point, the steep twists down to the safety of the Drumfrochar Road have already started, and it's onto the grips big time if you know what's good for you again (it's a 1:7). The Drumfrochar girlie is a side road at this point, but then carries you quite speedily down onto its main part, the B-7054, where it abuts with the wonderfully named Cornhaddock Street. A road sign points the way to the Old Largs Road at the corner, which is handy if you're coming the other way. Now, we have ridden the Drumfrochar Road home and back before, and know it leads down Baker Street, before running long and hard uphill on the Kilmacolm and Auchmountain Roads.

This is the way I would always head home if I had returned from Largs on the moor road. The reason being, it would provide a great day's climbing had I started

It's not only the high roads that can provide wonderful views, as this picture above shows, with a great look out over the water from low down on the A-78. Being totally flat between Largs and Wemyss Bay, it is far and away the fastest way to cover the Clyde coast run.

out over the Gleniffer Braes and then travelled over the Fairlie Moor Road. That's four big pull ups and gives you about 3700 feet of ascent. So, it's great to top out the Auchmountain Road after all that, and it's fine to make directly for home.

But today, I will take you on another back road; this one is the Dougliehill Road, which just happens to be the first road on the left when you reach the top of the Auchmountain (the B-788). This is also single track that was in a helluva state, thankfully it has been recently repaired. I have to say. I wouldn't ordinarily take this

A great halfway house between the A-78 and the Old Largs Road is the Routenburn Road, which is signposted for the golf club (Routenburn G.C.) as you leave Largs, heading for Wemyss Bay. It is also signposted for Meigle when coming the other way. The initial climb up from either direction is well worth the effort for the splendid views you get over the firth and her islands. We are descending into Largs in the photo above (anti), which shows the Millport ferry heading across in glorious sunshine.

Looking across the sheep fields to Great Cumbrae from the Routenburn Road, and what a pretty site she makes. Although it is a fantastic road to ride in either direction, heading south on it for Largs is undoubtedly the more scenic option. It's up there with the best of them for the pleasure and views it provides.

road if I was coming from Greenock, but the reason I mention it is because I will use it when I am doing a big climbing day when going in the opposite direction.

When you turn left off the Auchmountain, it's over a cattle grid and left through the moorland to sit above the coast again. Despite this road once being in poor nick, the views from it more than compensated for its lack of smoothness, and the scene right across into the Gare Loch is superb. Continue to enjoy long views of the Clyde upstream as the road drops and runs past the house at West Dougliehill, just before it turns inland slightly and the views become obscured by the waterworks. As you pass the house at East Dougliehill (which looks like a golf clubhouse), and ironically you're still in amongst the rough, the road then takes a sharp turn down to run onto the Dubbs Road, Port Glasgow.

Going as it does into the houses and factory buildings of the Devol Industrial Estate, this short sharp descent packs quite a punch when climbing it, and that is why I will take this road if I'm out for some serious climbing when going anticlockwise. The Dubbs Road will take you all the way down to the roundabout at the top of the Clune Brae, and even more climbing can be included if you want to approach Woodhall on the low road and batter up through it or even up the Clune itself, again when going anticlock. If you do intend to tackle the coast high routes anticlockwise, it means short tough starts to both the Largs and Fairlie Moor Roads. The big payback is the great long descents that you get into Largs and then Dalry.

In particular, the Largs approach down the Brisbane Glen is quite outstanding, just the way Arran shows itself early and provides a stunning backdrop the whole way down the lengthy descent. This is enhanced on the lower reaches by the church steeples of the town appearing as you bend and curve ever downward. It is an unforgettable stretch.

But in the meantime, it's back to the clockwise run, where just for the moment I will take you down the Dubbs Road only as far as the junction with Barrs Brae – not that far, as it's the next road on the left. And that is where we will emerge from our lower sweep of the whole coast. To continue on our way on that run, we must nip back to Largs shorefront.

COASTAL SWEEP CONTINUED

So we find ourselves back on the Greenock Road, Largs, just where we left it at Douglas Street, when we turned to go up the moor road. No sooner have we passed Douglas than we cross the Noddsdale Water, where we are immediately confronted with another high road option as opposed to sticking to the coast. This one is not easily missed, as it's signposted the 'Golf Club' and is the beginning of not one, but two higher roads, that can be taken from Largs all the

way to Skelmorlie, which makes for great scenic and quiet riding. But firstly, there is nothing wrong with holding onto the coast itself and attacking along the shorefront. This is especially advantageous if a tail wind is assisting your efforts, for there will be nothing to prevent it giving you its full oomph.

There's only a barrier at best between you and the sea breeze, so by all means make the most of it, as the flat 4 miles between here and Wemyss Bay is the fastest way to get there. We know this road, too, as we have returned from Wemyss Bay to Largs on it from the Rothesay run, and have enjoyed the taste of the salt air it gives, being down so close to the water all the way.

After leaving the pretty confines of the town of Largs, make haste along the early straights, all the time being wary of close passing traffic. This is almost a constant threat, what with the narrowness of the road and its busyness. But it's slow into the bargain, so is not as threatening as it first appears. The rough early terrain continues for some time, with the wooded bluff sitting inland from the road, running all the way down to just before Knock Castle.

This sits grandly above, a fair bit back from the road, high in among the trees and looks more showhouse than castle. No old stronghold this place; a baronial home, more like, as is its near neighbour Skelmorlie Castle, positioned just along the hillside. The fields take over from the bluff, filled with sheep and sprinkled delightfully in places with Scots pine. The old iron rail disappears about now, and doesn't make an appearance again till the run into Skelmorlie starts, while all the time the close proximity to the seashore provides ever-changing interest in its rocks and wading birds, along with far off views of Rothesay. Well, Bute, should I say.

The Routenburn Road can be added to in either direction by using the Skelmorlie Castle Road, which runs high above the Clyde in a similar vein and which begins almost immediately once the Routenburn returns to the A-78 at Meigle. It can also be gained by climbing the aptly-named Longhill in Skelmorlie itself, when going anticlockwise. It too provides great views out over the blue blanket that is the Firth of Clyde, and the above photo shows the stretch just after leaving Skelmorlie as you pass the caravan park making for Skelmorlie Castle itself.

The Cloch Lighthouse comes upon you rather grandly and unexpectedly as you contour round the coast on the great A-770 from either direction, but in this case we've come in from the Inverkip side (clock). What a fine site she makes; she impresses every time with her solid white walls and overall position.

Shortly, two roads are passed in quick succession – one signposted for Meigle, the next for Skelmorlie Golf Club. These are both used when running the higher route which I will come back to in a moment, but for now the first modern apartment blocks of the ever-stretching Skelmorlie can be seen ahead. And a final delightful flat purr along, between shore and field, leads into the village. Its tight old centre is marked by the redness of its traditional houses and buildings, most noticeably its grand church with tower. A little dingy and overgrown is Skelmorlie Main Street, what with its steep overgrown cliff face running alongside, all damp and vegetated. Still, it adds character to the place, no doubt about that.

Just before you reach the church which adorns the right hand roadside, the ramp-like Longhill rears up in front of you, disappearing round the bend in amongst walls and woodland. Now, if you went the higher route from Largs, this is where you would descend from.

This is a fantastic way to travel down to Skelmorlie Village from Largs Town, and begins also from the shore road (Greenock Road A-78) in Largs.

LARGS TO SKELMORLIE: HIGHER ROUTE

Head up the Routenburn Road (Golf Club road), by climbing and then turning left to shortly pass the clubhouse, continuing to ascend straight and true between the hedges. When you clear them, you sit above the greens and fairways, where the views already let you know that the effort to get up was well worth it, no two ways about it.

It is a great way to go, no matter which way you ride this road, but it's fair to say that it's probably more scenic and spectacular to come the other way, not only because of the stunning shape of Arran, which will then be right in your line of sight, but also Cumbrae and Co all come together in the long descent down towards the town. However, heading north isn't lacking charm, either, and it just keeps coming aplenty, even after passing the big black barns of Bankhead Farm. More climbing follows up this splendid narrow lane, bringing with it more open sea views to lift the spirits. The whole blue of the lower Clyde dominates the mid view over the sheep fields here, as now only southern Bute is present out there in its long low guise.

Only when you start the long, long, leafy descent down, do you fully realise just how much height you had actually gained in the first place. This descent plummets and plummets, past what I assume was the old stable block belonging to Knock Castle, which is itself just out of site. The stables – resplendent in their own right – are passed just before bottoming out, then another climb

The Cloch Lighthouse front from close up, and I think the ornate badge above the door showing a mini lighthouse makes a lovely touch.

begins. This comes rather easily at first, before more open farm land is reached and then it gets short, steep, and tough, as you pull up past Millrig Farm.

You're up so high again that the moor tops seem no higher than you now, as you look behind you. And at the same time into view comes Cowal, and most likely a show from the Rothesay ferry, if your luck is in.

Begin the steepish drop towards the waiting houses at Meigle; steepish becomes brutal, as you go in amongst the modern homes with their showy gardens, full on the brake levers to keep yourself from an overnight stay in the Sou Gen[6]. After which, glide nicely out of the lane and back onto the 78. You're on it no time before you turn right again, and head up the road past Skelmorlie Castle.

Now, this is a brutal wee twist and turn up behind the saltire-flying ramparts of this oversized room and kitchen. Force your way up its steep, short ramp till it lays back and you then pass the castle's quaint wee outhouses. Another enjoyable leafy lane pull up takes you out into the open. Now you're level with Toward Point across the Clyde.

The road continues to climb through the open scenes that we're used to by now, and the Rothesay boats may please as they ply through the glisten and shimmer of the flat Clyde below. Only when we reach the caravan park does the road level, but before it reaches there, it passes a strange-looking large rusty and fixed pump-like contraption, sitting in a field on the left under a tree. I've no idea what it was once used for, as it looks obsolete now. With the caravans on one side and the openness of wealth on the other, you only have a short stretch of flat to ride between the beech hedges, before the down slope starts slipping into Skelmorlie. The village is entered by a welcoming avenue of trees – most fitting I'd like to add – and then in you go on the Skelmorlie Castle Road.

You pass the modern homes first, but then as the road turns left and starts to take you down, expect to be charmed. By what? I hear you ask. Well, just the look of the place, to be honest; it's all old, and solid, and red, and homely. The Eglinton Bar on the left looks cosy, the small store across the road looks cosy. The houses look cosy; the whole place looks cosy. Yes, cosy is the one word that would best sum up Upper Skermorlie. For all the time you spend in it, that is. Because, although it does

6 - Southern General Hospital.

Although big nuclear submarines sailing down the Clyde do make a very impressive sight, don't forget you are looking at as-near-as-dammit Armageddon here.

bang into the hustle and openness of Wemyss Bay, with all its commerce. Ferry terminals, railway stations, cafes, shops, flag-flying car dealerships, there's some serious overload from the sparsity you've just emerged from.

COASTAL SWEEP CONTINUED.

There's plenty of opportunity to have your every need and whim catered for here, before continuing on and leaving it all behind. This starts when you duck under the rail bridge and climb, with some considerable effort, up and on towards Inverkip power station. You don't actually see much of the place itself, despite its size and girth – well, in the summer anyway – as the greenery keeps it hidden from view. Fast and furious is the 78 now, and so will you be as you drop back down to sea level shortly and then

undergo a name change in places from time to time, you are principally on the Longhill all the way, which will run you down to the bottom of its ramp, where you meet the 78 and join with the coastal route again.

On the way down, you pass between beautifully built garden walls, six or seven feet high in places, and finally round a fast-flying left hand bend, where glimpses of the Clyde can be seen through the trees. It is probably best to ascend Longhill, just to be able to take in all the wonderful surroundings at a more leisurely pace, and as you do so on some future run, you will come to realise that the bloke who named it Longhill, was the sort of geezer who called a spade a spade.

Now, once you hit the 78, you quickly emerge from the dank of Skermorlie and are over the Kelly Burn right slap

Fast descending down into Greenock (anti) on the great Auchmountain Road (the B-788) makes for a very exciting entry into this once mighty industrial town. These steep high early bends aren't overly technical, but due to the quick increase in speed they do require your full attention.

Sailing along Gourock's glorious shorefront on Albert then Ashton Road (clock). A more pleasant purr would be hard to find, especially on a sunny summer's day. The white buildings that line the road give the appearance more of an English seaside town than a Scottish one, I always think.

fire as fast as you can between Inverkip on one side and its glistening marina on the other. It's so fast at this point, with the vehicles I mean, that it's no pleasure to ride this section despite the striking surroundings, especially the hillsides ahead on both sides.

So I always find myself going flat out till I reach the large Bankfoot roundabout where things start to ease off a bit. In the past, we have gone straight ahead into Spango Valley and past the long IBM plant, but not today. Today is Gourock, and we shall approach it by the splendid Cloch Road. So turn left and climb just a tad, past the entrance to Ardgowan House, and begin a most enjoyable swerve and a curve of a descent round wide bends, green and fair. The sign says 3 miles to the

Looking out over Greenock's docks shows the Arrochar hills and the Gareloch from the top of the Auchmountain Road (anti), and it's this instant full-on view that hits you almost immediately the moment you swing round off the moors. What a bang it hits you with. It's simply stunning.

Argyll ferry and it means we're back on the A-770, but on it for the first time from this direction. It seems all quiet compared to the much busier 78, so it's got that in its favour as well.

You travel down safely, all very gentle stuff, till the coast puts in an appearance in the shape of Lunderston Bay, lying across the low fields to your left. The road continues to flirt with the shoreline for a short while, before pulling back inland slightly and continuing flatly and sleekly, always broad and quick, till it hits the coastline again. Across from you now is the Dunoon fellow, and the width of water when you draw level with it does tend to have an impact on you; one that gets you every time. However, it's not just natural wonders that impress on this famous roaring road. Shortly, there is a man-made one about to impress as well.

A fantastic view of old Greenock Town from near the top of the Auchmountain Road. In the distance can be seen the entrance to Loch Long.

The fun's just about to begin now that the top of the Auchmountain Road has been gained (anti), and the next mile or two will be not only thrill-a-second but completely effort-free into the bargain. It's taken quite an effort to get here, so the reward always feels well earned.

You first see its white tower with black stripe before the rest of its accompanying white walls and buildings; the famous Cloch Lighthouse, of course. I've said this before, but I'll say it again, they are in my opinion – and many other people's opinion, too – magnificent buildings. This one is no exception, and is even older than its near neighbour across the water at Toward.

August 1795 saw the first light shine from its glass, and it's been doing a sterling job ever since. The whole setting of the place is just magical, what with the white of all the buildings. The old keepers' houses, both of them, cut a fine dash, with the older one especially striking. Its

Just a glimpse of things to come can be seen beyond the Greenock Town sign, which sits under the shade of a tree at the highest point on the B-788 where the Auchenfoil Road becomes the Auchmountain (anti). Great anticipation is always felt here, as the fantastic long fall down into Inverclyde begins right round the next corner.

stepped gable ends and the miniature lighthouse shield above the door are the icing on the cake.

Built here at Cloch Point to warn ships of the nearby Gantock Rocks, it's now fully automated, of course, as are all the others, but that still doesn't detract from its charm. The countdown markers into Gourock begin almost immediately after you leave the lighthouse behind, and the early mixture of different houses soon gives way to the long row of white walled, red roofed semis that not only run you up to the Western Ferries, but are colour co-ordinated with it. From here on back into Greenock and Port Glasgow is a route we've travelled well, and I want to be repetitive as little as possible, so I will simply say that it is a classic return route the old A-770, and one I delight in every time I ride it.

On a super sunny day with the yachts out playing on the firth, if it wasn't for the Cowal Hills across the water, then Gourock front could be mistaken for any southern English seaside resort. Further on, the sandstone villas that line the surrounds of Eldon Street, on the Greenock centre approach, are ones I never tire of admiring. And the gentle rises and descents of the road here add to the effortless feeling it gives for the not-too-tired rider.

The next stretch of road after Greenock town centre, is one we also know well, the busy A-8, but I will take you along it just one more time as far as Port Glasgow. For there is one more route that climbs out of Inverclyde to take us back home which we haven't covered yet, so that will be the way we return on this occasion.

Batter along the busy dual carriageway till you come to the large new roundabout as you near Port Glasgow. Up until now, we have always turned left here, to run ourselves down to the waterfront on the new road. But not this time, no; this time we will charge straight ahead into the Port's centre, till we come quickly to a wee mini roundabout. At this, we turn right and go under a great arched rail bridge onto William Street, where then follows a left turn, which runs us behind the back doors of the old Port's tenements.

All good stuff ,I must say, as I like the old. The end of this street (Glen Avenue) sees us meet the start of our climb, in the shape of Highholm Avenue. This point can also be reached by not turning right at the mini roundabout, but by continuing on and taking the next right onto Balfour Street (signed Park & Ride for the station), which also runs onto Highholm.

Looking right into the mouth of the Gareloch from the high Dougliehill Road, which runs from the top of Port Glasgow over and across to the Auchmountain Road and joins it near Knocknair's Hill Reservoir. I mentioned in the Kilcreggan run how tight the mouth of the Gareloch was, and how difficult it must be to manoeuvre a big submarine in and out of it. This photo shows exactly what I meant.

Another view of the Clyde from the Dougliehill Road, and although the views are great the going is tough, the road surface rough, and the surrounding terrain duff.

This route has the advantage of running past Ramsay's General Store on Shore Street, which opens late on weekdays and can be the last stop for a while to grab some grub or juice. Anyway, whichever route is chosen you need to get the climbing legs going now for what is a great climb ahead, full of interesting twists and turns that take you steeply, but quickly, up to the top of the port. Yes, you'll find the early stages steep indeed, as you follow the double yellow lines up past the station car park, leaving behind as you go the lower older parts of Port Glasgow, with its aged buildings and church steeples. And you'll also find yourself straining your neck a bit to look up ahead, so fierce feels the gradient early doors.

But this pales into insignificance when the junction with Glenhuntly Road is reached. Don't panic, for it looks

Just about level with the Port Glasgow dock cranes. If returning, when going clockwise, it now means you have a very long steep and sustained pull up in front of you to reach the high ground before making for Kilmacolm.

doing yourself a disservice if you don't see Barrs out to the end, which isn't far away at this point.

Shortly into view will come the first factory building, standing out in white with its square chimney above its zigzag edges. And this means you're almost there! Out of the greenery you come, then past the factory and, boom, it's all over. You've made it. Well up, and all that jazz. Next, it's breather time, for it's all downhill when you turn left on the Dubbs. You have the whole of that road to run, as the Barr Brae emerges at the far end of it, just as it meets the Dougliehill Road. And, pumped up to hell, you fire down it, feeling on top of the world after clearing your last major big climb of the day, which is always a nice feeling.

A long enjoyable straight, then swinging big curve, takes you down through all the houses and factories of this high sitting estate. You pass another opportunity to join the cycle track further down, as the road plummets you towards the Clune Brae roundabout. But you don't go quite as far as it this time, because when you come level

much worse than it really is. Having said that, it does look fearsome the way that it doubles back hard, with its steep grass slope coming towards you and topped by its metal crash barrier. Bank hard right to go up it. It's fairly tough, but only at the start, for when you ease your way round the next left trending switchback, it eases off quite considerably and there then follows a straight tight climb. Tight, because of the cars parked along the right hand side, as you wheel your way up in amongst the grey modern houses. This is a good time to get into a rhythm to aid recovery and make what comes next much more manageable.

That's because shortly the road will swing right and up at a red brick wall, signalling the start of Barrs Brae. This is the third stage of this climb and the last, taking you up onto the Dubbs Road and into the Devol Industrial Estate. It also starts steeply, but you're over it quickly and soon purring your way up. At about halfway, you meet the cycle track crossing over the road, and it is possible to join it here and immediately come off the steep stuff. That is perfectly fine, if you want to, but you might feel you're

Looking back down the steep Glenhuntly Road towards the dock cranes, after pulling up through Port Glasgow's town centre. You can either make straight for the top of the Clune Brae along Boglestone Avenue or turn right up Barr's Brae and go through the Devol industrial estate.

Heading onto the Auchenbothie Road (clock) just after leaving the Bardrainney area of Port Glasgow, and the return home starts to be made in earnest. It is a fine return road that will carry you quietly and picturesquely back towards our own millionaires' row, Kilmacolm.

Approaching Kilmacolm on the Auchenbothie Road (clock), where you have the option at this point to either return on the great but busy A-761, or jump onto the cycle lane for the quiet life.

with the shops just before it, you take a right onto the Auchenbothie Road. This great road runs you just about all the way back into Kilmacolm, and is about the only way we haven't come so far, so here goes. It does climb up at first, though nothing too terrible. Up through as much greyness of sixties-style housing as you can shake a stick at, levelling out just before the country stretch of the Auchenbothie shows itself, with the two obligatory national speed limit signs either side.

Then it starts with the pleasant stuff, as into the fields we go next. There is a certain roughness about the first ones, despite some cattle being in them as opposed to sheep. The striking yellow gorse is present amongst the mud and pylons, as up ahead a small conifer plantation draws you towards it and into the softer-feeling farmland. It gets very nice about this point, because it just so

happens you are sitting on top of a fair bit of height now, which is just about to propel you down into the bends below, going through the fields and along the hedgerows, and finally running beside the old rail-line cycle track.

All pastoral now, as thoughts turn to the best way home, and there are two main options from here: the cycle track is the easiest and most convenient; the other is to head into Kilmacolm on the road and head back through Bridge of Weir that way. Both routes we have used in detail in previous runs, so I won't go over old ground again, but suffice to say how you are feeling along with the weather, wind direction and strength, will determine which one you take. Even these two routes will have options almost right up to the end, and that is a fitting end to a run full of variations.

So there you have it, as I approach my front door again, returning from another great and enjoyable day in what I regard as my back yard. Sometimes extended this run, but often cut short for one reason or another, but that is one of its strengths, the amount you can vary it to suit your need any time of the year. That is the reason the writing for this run was a bit longer than usual, as I wanted to include as many variations as I could.

There is plenty for you to work with to start building up the old endurance, and you won't find a better place to do it. Trust me…

Liam Boy

ROWARDENNAN

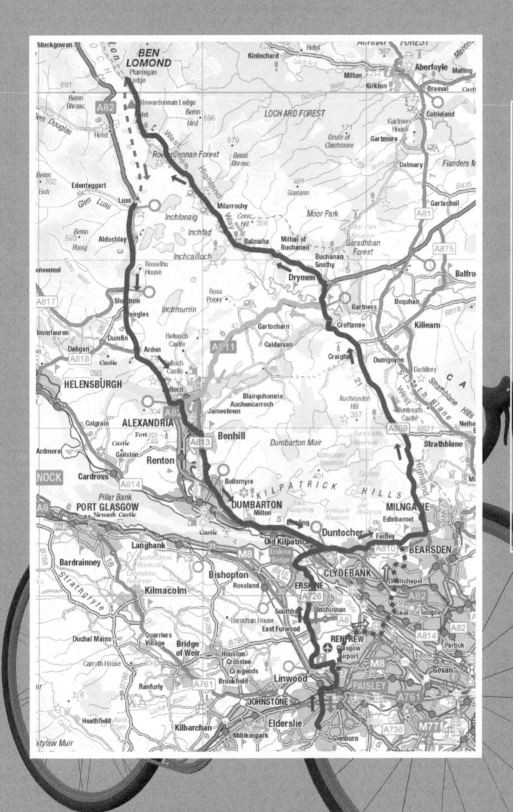

GARTOCHARN RETURN

71.9 MILES
4.44 HOURS
ASCENT 3340 FEET
2536 CALORIES BURNED

LUSS RETURN

63.3 MILES
4.03 HOURS
ASCENT 2620 FEET
2022 CALORIES BURNED

LOCH LOMOND CRUISES
TEL NO 01301-702-356.

O/S LANDRANGER
MAPS 64, 57, 56.

ROUTE SUMMARY

Erskine Bridge
Duntocher
Baljaffray Road
Stockiemuir Road A-809
Carbeth
Croftamie
Drymen
Balmaha
Rowardennan

ROAD RETURN

Balmaha
Drymen
Gartocharn
Jamestown
Bonhill

LOCH LOMOND CRUISES RETURN

Ferry To Luss
A-82
Balloch
Alexandria
Bonhill Bridge

BOTH ROUTES RETURN

A-82 Or Dumbarton
Dunglass Roundabout
Bowling
Old Kilpatrick
Erskine Bridge
Paisley

TAKE THE HIGH ROAD

'By yon bonnie banks and by yon bonnie braes', so goes the famous old song and so do we on this run, as we take the road up the east bank of Loch Lomond to its termination at Rowardennan. It used to be that for most who did this run, myself included, this would be the end of the line and therefore a case of retracing your tyre tracks back down the road to Drymen. However, that needn't be the case now, because in the summer of 2014 additional sailings were introduced by a small ferry that sails from Rowardennan Youth Hostel across the loch to Luss, and this can be used to make a circular route. Please note that the Luss ferries may only operate in the summer, so no circular option might be available in the winter time[1].

---

1 - It is advisable to phone Loch Lomond Cruises if you intend to do a circular winter run, to find out about their sailing times out of season.

There is also a ferry that crosses over to Tarbet which used to sail twice a day, but this has been reduced to one crossing now, leaving the youth hostel at 4.45pm. This can obviously be used by anyone wanting to include Tarbet as a circular route, as opposed to Luss, but I found this service's times weren't suitable for my needs and therefore I never used it in the past. Either the 10.45am or 3.30pm to Luss is catchable, depending on whether you are a late or early starter, and makes for a great day out. I thoroughly recommend it.

If you just so happen to live a bit closer to Rowardennan than I do, in around the north end of Glasgow, Milngavie or Clydebank and the likes, then it is certainly feasible to make the 9.30am boat and make a great circular day out, and one to really enjoy using that one.

However, even if I do go straight up and back down to Drymen, I can still turn the vast majority of this route into a circuit by going out the tough Stockiemuir Road from Milngavie, and returning by Gartocharn, back over the Erskine Bridge via Bonhill. So for me the ride will entail: heading over the Erskine Bridge and gaining the Stockiemuir Road at the far end of Baljaffray, then riding north to Drymen, before taking the long road all the way up the lochside for 11 miles to its termination at the Rowardennan carpark. The carpark itself is the main starting point for hillwalkers doing the mega-busy Ben Lomond, so expect a fair wee bit of traffic on the road up, especially if you're heading that way on a sunny weekend. The road, incidentally, is wide enough to handle it all, as it isn't narrow single track at any point, so jams are rare.

When you do reach Rowardennan, you can either return by the way you came or cross the loch to Luss. Please note that the ferry boat doesn't actually leave from Rowardennan pier itself but from the Youth Hostel pier, which is situated approximately half a mile further north and is gained by following a Land Rover track and not a tarmacked road. So mind how you go on your roadie. Many saloon cars, and not just four wheel drives, use this track to gain access to the youth hostel, so it is rideable on a road bike, but I don't like taking my best machine onto tracks, to be honest. It is more than passable with a bit of care, however, and is very pretty, being lined either side by Scots pine.

If you do cross on the ferry, then simply return back down the A-82 Loch Lomond road, or alternatively head up the Loch Lomond road to Luss first, if you fancy doing it the other way round.

Now if you don't take the ferry, then head back down to Drymen and, after leaving that village, it is easier for me at least and also a bit different, to return home via the A-811 towards Bonhill, than it is to return along the Stockiemuir Road, the A-809. I will then re-cross the Clyde on the Erskine Bridge and make my way home. If you do prefer to return back by the Stockiemuir Road, and depending on where you live, you might want to cross the Clyde on the Renfrew ferry, which is approached down the Peel Glen Road and accessed through Drumchapel.

So there you have the Rowardennan run in short, covering approximately 60 to 70 miles in beautiful scenery, and giving an option or two depending where you live, or even a very scenic ferry trip.

So to the Erskine Bridge we head, and into new territory once we get ourselves over that glorious expanse of steel and air. I have really only one way to get there and

have covered it before, but I'll give you a quick reminder. On leaving Glenburn I'm off down through the west end of the town, then firing down Greenhill Road on my way to Saint James interchange. Once over (thank Christ!), its fly down the Barnsford Road and on through the Red Smiddy and the remainder of the numerous Erskine roundabouts, till I'm under the Golden Gate girl herself.

I gain her via the awkward cycle lane approach, and am shortly into the long, fairly easy-angled climb that draws me up onto her middle section, allowing me the chance to admire the westward sea views of the Clyde towards Dumbarton Rock. A great long meandering view away to the Cowal Hills, guided by Old Man River, is what you can expect every time you cross the Erskine. Sometimes when the tide is out, the green marker buoys which form a line out to sea are more easily seen. Though they're not so much needed nowadays, they are still used, and the maritime history of the Clyde is second to none.

Now begins the charge down the other side, fast approaching the glorious green flank of the Kilpatricks. At the bottom of the cycle track, a tricky manoeuvre is required to get us across to the carriageway that will take us east-bound towards Clydebank. After a careful check over the old right shoulder, away you go, quickly into the cleats, followed by a head-down charge. Shortly you'll swing onto the mighty A-82, all dual carriageways and then some here, as lanes break off left to take you up and over the Mountblow Road and down into Clydebank and Dalmuir that way. We don't require the break-off lanes, but can use them for safety for a while, as we still charge straight on and take the first cut-off left and dive into Duntocher.

Feeling a bit relieved to be leaving the 82 behind, you ride along Dumbarton Road and past what seems to be more pubs than you can count, along with all the other amenities belonging to this old place, as all their eggs are in one basket down here on the Dumbarton. Across the road, the village green adds some pleasantness. Unwittingly, you cross the course of the late, great Antonine Wall here — the northernmost frontier of one of the world's great empires — and then, with a rise, you're passing a string of garages and a filling station, on the way up to the big Hardgate roundabout at the top of the famous Kilbowie Road.

Straight ahead we go, officially on the A-810, and gently rise after making our way through the older white — former, I dare say — council houses of old Hardgate, leaving its bustling wee centre of commerce behind. All the time we are making for the green belt between here and Bearsden, which has a bit of an extension in the shape of Clydebank and District golf course, which sits down on the right. Into some greenery you ride, but before you hit the fields proper, you pass the entrance to the outlying Faifley estate, which is really an outlying scheme of Clydebank. This whole area does have a look of desperation about it, not so much Duntocher, but certainly Hardgate and Faifley.

The area did prosper with cotton mills for a while, but the American Civil War put paid to that enterprise. Obviously Abraham Lincoln didn't have any shares in the cotton business. So behold the quaint East Dunbartonshire Council sign, with its wee Roman Soldier and the rest. It lets you know another boundary has been crossed, which is always good to know, being another psychological boost. And with that we pass the Cochno Road coming in from the left, where next it's the turn of the Baljaffray. The nearly new Langfaulds roundabout is where it now begins, so turn left when you reach it.

The roundabout's name comes from the nearby farm, and sitting behind in the distance is Castle Hill, so-called because a Roman fort once stood there — all part of the Antonine Wall's defences. It's quite an interesting stretch of road, the one that approaches Baljaffray, as it affords a fair wee panorama of the city from its height. This

After quite a long toiling gradual ascent all the way from the Baljaffray roundabout to the Whangie carpark on the A-809 Stockiemuir Road, it's chocks away! And the long, long drop begins, throwing you down in the direction of Croftamie. There's no turning back once the fall starts, and be prepared to be amazed at the length of the fall and the great views that open up northwards to you as you plummet down. Above, Ben Lomond is prominent in the distance.

continues with the pull-up over Baljaffray itself, where halfway over it the green fields give way to grey walls. You've just met Bearsden. No sooner are you up than the long, long descent down begins, with the Campsies coming into view away in the distance.

At the other side of Baljaffray Road (the B-8050), is its namesake roundabout and a sign saying 11 miles to Drymen. This is the start of the A-809 Stockiemuir Road, and it's tough. No doubt about it, it's tough. Maybe not so much going north, I have to admit, but when returning on it the other way, you'll soon find yourself digging deep just to keep yourself in motion, never mind anything fancy.

So from the Baljaffray roundabout, a wee rise — just to let you know what to expect — and you're off and running. It's all very pretty, though, I must say. Now as well as being tough, it's also bloody dangerous, so say the statistics anyway. This is the case for cars more than bikes, I hasten to add, as the Stockiemuir is one of Scotland's most dangerous roads.

Still tightly hemmed in by the greenery, you round Crossburn roundabout and rise again. This time it's longer than the last and staying closed in till you meet with the entrance to Balvie Farm, where things open up a fair bit, on the left side anyway. The openness of the sheep fields and conifer hillside behind really jumps up at you, after all the enclosed road riding you've just covered. Soon you're firing down and through tiny Craigton, where you're out into the open fields and meadows by this time, and it's green galore. Those dangerous Stockiemuir double bends are met for the first time, before a slight rise takes you past the clubhouse of Hilton Park golfie, at which point the distinctive shape of Dumgoyne plug shows itself briefly across the strath.

Gamely soldiering on, we meet another double-bending diving descent and find ourselves down among the meadows. Rough rush-filled meadows at that, and low and still, they form a quiet sheet. By a low stone bridge, you cross the Allander Water and find yourself in Stirling District — another boundary crossed. You're barely up the road any distance when you pass the iconic Carbeth Inn sitting in its spot, as it has done since 1816. It has always been a mecca for the motorbike team, not so much for us clean-living lads and lassies on the cycles, so we'll leave the leather-clad brigade to it and push on. Just as well we're sober and focused, because a long arduous pull-up lies ahead of us.

But before we pull up and out of Carbeth, keep your eyes open for some of the famous huts that hide within the woods here, as they are a bit of a rarity in this country. In other rural countries, like in Scandinavia, hutting is an established way of life. However, in Scotland, the Carbeth hutters are a breed alone. These hillbilly-type shacks were first erected here in the 1920s and 30s, and have been popular weekend retreats for their owners ever since. A lot of them come from within walking distance, from the Clydebank area and the likes. Some people actually used them to escape the Clydebank blitz in March 1941 when the Luftwaffe hammered the town in two massive night attacks.

The Gerries were after the shipyards, of course. But despite 439 bombers dropping over 1000 bombs, my old man assured me that all they hit was a half-finished submarine. This would have been lying in John Brown's yard, I assume. Sadly, it was the town and the people who took the brunt, with 528 people killed and hundreds more injured. 35000 people were left homeless; out of approximately 12000 homes, only 7 were left intact.

So it was towards Carbeth a few came for sanctuary. Since before and after the war, hutters had paid a nominal rent to the landowner for their hut space. All was well until the about the mid-1990s when the land around here started to become worth serious dough, and the then landowner, Allan Barns-Graham, tried to have the hutters removed from his property.

It was a classic David versus Goliath struggle, with the hutters being made up of working class people, and Barns-Graham being a rich landowning part of the establishment. At one time he was actually an election

agent for top Tory Michael Forsyth, one of Maggie Thatcher's key men north of the border.

It was a bitter and lengthy battle, with the legal wrangle lasting around 15 years, no less. It was finally settled in 2010, when the hutters were given the chance to buy the land themselves. During the dispute, the huts of the men leading the protest were mysteriously burned down. All's quiet now, I'm glad to say, and as you cycle past the place, you'd never know just how much animosity had been brought to this leafy green spot in the past.

So anyway, onto this long climb now and it rises and rises till we pass the entrance to Auchengillan scout camp. The landscape opens up to a fair old width here

Once the cut-off to Killearn is passed, the A-809 levels off for a short while and gives good views of the Loch Lomond hills ahead. Then much to your amazement, the road starts to fall again, for quite some length, right into the village of Croftamie itself. It's only then you realise just how much climbing you had previously done, more or less from the Erskine Bridge, and the height you were up.

before levelling out and passing along through the heath. The heath itself is a bit of a giveaway to the actual height you are up now, which you may not be aware of till you approach a well-signed, swinging right hand bend that sits above the Whangie carpark. Behold the view in front of you. It's about to get seriously good here, mark my words! A long, and I do mean long, descent tis about to start, and it has everything to entertain and excite. So away you go and enjoy your payback for all the climbing you've done since leaving the Erskine Bridge.

A dramatic start sets you off, airily passing the yellow gorse bushes that cling to the mounds aside the road, and as you go, the view of the mountains away to the north is truly spectacular. A skirting fairly flat start takes you round the right hand side of what is in essence a large bowl, taking you ever closer to the beginning of the drop.

All the Luss and Arrochar hills line up behind the mighty Ben Lomond, which steals the show with its massive isolated bulk. This is the first sight of the Beacon Hill this day, and its lower flanks will be the termination of today's run, of course. To give the mountains added stature, away to the right will be the broad flat of the Flanders Moss, enormous to the eye at this point, as we find ourselves hurtling down towards it.

With the Stockiemuir itself on our left, we start to descend steeply down through open fields at first, before entering into the lower bends among the trees and pastures. The descent here lasts so long that at one point you actually think it has finished, when you level out by some fairly enclosed fields, only to realise when you re-enter the woodlands that it's not all over yet, and off you go again. You find yourself diving round sun-dappled bends, as the trees allow through only partial sunlight. This can make spotting potholes and suchlike difficult, but that's not too much of a problem here as the road for the most part is in good nick. Eventually, and I do mean eventually, the road levels out just before it reaches the cut-off for Killearn, which after all that descending actually requires a short rise to reach.

Now we're not taking the Killearn road today, as that will be left for the Trossachs run. Instead, keep going straight ahead, where the sign says 3 miles to Drymen.

Just before the fall down to Croftamie begins, you nowadays enter the so-called Loch Lomond and the Trossachs National Park.

And now we're back out into the open, running along between the hedgerows, where Conic Hill starts to make its presence felt and obscures all but the top of Ben Lomond ahead.

Shortly, you enter into some lovely tree-lined road and also into the Loch Lomond and Trossachs National Park, where incredibly there is even some more great descending to come. Once again, it's curve down through the big beech hedges and the like, before finally coming out of the bush when you cross the picturesque Catter Burn and enter the equally picturesque Croftamie.

A big dramatic right swing in the road runs you into the main part of the village, but not before you pass the quaint village store on the left, looking resplendent in its black and white garb. Even along the Main Street, white-walled, red-doored farm barns stand cheek by jowl with the houses. Go over the rise, and more shacks to delight will line either side of the road, some built in near dazzling red stone that literally shines. You're almost at Drymen now, as the sign back at the big bend tells you it's only 1.5 miles to there; in fact, Croftamie is so close to Drymen that it used to host its railway station in days goneby.

Only another slight drop leads out to the bridge over the Endrick Water, and here you find lush meadows filled with the yellow of buttercups to the right of the splendid, solid, low stone, brown bridge that carries you over. To the left is a totally different scene, where the Endrick has cut dramatic curves and sways out of the banks by its years of gentle meandering. Six foot high, sheer earth faces line the river bank, above which the cattle graze in fields dotted with specimen trees. These are old and grand, isolated from one another in such a way as to suggest to me that this is land belonging to Buchanan Castle, at least at one time.

You then pass the entrance to the castle and its namesake golf club. And it's interesting to note that no Buchanan ever lived in the modern baronial pile that stands there now, as it was built by a Graham, the 4th Duke of Montrose, in 1854, and was used as a hospital during World War II. Its most famous guest was one Rudolph Hess.

After the castle entrance, climb slightly up and shortly turn left, to climb slightly again and enter the gardens of Drymen. The white sentinel of the Buchanan Arms Hotel greets your arrival. Up the normally busy Main Street you cruise, avoiding tourist after tourist, who will be in evidence — or my names not Liam Farrell.

At the war memorial in Drymen you make the turn to take you onto the B-837 for the 3 miles to Balmaha, before continuing on up the lochside on a minor road all the way up to Rowardennan, 11 miles away. Drymen will please in its prettiness, and acts as the gateway to Loch Lomond's east side. This village was once a favourite of Larry Hagman, who played the dastardly J.R. Ewing in the 80s TV series Dallas, no less.

The row of shops on the left, made from the same impressive red sandstone as the Croftamie dwellings, has gone for an overall arts and crafts sales pitch. So much so that in one, which sells whisky amongst other items, you can find out what is the malt of the month. It was a Bowmore the last time I passed, in case you are interested.

Turn first left at the war memorial, and the village store is just across the road, if you need ought, where the sign says its 4 miles to Balmaha and 11 to Rowardennan. It's all really good stuff to come, particularly the first 4 miles to Balmaha, which you will really, really enjoy. It's a stomper of a bit of road, no kiddin'. This is you on the B-837, by the way, and the B-837 won't disappoint, I promise!

As you glide round the bends while taking your leave of Drymen, you'll pass one or two new houses still being built, and at the same time pass some that are on their last legs, before you emerge out into the fields. In many ways it's a real mixed bag, the old Drymen lady, as it's not only the houses that are real old and new, but also the old agricultural ways are now becoming surpassed by the modern tourism industry. So what is so good about this road? you are entitled to squeal. But before you can ask that, you almost instantly find out for yourself. As soon as you leave Drymen, the dramatic Conic Hill strikes from the side, and its green flank stands out even more so by the fact the white linen walls of Buchanan Smithy's cottages stand in the forefront.

All neatly lined up like soldiers on parade are the Smithy's row of former workers' houses, built by the 3rd

Duke of Montrose, James Graham, to house workers for his estate. Three blacksmiths lived there, hence the name given to this tiny hamlet. All look chocolate box-pretty, I must say, with their solid chimneys and black-trimmed windows. The leafy setting doesn't do the look any harm, either.

So giving a wee admiring glance as you pass by, the road just gets better and better now, as it will become a long, straight, leaf-enclosed lane. This tunnels you forth, before starting to descend and bend, opening up just before coming into Milton of Buchanan, which is almost a take two of the Smithy.

More picturesque white houses greet you and once more it's Pleasantville. This whole area was a stronghold of the Clan Buchanan, hence the name places, but the Grahams supplanted them at one point. After a dip in the road and a climb and bend out, you find yourself on another long leafy enclosed straight, as you start to home in on Balmaha. A better run in to a village, I doubt you will find. For as you come out of the initial trees, you spy the mighty Loch Lomond for the first time, lying low, away across the fields to your left. But from this vantage point, it's difficult to gauge its true size as it's 5 miles wide at this point.

To your right is a magnificent large white house and even larger garden, where the owner has turned his somewhat sprawling lawn into a mini golf course. But it's the view across the field on the right coming up next that steals the show here, in my opinion. Conic Hill has been coming closer and closer and so, too, have the lesser, though no less dramatic hills that sit to its left. Pointed and sharp, with sharper pointing conifers on top, they give the field in front of them, containing cattle and sheep, an almost Alpine appearance. This is quite an unexpected scenario from a road that can be no more than 20 metres above sea level.

From here, the great rush down into Balmaha, again straight and again leaf-lined, finishes off a most pleasant and as enjoyable a stretch of road as you are likely to find anywhere.

Also, expect to be charmed by the watery scene that will greet you when you do level out. This is just after this village's local store, coffee machine et al. This is the last chance saloon before the 6 or 7 miles up, then 6 or 7 miles back from Rowardennan, there being nothing further up the road in way of succour.

Just offshore sits the impressive hump-backed Inchcailloch (Island of Nuns), very dramatic in its wooded and steep-sided persona; a sizeable flotilla of small craft cram the bay in front of you, taking advantage of the protection the inch provides. And with this most tranquil scene serenely spread in front of you, it's time to begin the final leg of the tour.

The warning triangle alerts you to what's to come, showing 15% inside its red confines. A quite sensational swing in the road brings the brutal wee climb into play, so get into your lowest gear and get ready to attack the pedals, but not for long, for it is a short one, thank God. The road almost immediately levels and runs alongside an old stone wall, where the height just gained by the climb allows the loch and another of its islands,

After 3 miles of unbelievably leafy-canopied chocolate box-pretty riding, you arrive in Balmaha, which matches the road just ridden for attractiveness. The view out over the bay into the loch could grace the cover of any Scottish calendar, and the small craft on the water, sitting still and quiet, are the icing on the cake.

Inchcailloch's near neighbour Inchfad, to be admired at your deep breathing leisure. (Inch is old Scots for island, in case you are wondering.) So after the up, the road will now down.

This down deposits you behind Conic Hill where, above the pretty sheep fields, the path belonging to the West Highland Way can actually be seen as it trickles down the hillside. The road now starts another toughish wee climb back into the woods, and then in similar fashion on the other side, drops you back down to the lochside, this time at Milarrochy Bay. The road can be busy all the way up and back, but it's broad enough for its entire length for traffic to keep moving in both directions. Also the road surface is mostly excellent all the way, too, except when

A closer view of the steep rugged side of Inchcailloch from Balmaha, which sits just offshore and provides a wonderfully dramatic backdrop to Loch Lomond's flotilla of small craft. Get ready now for the brutal short rise that you must take to lift you up and away out of Balmaha and on to continue to Rowardennan.

needs an effort to take you up and over to heavily-wooded Sallochy Bay. In here, you can find yourself among firs and ferns or trees that are a bit more native and deciduous. It can be a real special moment to stop in the forest here and just listen to the woodland song birds sing. This will be a lot easier to do on a week day, as opposed to Saturday or Sunday, as there will be a lot less traffic around.

Although it will not be possible for a lot of you, as the weekend is the only chance you may get to ride, it is better to do this pretty route on a quieter week day because this road is so popular at the weekend.

A less strenuous rise takes you past the entrance to Glasgow University's ecology hot spot and also the small and lily-covered Dubh Lochan, only just recognisable through the trees. Gleefully, keep flying through all this bird-whistling woodland till the entrance to Blairvoickie

you really need it to be — i.e. on the short, steep descents that you meet from time to time, especially the second one. Here, you will find on the way back, the surface is positively dangerous, so be particularly careful.

At Milarrochy, you'll find the tourist information centre and carpark, followed shortly by its large campsite. So there's always a bit more happening here. After a bit of flat riding beside the fields, the second and toughest wee climb of the whole stretch comes into play, and you will see the poor road surface I talked about earlier as you strain your way up it. This is the one to watch on the way back. It's bloody awful! You come down just as fast on the other side, after some nice wooded riding, and are deposited at Cashels. This is nice, flat, and straight here, and continues on like this till you're right alongside the loch. It's a fairly quiet spot, save for the numerous West Highland Wayers you're bound to encounter enroute. The Way runs alongside the road at this part, so be ready to say hello in at least twelve different languages.

The distinctive top of Ptarmigan ridge on Ben Lomond shows ahead and a pattern of woods, then water riding, sort of repeats itself all the way up, though interestingly enough in slightly different guises. The next woodland you enter is Rowardennan Forest itself, just after Anchorage Cottage, and once more another wee rise

The sheer breadth of the bottom end of the loch does become apparent from time to time on the road up, whenever the views across the loch present themselves, and it is a very, very impressive sight to behold. Despite that, it isn't Loch Lomond at its broadest, not by a fair margin. That part will sit to the south of Balmaha, which is behind us now as we make our way up the east side.

The sunlight coming through the Sallochy woodlands makes for a most delightful dappled dally as you donner up.
This stretch, I have to say, ranks as my favourite.

It simply couldn't get any prettier than this, as a leaf-covered cottage is passed just as we enter the final woodland before Rowardennan. That is another delight to come, but so, too, are the fields and meadows that have just gone before. Beautiful broad meadows of yellow buttercups, with dancing dragonflies and butterflies, have been seen enroute, and their sheer scale makes for another wonder.

Farm means you're out in the fields again for a bit. Loch Lomond itself is obscured from view on this stretch, but above the trees, you get a great sense of the way the mountains criss-cross each other towards the top of the loch, forming the narrower half of this great water mass.

This open stretch comes to an end when you pass a quaint grey cottage on the right, where it has to be said the fields around it are mega meadow-sized to the point of inspiring. Another climb and another great straight bit of diving through the woods follow, but not much further now. For when the trees give way on the right shortly after, Ben Lomond seems close, very close, and you know

This is the woods before making the final approach to the Rowardennan Hotel. It is a fitting finale and the telegraph poles give the game away that you are close to your destination, as they are the ones that service the hotel itself. A delightful wee drop down deposits you in Rowardennan.

the end is nigh. It is the telegraph poles leading to the Rowardennan Hotel that guide you along, and a final dive into the woods brings you out at the white, semi leaf-covered hidden hotel itself.

There's very little in Rowardennan, save for the hotel and some wooden holiday chalets nearby. These aren't too intrusive, however, and you're passed them and the hotel in seconds. There is just a final skirt round a small white curving pebbly bay, which shows off Rowardennan pier to its best, before you finally arrive at your destination.

Now there isn't much to the place in a way, to be honest. It really is just a large carpark, pine-sprinkled and pretty all the same, with a rather well designed large toilet block (always handy) thrown in for good measure.

But, and it's a big but, that description would not do

Rowardennan beach and pier on a very quiet day, and you can be sure it must be a week day. It is a most beautiful spot to linger awhile, and I like to sit on the pier all by myself and listen to the waves lap against the shore. It can regenerate a fatigued mind and legs before beginning the long journey home.

this picturesque and serene spot justice, because it is a most delightful and tranquil place to linger. So by all means, sit on the pier and enjoy a most calming dose of gentle water lapping that only a loch this size can provide in such measures. And it is only this loch that can provide such measures, for Loch Lomond is the largest mass of freshwater in the whole of the British Isles. 5 miles wide at the bottom, as already stated, but still holding a distance of over 1 mile wide for most of its length — and what a length at that, 24 miles long. Chances are, the carpark will be well used even on a week day, but most of the drivers will have come up to climb the Ben, whose summit in my opinion provides the best viewpoint in the whole of the Southern Highlands.

In complete contrast to a quiet Tuesday or Wednesday, the carpark at the weekend can look more like Renfield Street than Rowardennan. Don't worry, though, for most of the people parked here have come to climb Ben Lomond and it can still be possible to find a quiet corner to sit in.

Even this busy place can go all quiet and tranquil for a time midday, and so that makes it a good time to be there and to allow you some quiet time to yourself. A bonnie view up the loch from on or near the pier can be had, with the top of Ptarmigan ridge sitting above the youth hostel and the conifers that cling to its steep sides. A real wildscape is the best word to describe what you see when looking north from here, and the mountain ridges, all one after another, dive fearlessly into the cold hard water of the loch, which doesn't do the soul any harm.

ROWARDENNAN-LUSS

SAILING TIMES: 9.30am, 10.45am, 3.30pm.

ROWARDENNAN-TARBET

SAILING TIMES: 4.45pm.

Now, as I stated at the start of the run, there is a possibility that you can cross the loch on one of the ferries provided by Loch Lomond Cruises, that leaves from the youth hostel pier every day. Either of these two ferries will escort you across the water to Luss or Tarbet, and takes 45 minutes[2] to do so, this at a cost of £8 for

an adult and £5 for a child single, and the bike costing a further £1. From previous experience using the ferries to and from Inversnaid, I can assure you the staff on board are really brilliant, especially the female crew. The service was available from early April to early November in 2014, which gives a good idea of how much the ferries sail in any given year.

Now if you're an early riser, or stay a bit closer than I do to Rowardennan and can make say the 9.30am sailing, then by all means use that option to cross the loch, if you fancy it. I tend to work late most nights, so getting up early doesn't fall in well with my usual routine and I'm never able to make that one. Also the 4.45pm sailing to Tarbet doesn't suit, either, as I would be docking at 5.30pm and then have to begin the long journey back to Paisley a little too late for my liking. So it will be between the 10.45am or the 3.30pm sailings to Luss that I will aim for, then gingerly trundle up the Land Rover track to the youth hostel[3] to await the craft.

This will come in the shape of the *Lomond Warrior*, a fine sloop if ever there was one, and up till now punctual to a fault. You will have a quiet bird-twittering wait by the side of the loch, as you await the boat and once on board you will find there is a great wee bar selling teas, coffees, and shortbread, as well as the hard stuff. Let me tell you, crossing the loch and making a round trip of it is a great way to spend your day on the bike, having done so many times on the Inversnaid run, which is coming up next. In my opinion, the views on the Luss crossing are even more impressive than on the Inversnaid one, especially the view you get back to Ben Lomond.

2 - The 9.30am sailing to Luss takes only 30 minutes.

3 - Remember the boat leaves from the youth hostel pier, not Rowardennan pier itself.

One of the Loch Lomond Cruises boats leaves Rowardennan youth hostel pier heading for Tarbet. That's not the one we want, however, for we're after the new service that will take us over to Luss. It's only a Scots pine-lined bumble along a track to that pier from Rowardennan itself, and as it's not tarmac mind how you go on your best roadie.

This is followed by a picturesque approach and docking in Luss itself, with clear waters and dabbling ducks all there to greet your arrival. As stated earlier, it is more than feasible to do this run in the opposite direction, and just like the Inversnaid run to follow, it would, if you were doing it for the first time, give you an accurate time and distance from Rowardennan to your home so you could time it for a ferry when going anticlockwise the next time. The ferry times from Luss to Rowardennan are as follows:

LUSS-ROWARDENNAN

SAILING TIMES: 10am, 2.45pm, 4.15pm.

LUSS RETURN

For me, it's around the 26 miles mark back to Paisley, and it starts by a run up through and under the high chimney pots of the cottages leading down to the loch. The end of the pier road meets the old A-82 at the Loch Lomond Arms Hotel, and a left turn finds us on the road home. The early stages of this return will be a trip down memory lane for the older car-driving riders among you, who, like most nowadays when motoring up Loch Lomondside, will stick to the modern A-82. You soon rejoin the modern road shortly here, but not of course as previously mentioned in the Dunoon run, before passing the beautiful watery scenic stretch at Aldochlay.

The boats sleeping still in the water just in front of the steep wooded Inchtavannach never fail to impress.

A few wooded moss-covered wall curves later finds you back on the big modern. It starts off with a couple of flat, fast, sweeping bends, also fairly enclosed by summer foliage, that will take you to the start of the long straightish section running you down all the way to the big roundabout at Arden. Keep yourself tucked in safe just outside the white line of the main road, and I myself tend to stick to that as much as possible. However, if the tarmac is better on the road proper, then I will nip inside and take advantage of any smooth stuff going. Don't forget to keep your fuel levels high with hydration and grub, as a long return journey can often be the most arduous stage when fatigue sets in from the many tough miles gone before.

Once through the Arden roundabout, purr along nicely till you come to the road leading into the Duck Bay Marina, at which point you have two options. You can either stay on the main A-82 — not recommended, because the road becomes mega-busy and fast here and our safe haven, the unofficial cycle lane, has disappeared. Instead, it's better to take the stretch of old road past the

Rowardennan youth hostel pier waits patiently for the arrival of the Loch Lomond Cruises boat that now allows the Rowardennan run to become a circular route. On a good day it is an idyllic spot to linger by and marvel at all around you.

The small nippy Lomond Warrior is the craft that carries us in quite some style across the loch to Luss, and right on time here she is berthing at Rowardennan.

Looking back to Rowardennan youth hostel from the Lomond Warrior as she starts to head over towards the west bank. Settle in for a most scenic and enjoyable wee cruise, and don't forget there are refreshments on board.

Duck Bay, which is quiet, scenic and safe. It also very conveniently leads to the pavement section of the official cycle path, making it easy to join it at the entrance to Cameron House Hotel. I always mount the pavement there and break off left on the official cycle lane, which takes me down the Old Luss Road into Balloch.

Now, you can access Balloch by staying on the A-82 and climbing up to the big Stoneymollen roundabout at the start of the real fast dual carriageway section and drop into Balloch that way, but I feel it's a lot of effort for nought, as the Old Luss girl takes you to the same place by a gentle leafy descent. I've stated before that I usually avoid the dual carriageway section of the 82 where it is national speed limit, as it feels just too hairy for my liking, so I won't recommend it to you. Instead, I will take you back over the Erskine Bridge through Balloch and Alexandria.

So once again, not for the first time, we are into the Vale of Leven, and also not for the first time we find ourselves on the Luss Road, Balloch (a continuation of the Old Luss Road), but this time we are going in the opposite direction and heading south. The early Balloch bungalows disappear as the old Argyll Motor Company building looms into view, and we continue straight on till we come to the large fancy water fountain that refuses to spout. This time, take the left fork and fall down in among all the modern bypass stuff.

This will lead you to the beautiful Bonhill Bridge, that prize-winning specimen of architecture that Charles Rennie Mackintosh would have been proud to construct. I'm sure he would have approved of the yellow and red contrasting finish that certainly shows off its shape. When we get over, we will — if we look to our left — see the road we would have come down had we not taken the ferry, but instead returned by road and come back

via Gartocharn. This route is also recommended and, of course, starts back at the popular and picturesque Rowardennan pier

ROWARDENNAN ROAD RETURN

It is a bit of a wrench to pull yourself away from here on a really good day, but it's a fair old haul back to Paisley for your old mate, Liam boy. And bear in mind I'm not getting any younger, so the sooner I start, and all that. It is just as enjoyable to reride the road back down to Balmaha and enjoy the serenity of the 6 miles of woods, lochside, and pastures that you have just had your fill of on the way up. Again, going in the opposite direction on any road opens up new and different views to you; the ones you had your back to when going the other way, of course. So make the most of the return journey and

Looking back across the loch to the mighty Ben Lomond, and it's only one of many interesting and stunning views you will get on the sail over.

Approaching Luss village on the ferry and arriving by boat does, of course, provide views that you simply can't get from anywhere else.

on this one, as a lot of road will be going back through enclosed woodland which can have an overall same look to it whichever way you ride it, just ease up a bit and look for the subtleties. They are there alright.

For soon you'll be enjoying the vast sweeping meadows again, once you emerge out of the initial woodland, glide and cross the burn running down the Caol Ghleann, just at the wee grey cottage. But I must be honest and say that I enjoy the Rowardennan Forest the best at Sallochy, with all its strength and gentleness. The strength and solidness of its pines, the gentleness of its ferns and songs. Dappled sunlight on the tarmac does delight, as it moves and sways with the motion of the leaves and keeps one cool on a baking day. So, too, will a shaded light breeze, as it finds its way through the bark to your motionless body, if you've stopped once more, only briefly to absorb the silence.

And so onward and returning, curving and climbing, till the passing of Anchorage Cottage means we are on the loch again and admiring its numerous Inches. These

No prizes for guessing we're at Luss pier, and today it just happens to be a scorcher. This is no quiet backwater, you will be quick to realise, and the contrast from the east side couldn't be greater. We have now arrived in Touristville.

seem to be easier to appreciate on the return leg, and quite a spectacle they make. All seem heavily wooded and most striking at times, where one has to look hard to see any sign of settlement on them, which I assure you there is. Back through Cashels you go, and get ready to take the tough wee rise that hits you when you re-enter the woods; be wary of the poor road surface on the descent. It really is bloody awful, so a bit of caution should see you down safe and well.

The fields before Milarrochy follow next, before the campsite and then Milarrochy Bay follows them, as does the next rise — again in the woods — to take you out into the brightness. It's beautiful brightness at that, because pastoral fields sit high above the loch here and, with hard-won height gained, a quite special look over to the shapely and striking Inchcailloch is your reward for

Just about to pedal up, if you can find any room to do it, on the first street in Luss that we come to. It's still a pretty wee village despite the hordes, but I for one can't wait to get away from the crowds.

all your efforts. It certainly is a most impressive sight, so steep and wooded that it reminds me of something more akin to Thailand or a South Pacific island, perhaps. Its overall shape adds to its appeal, as it has a similar profile to Suilven in wild Assynt.

You're almost back in Balmaha now, which you reach by dipping slightly into the remaining sheep fields and, whilst enjoying the last view you see of the shapely Conic Hill from this side, a final stone wall-guided glide up brings you above the brutal short rise out of Balmaha. Heavy anchors on the way down, of course, or there is a chance of an early bath in the loch itself, so ferocious is the drop. But once down it's all easy again; easy street in the village street.

Fancy a coffee? The village store, with outside tables on the right, has a wee machine and muffins and cookies to temp you. Not that I ever give in to temptation, you understand. By the way, I realise I've mentioned the coffee machine twice; it's just that I like a coffee!

If you didn't get a chance to fully appreciate and enjoy the tree-lined descent into Balmaha, then you will on the rise back up. The long straight avenue draws you back along as far as the eye can see, till the road bends right,

mostly be effort-free riding down through the streets of this pleasant place. After leaving Drymen, you will soon find yourself approaching the Endrick Water again and its splendid old bridge, its several arches allowing the soft flowing river to pass unhindered underneath. No problem to cross the gentle slope that takes you over, as you do come down a hill approaching it and the momentum allows a fairly effortless crossing. This allows more time to admire the yellow dotted meadows upstream and the grand trees adorning the fields down.

All this easy slow stuff is good at this stage, for me anyway, because now I have a decision to make as to which road to take on the return journey. That's because branching off to the right is the A-811, allowing passage to the Vale of Leven and a different way back, or I can retrace my way back home by taking the Stockiemuir again. For the purposes of making it a round trip and to make you aware of another route (no bad thing), I shall take the 811, but of course it might not be the best option for you.

If going back over the Stockiemuir Rd (the

The old road that carries you south for a mile or two from Luss, before the new road is hit, is still an old-fashioned gentle gem. And no more so than at Aldochlay, where the view of the boats in the bay with the striking Inchtavannach behind is always picture postcard pretty. Soon you will be on the more modern A-82 which will lead you through the Vale of Leven towns. Once you cross the Leven on the Bonhill Bridge, you will meet up with one of the road route options which you can use to return from Rowardennan, should you so wish.

just before you enter Milton of Buchanan. Then, after the brief sortie down and up through the hamlet, it's on towards the Smithy. Just the way the trees border the road here practically equates to a canopy at one point, a most long green elegant corridor that I don't think I've seen the likes of anywhere else. This is followed eastwards now in wonderment and full enjoyment, before the white walls of the Smithy's cottages signal the all-too-soon end to this glorious glide.

Now it's only a short hop back to Drymen, which is entered with a descent and a smile. That's because it will

A-809) is your best bet or shortest way, be prepared to dig in deep for a tough and hard climb back home. This will be especially so after the side road to Killearn, where the long haul back up will not ease again till you pass the Whangie carpark, and even then there are pull ups after Carbeth and the Hilton Park golfie. The deceptive climb back over the Baljaffray can also feel like tough going, just so you're ready for it, and I'm always glad when I clear the bugger.

For me, it's back to the right turn onto the Gartocharn road (the A-811) and here is, what I must say, a most

If you decide not to use the ferry, but instead want to return the way you came, then you will find the road back down to Drymen is just as much a pleasure to ride as it was on the way up. Here we are once more enjoying the wooded delights of the forest at Sallochy.

impressive scenic start to this road — and what a contrast, too.

In the foreground is the billiard table flatness of the fields that border the Endrick, all vast and spreading at that. So much so, they remind me of a Texas cattle ranch, except a bit greener. Beyond that, however, is the height and drama of the Highland mountains, all a distance away, yet close enough to impress nonetheless. The shapely pyramids belonging to the Arrochar Alps make their presence felt and, mixed with the contrast of the near level foreground, it makes for quite a striking scene. It's just a little difficult to take your eyes off it, so it's just as well the road at this point isn't too technical or tricky.

In fact, it is fairly flat and straightforward to begin with, as you start to cover the 6 miles from here over to Balloch. There is a slight rise in the road as you make your way into the trees and, still long and straight, it goes up past the hidden Kilmaronack House. But the straight stuff soon stops just after Badshalloch Farm, where the bends start and it becomes nice and interesting. By this time you have crossed into West Dunbartonshire, there now begins a couple of miles of similar riding that rounds fast sweeping bends, some with double white lines in the centre such is the severity of them — for motorists, that is.

Officially the old 811 is a primary route, but even on a week day I haven't found it too busy, and if you do most of your long rides at the weekend, especially a Sunday, then traffic shouldn't be a problem. I've never felt threatened by cars or trucks on the continuous bends that lead towards the village of Gartocharn. The bends flow

low, always among the strong greenery, never rising nor dropping too much, as they bring you to the countdown markers that herald your arrival. So, too, does the distinctive mound of Duncryne Hill sitting behind the village, which is seen before you arrive and also lets you know you are close. A little bit of respite is earned as you fall gently into its Main Street.

Gartocharn was put on the map a few years back when Scottish national treasure wee Tam Weir took up residence in the village. Most people will have gotten to know him by his excellent 1970s programmes *Weir's Way*, by which time Tommy was in his later years, but still very active. With his woolly hat and red nose, he did come across as a bit of a rambler who enjoyed a donner, but nothing more. But don't let that woolly old exterior fool you. Let me assure you, he was an excellent mountaineer in his day and a pioneer to boot. He did things back then that a lot of mountaineers today, with their modern equipment, would struggle to do in this day and age. For example, he once tackled all three big ridges on Ben Nevis on a winter's day, and that is some going, let me tell you.

The village also plays host every year to some evangelical gathering of Truthers, but as I'm not one of the flock I don't know much about it, you'll be surprised to hear. Now you fly past the gardens and bottom out in the centre of the village and then start the descent out, passing some mucky old farm buildings as you go. The pull out is a long drawn-out job, which thankfully isn't too fierce and so you can still keep up a fair wee cadence even at this late stage in the day. Mind you, this bloody

Riding past the row of quaint white houses that more or less make up the hamlet of Buchanan Smithy. The previous leafy canopy-covered stretch of road has just been enjoyed to the full. We're almost back at Drymen.

We're just about to recross the Endrick Water by its most fine old bridge. The buttercup-covered meadows are in full bloom at this point, as this is a run being done on a beautiful glorious June day. Once over the bridge, you may be faced with two options (depending on where you live) on which way to return home. The first option is to go back the way you came by using the A-809, but this means a long hard climb back up the Stockiemuir Road to the Whangie carpark, or to take the first right just after the bridge and return via Gartocharn on the A-811 and then the Vale of Leven.

The steeper descent you hit just after the farm, passing Ashcroft House, doesn't do your morale any harm. The road levels and straightens for a bit, passing a bird of prey centre (could be worth a look?) before the final rise on this road is encountered, coming at you at quite an interesting spot. A staggered junction here allows side road access into Balloch by the back way, and a number of large sheds belonging to a country store suppliers sits on the left.

These are solidly built concrete structures, decked out in cream and blue trim. This place used to be a bus garage, if my memory serves me right. So Tally-ho! Onto and attacking pedals for a last hurrah, it is, as up and over we go, through a pleasant tree-lined rise. Big deciduous jobs stand either side of the road and welcome you into the Vale of Leven. The top houses of Balloch sit across to your left as you begin a most worthy descent down, one that

climb does overstay its welcome by a fair old bit as it gets you back up in amongst the pastures. Still, it's always good to have some height in the bag which you know you will be able to cash in sooner or later, and that is the case on this road.

After a clever bit of energy-saving, by pacing yourself well all the way up through the long gradient on this one, you find yourself back amongst more fast sweeping bends when it does finally level out. It's more open this time, due to the extra height gained, and all around the softness of the lower Loch Lomondside terrain is in evidence. No steep or harsh hillsides here, far from it, it's rolling ruralsville you find yourself in. Feeling fast and flash after getting pumped up by all the climbing, you whizz round these corners, passing various isolated houses and places as you go, before you see Ashfield Farm, red and white, sitting ahead on the right.

Height will start to be shed at this point, only slightly at first, till you're past the farm, which incredibly has a traffic light set up controlling the main road, which was put in place to allow the cows to cross over. I was tickled pink when I saw that for the first time, I must say.

The Strathblane hills show well as you crest the gentle rise on the Endrick Bridge itself. I'm sure you will find that the bridge makes for a most picturesque and pleasant crossing of this quiet murmuring water.

On the return journey back along the A-809, Croftamie will soon be ridden through and then the climbing begins in earnest. The picture above shows the road just after the initial climb out of Croftamie has levelled off and you're leaving the National Park behind. There is still the long hard climb back up to the Whangie to come, but even after that there is still much upping and downing all the way back to Baljaffray. It's a tough return route, no two ways about it. Make sure you've got plenty of water and are well hydrated for this one if it's a long hot summer's day, as you are going to need it.

would do any town proud. And on clearing the last of the trees, Balloch's homes and roundabouts open up to you. Turn left at the first roundabout, to take you onto the Carrochan Road (the A-813), which will shortly flip you into Jamestown.

It's difficult to know where this small settlement starts and ends in places, and I think a major fear of the residents here is that sooner or later they may get swallowed up by Balloch on one side or Bonhill encroaching from the other. The grand spectacle of the Jamestown Parish Church holds court as you pass through its small centre, and on along Main Street you continue, running alongside a low stone wall that separates you from both the Vale and the River Leven itself. Through the trees can be seen the very large factories that occupy the vale — Polaroid was a major player in there for a long time, but so, too, were many others. Many big hitters still have bases there and it's these you see as you skirt along.

It has to be said that, like the salmon fishers you see casting the Leven who look out of place in such an urban environment, so do the manufacturing complexes that sit in this green and pleasant vale. To my mind, there has always been something out of kilter with the way that industrialised Scotland meets its beautiful natural green self here. Anyway, just to reinforce what I was saying earlier about Jamestown's threatened identity, before you

know it the street sign tells you that you are now on Main Street, Bonhill. Route-finding along here is absolutely no problem, as you will continue on the 813 straight along, right until it meets with the A-82 just outside Dumbarton.

Before we meet the 82, though, we come to the bonnie Bonhill Bridge, and this means that both the road and ferry return routes have come back together as one. What can I say about the Bonhill Bridge? It won't be winning any awards for its appearance, that's for sure. Had they run a competition to build the ugliest bloody bridge imaginable, then the Bonhill baby would certainly be in the top three, if not the all-out winner. I would be willing to risk a small wager on it, and I'm no betting man. The semicircular steel structure has been finished off in a yellow and red paint job, just to give it that 'Dear Jesus' look[4]. Anyway, that is the least of our problems at the moment, because just after the bridge a taxing wee climb comes into play and is one I always hate, to be honest.

I will guarantee you that when you start to ride longer yourself, you will begin to accumulate bits of road that you love and others, usually climbs, which you hate. This one is most certainly in the latter category. It pulls you up into the road running below all the grey 60s and 70s built schemes of the town, which were constructed to house the Glasgow overspill, as they came to be known. These

4 - Just in case you're wondering, all that stuff I said earlier about Charles Rennie MacKintosh, I wasn't being serious.

The Endrick Water from the start of the A-811 looks tranquil and pastoral as the route back continues now in a westerly direction, if the right turn has been made after crossing the Endrick Bridge. This is a much flatter and therefore easier option to the Stockiemuir Road, but that's not the reason I like to come this way. It's because it makes the Rowardennan run still mostly a circular route even if the ferry option isn't taken.

Beautiful big broad bright buttercup meadows can be seen as the A-811 is ridden in the direction of Gartocharn, and what a delight they are to witness. They enhance the pleasure of any run any day.

were the poor sods who had their tenements pulled down in that era, tenements that admittedly needed pulling down, but instead of rehousing people back in the area they grew up and the only place most of them knew, they shunted them out of the city.

These developments swelled the size of Bonhill in sheer number of residences, but not in facilities or amenities, as there wasn't a lot built to make life any sweeter for the new arrivals.

The next roundabout you hit seems to lead into a number of these estates, all sitting above you high on the hillside. We don't enter any of them, though, but plough straight ahead and leave battleship-grey Bonhill behind, way behind. For a short stretch you're back into the fields again, but not for long, because a wee dive down soon takes you out at the roundabout which leads into the industrial estate itself.

The massive Aggreko plant sits dead ahead, and it's going round the side of it that will take you out at the new roundabouts on the A-82. Turning left and running along towards the Bonhill Road roundabout, means a choice has to be made. Previously, I have advised that going through Dumbarton — as opposed to running the 82 direct — is preferable, as it is quieter and safer. Especially so as the Loch Lomond cycle lane can be picked up and followed back to Bowling. By all means turn right at the roundabout and go that way if you want to. However, taking the A-82 instead is by far and away the fastest way back to the Erskine Bridge, and as there is a 30 or 40 miles an hour speed limit on this stretch then it isn't too frightening, unlike the stretch further north.

So if you want to get back fast and take the shortest route, go straight onto the 82 and start to make your way along past the north end of Dumbarton. Most of you reading this, but not all, will have driven this road many times. Personally, I couldn't even hazard a guess as to how many times I have travelled down it, returned from the mountains, over the years. The good thing is it is flat, fast, and furious, as most dual carriageways tend to be. Fast and furious, not flat that is. Soon you are making you way under the striking height of Dumbuck Quarry and going through the lights and on past the Milton Inn, where another mile or so of the furious stuff sees you up at the girth of the Dunglass roundabout and right into the sanctuary of Bowling. Phew! I say again, phew!

Just to help you get your breath back, and anything else you need to get back, it is a short downhill stretch that welcomes you into another old backwater sort of a place. Bowling is now commutersville, its heyday long passed. But not a problem to your average bike rider who likes it quiet, of course. Our course to carry us over the Clyde soon appears, dramatically spanning the river. The Erskine Bridge is no eyesore, that's for sure. This is the first place you spy it from when returning this way, which is just before you reach Bowling centre; a centre that contains nothing but houses and tenements, along with the occasional boozer, though some of these (tenements) are of an impressive age. The date of construction is

Heading along the main A-82 at Dumbarton and approaching the striking lump of rock that is Dumbuck quarry. Whether you returned by the ferry or Gartocharn, both routes will have re-joined by now a few miles back on the A-813 at the bonnie Bonhill Bridge. As for the mega-busy A-82 itself, I only use this stretch at quiet times because it is flat fast and convenient. It will carry you back to Bowling and the Erskine Bridge a lot quicker then meandering through Dumbarton, but the safety of the cycle lane is just to the right of the road if you prefer to use that.

Crossing the Black Cart on the Barnsford Road behind the airport, on the approach to St James interchange. Soon another great summer's day run will be over and reduced to a distant memory, so just remember that when doing these runs it's all about living for the moment.

stamped on some and it's always interesting to see when a thing was built.

It's not long until you find yourself out the other side and climbing up the swaying road into Old Kilpatrick. An iron sign now lets you know that it was 142AD that the legions from Rome set up shop here. Then you hit the first houses and fly down through the Main Street till you're under the bridge. Despite the impressive structure of the bridge overshadowing all below, the old tower of the parish church holds its own against it, with its blue clock face. Just for the record, its time is accurate.

You know the drill by now for getting across: it's up Station Road and then all the carry on round the side of the bowling green till the cycle lane is gained. Just be gentle with yourself while you allow tired legs to get into a rhythm as you make your way back over and take in the view upstream of Glasgow, as you crest the bridge.

It might not be as dramatic a scene looking upstream as it is looking down, but the scale of Glasgow, with its uncountable number of high flats, is still an impressive sight. Just recover on the fly back down the other side.

On decanting the bridge, I've got the modern styled A-726 to follow back up through the roundabouts of Erskine, to run me up the back of Glasgow Airport on the Barnsford Road. There's nothing much to see as you return, save for some brand spanking new white flats at the Bargarren roundabout. The rest of the scenery is the tightly packed scatty trees and undergrowth that abounds either side of the road till you climb up to and through the Southolm roundabout.

This leads a lot more openly through the fields to the Red Smiddy, and it is worth saying that when you shortly cross the River Black Cart, the view downstream is one of a most pleasant pasture, despite me previously knocking it.

So now it's up to the airport's perimeter fence, just about where the fire boys do their training at the well burned-out replica of an aeroplane. And across the sway of the flatness of the meadows inside the fence, the multicoloured tail fins of waiting planes sit in line, awaiting their next holiday destination. A most grand spectacle does Glasgow Airport make, even from this distance.

Often when going along the stretch of road that starts at the windsock, you find yourself exposed to any south westerly wind, as there is no shelter from one whatsoever at this point. It often pecks you out if you are against one, as more often than not you can be on your last legs at this stage.

Then the final bending rise brings Saint James interchange. Once through, I have my own way and shortcuts back up to my home in the Glenburn area, from the north end of the town. Greenhill Road is my normal artery there and back, and from the Greenock Road side it begins with the Carlton Die Cast Company building, which I think I'm right in saying was designed by the same bloke who designed Stalingrad.

There is a lot of old stuff like this down here, but not as much as there was. The new has also taken hold, most noticeably the football ground. Still, the top end of the road holds its own in grey days gone by, with the old gas works being the icing on the cake. No doubt you will develop your own preferences and shortcuts as you reach the final furlong or two on your own patch.

It makes for a familiar and quicker finish on occasions, and is a nice way to end any run, I think you'll agree.

Thanks for coming again... Liam Boy.

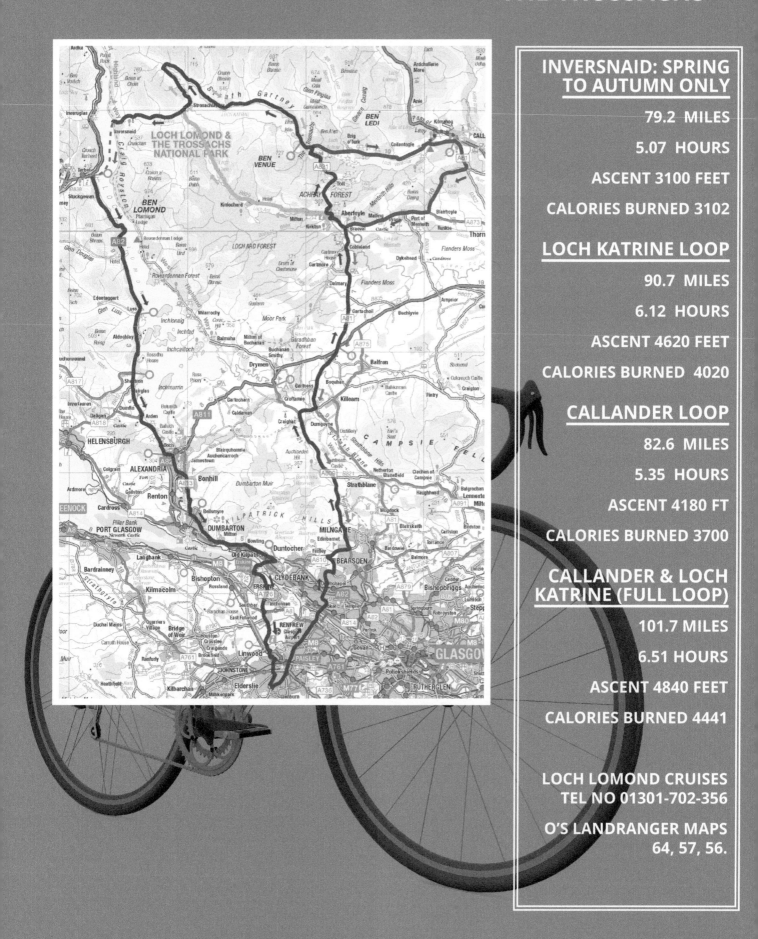

THE TROSSACHS

INVERSNAID: SPRING TO AUTUMN ONLY

79.2 MILES

5.07 HOURS

ASCENT 3100 FEET

CALORIES BURNED 3102

LOCH KATRINE LOOP

90.7 MILES

6.12 HOURS

ASCENT 4620 FEET

CALORIES BURNED 4020

CALLANDER LOOP

82.6 MILES

5.35 HOURS

ASCENT 4180 FT

CALORIES BURNED 3700

CALLANDER & LOCH KATRINE (FULL LOOP)

101.7 MILES

6.51 HOURS

ASCENT 4840 FEET

CALORIES BURNED 4441

LOCH LOMOND CRUISES
TEL NO 01301-702-356

O'S LANDRANGER MAPS
64, 57, 56.

ROUTE SUMMARY

ALL ROUTES OUTWARD

Renfrew Ferry

Yoker's
Kelso St.

Drumchapel's
Kinfauns Dr &
Peel Glen Rd

Baljaffray Rd
Stockiemuir Rd A-809
Carbeth
B-834 (Killearn)
Blane Smiddy Roundabout
A-81
Aberfoyle

INVERSNAID ROUTE

Kinlochard
Inversnaid Hotel
Ferry To Tarbert

LOCH KATRINE LOOP

Duke's Pass
Loch Katrine
Stronachlachar
Kinlochard
Aberfoyle

CALLANDER LOOP

Duke's Pass
Brig O' Turk
Invertrossachs Rd
Or Callander
Port Of Menteith

INVERSNAID RETURN

A-82
Balloch
Alexandria
Bonhill Bridge
Bonhill
A-82 Or Dumbarton
Bowling
Old Kilpatrick
Erskine Bridge
Paisley

KATRINE AND CALLANDER RETURN

Reverse Of Outward Route

INVERSNAID & THE TROSSACHS

ROB ROY COUNTRY

J ust to the north of Glasgow lies an area of outstanding beauty and grandeur, which was made most famous by that unashamed pro-English Uncle Tom, Sir Walter Scott, with his poem *The Lady of the Lake*. This was centred round the beautiful Loch Katrine. To make a day of it, cycling up from the central belt in and around the lochs and mountains of the Trossachs will give you a fantastic run and memorable day out all in one. Many people will drive up to the large carpark at the eastern end of Loch Katrine itself and get the bikes off the back of the car, or hire a bike and cycle round the traffic-free road from there – and that is absolutely fine.

This is especially good if you have kids, for the first 2 or 3 out of 10 miles round to Stronachlachar is not only gorgeous, but is mostly flattish and, as already mentioned, is without vehicles to pose any danger. You will pass many adults as well as little ones, all enjoying the wonders of the place, if you decide to make your

way around the Katrine on your run. Taking the official cycle route round it is only one of several options open to you, once you make your way into this most beautiful area. For me, or anyone else coming from the south, there are two main overall options when touring the Trossachs, though even they have variations just to keep it interesting time after time.

These won't go to waste, I assure you, because once you've entered the confines of this wonderful, though often wet corner, you will be drawn back to it again and again. The main approach route from the south will be the deceptively delightful to ride A-81, after which a loop around numerous lochs can be made – often, though not always, involving the Duke's Pass – and then returning back the way you came. Or alternatively, you can return by the ferry boat that leaves from the Inversnaid Hotel and crosses Loch Lomond to Tarbet, and return back via the A-82. There are usually 3 sailings a day from Inversnaid, and fortunately two of them are well suited for our purposes, running as they do in mid-afternoon.

Just approaching Renfrew Cross enroute to the Renfrew ferry, which is a great way to get across the mighty Clyde and, without doubt, the easiest. It is the gateway to many great northern routes, and today's destination will be the wonderful Trossachs... Enjoy.

That way, you will learn the distance and time from Inversnaid to your home, so you can judge it accurately when you come to do the run in the opposite direction next time.

That is the way I worked it at first, and found out by taking the most direct route home through the Trossachs that it was 47 miles back to my front door, if I returned over the Erskine Bridge. Now, I mention the bridge intentionally here, because although it is perfectly feasible to go and return via that way, there is in fact a shorter alternative, at least for me. The Trossachs sortie follows the same route out as the Rowardennan run, all the way out along the A-809 Stockiemuir Road, till it meets with the B-834 leading to Killearn. By all means, if it suits your needs, use the Erskine Bridge, then follow this course to that point and similarly return by the bridge on the way home.

However, there is a fairly forgotten old stalwart that can also be used to ferry you over the Clyde, can save me 3 or 4 miles of riding, and about 200 feet of ascent. That old stalwart is none other than the Renfrew ferry. This is the only one of the upper Clyde ferries remaining; at one time there were another five similar ferries all operating between Erskine and Finnieston, which were mainly used by the shipyards' workers. All the rest were eventually replaced by tunnels or bridges, but Renfrew wasn't suitable for either, so I'm glad to say the old ferry remained.

A survey in 2007 found that a replacement bridge here would cost £15million, as it would need to lift up or be high enough to allow ships being built or serviced upstream (mostly Royal Navy) to pass underneath.

So, it is to this point on the banks of the mighty River Clyde that I will point my front wheel and handlebars, as

That said, they are spaced quite far apart, so if you miss the 2.15pm, for instance, you will have over 2 hours to wait till the next one. Now, if you are unsure of the distance between your home and Inversnaid, and are worried about getting stranded there or being faced with a tough long ride back the way you came if you miss the last ferry at 4.30pm, then initially it might be a good idea to do this run clockwise and head for Tarbet first.

Immediately after the fantastic full rush of the long descent down the Stockiemuir Road has ended there then begins a slight pull up to the B-834 Killearn cut-off, which is the road we want to take on this occasion.

I head out the door and prepare to smother myself and my machine in some highland happiness in and around Loch Ard, Loch Katrine, Loch Arklet, and several other glorious Trossachs waters. This time I'm still heading north, though not making for the west end Maxwellton area of Paisley, but rather the town centre itself. This is a very fast course down into the town, because after only a couple of short warm-up rises on the Stanely Road, passing football parks and some grand houses and gardens, you shortly take a mad diving descent round and down the Munt.

This is the name given by locals to the short steep hill and its helter-skelter bends on Park Road, and caution must be shown particularly on the second bend, a tight hard left-hander, or there is a good chance of meeting a car head-on coming the other way uphill. In fact, the stone wall with iron railings built in, which faces you on the first of the bends, has had more hits than John Lennon over the years. Once round this hairy wee challenge, there is a great firing descent down into Causeyside Street on the Calside, which joins Causeyside at a prominent V junction overlooked by the Craig Dhu pub. After this, a busy but leisurely mosey can be had between the tall solid stone tenements on one of Paisley's best loved streets, right down to the mega busy crossroads with Canal Street.

It's best to go straight over and finish off the rest of Causeyside, before rising up Saint Mirren's Brae and reaching Paisley Cross. Now, the most direct way to Renfrew, as there are a couple of options, is just to head straight down the Renfrew Road (the A-741), which is probably the busiest road in the whole of the town, as it is the main artery to and from the motorway. However, it is a fairly short excursion along it, and if you hit it after the morning rush hour it's not that bad, being dual carriageway and a 30 mph limit. It's soon gained after weaving round past the town hall and then banking into Smithills Street, now part of the limited access to vehicles part of Paisley centre.

Poor old Paisley. The heart, the life, the hustle and bustle have all been ripped out of it by pedestrianisation. It feels like a ghost town now when you walk up the once busy High Street. The massive Braehead shopping complex has torn out the retail heart, and the lack of buses, buddies, and bustle has removed the life. Now it seems that empty stores, charity shops, and drug addicts are the three fastest expanding commodities in the town.

A glorious tree-lined avenue that falls long and fast in its top end is what you'll find on the B-834. It will guide you quickly down to, then over, the Endrick Water, before rising up to the Blane Smithy roundabout, and ultimately the great A-81. Then you're motoring north.

You find yourself skirting the one way system of the Sneddon, once you clear Smithills, and soon you're up and past the Reid Kerr College[1] and Renfrew-bound. The college, then Chivas Brothers bottling plant, both dominate the left hand side of the road for the most part, with the Gallowhill housing scheme doing the same on the right, before the motorway is reached.

It's straight and flat all the way to the bridge over the M8, and once into Renfrew, the road continues in a similar vein. You do, however, notice a definite drop in traffic volume, which is always welcome, and the road still continues long and straight all the way down, literally to the ferry itself. In the old days it was a real flyer all the way, but every time I enter Renfrew now they seem to have added another set of lights. So much so, I actually lost count of them last time I went through. I think it's up to eight sets now, which will be the only temporary obstacle to slow you up on the way down this glorious long avenue.

With its long row of impressive sandstone tenements that follow Robertson Park, all sitting left side, the Paisley Road makes a fine sight, making it so easy for it to pull you down. Then the striking town hall comes into view – another grand sight, in its dark coat with impressive multi-turreted tower. This one was finished in the April of 1872, and replaced the original. The original doubled as the town jail, though not very successfully, for escapees were numerous.

---

1 - It's now changed its name to West of Scotland College.

Go right below it, as on towards the ferry you slip; not much further now to the ferry slip. The area down by the waterfront does still retain a look and feel of the old world, despite the massive encroachment of the new flats of the ever-expanding, so-called ferry village, creeping in from the right.

Nowadays, the crossing is operated by Clyde Link and they do run a good show, in my opinion, having taken over the job in 2010. Monday to Saturday they run from 6.30am to 9.20pm, and on Sunday it's from 10am to 6.30pm. Officially, they cross on demand during peak times and every half hour at others. Most bike riders will arrive outside peak hours, but don't worry, I have been assured by the crewmen that they don't leave anyone hanging around for half an hour, and this has been my experience whenever I have used them. There is a bus shelter either side to protect you from the elements, and when the ferry does come in, make your way down the old cobbled slipway rather gingerly if you're wearing cleats, and hop aboard. It's £1.70 for an adult and 80p for your little yins, each way.

So once on, bear in mind that you are using a ferry crossing that has been here for around 200 years,

Looking back after riding the first mile or so of the long, easy, early bends of the A-81, and already at this point you will know that you are on a real road to savour. The A-81 heading for the Trossachs is just about as good as it can get for a roadie.

and in fact has operated for longer, as it used a berth slightly upstream before that. At the time of writing (July 2013), Clydelink are reintroducing the Govan ferry on a one month trial period to see how it goes. If it proves successful, then that will be another way to get over the river if you stay in that area; only time will tell. Here's hoping[2].

In no time, you're across the 200 metres of water and stepping onto Yoker cobbles, before precariously exiting the slip and then riding up Yoker Ferry Road. Its old red sandstone tenements greet you as you approach the junction with Dumbarton Road, and after taking

<hr>

2 - Unfortunately this ferry service was stopped after the Commonwealth Games.

Kelso Street straight across, you're soon up and over the rail bridge and heading for the roundabout at the western extreme of Knightswood. On turning left at the roundabout, you're onto Dunreath Avenue and you follow this round, leaving the last of the houses, before passing over the pretty Forth and Clyde Canal and A-82 in quick succession.

Now, the plan here is to make our way up to the Langfaulds roundabout at the beginning of Baljaffray Road, where we will meet up with the other route we can use, if coming over the Erskine Bridge. After this, we follow the same course we did on the Rowardennan run, out the Stockiemuir Road till it's time to cut off for Killearn. It is actually very straightforward to negotiate your way from the Yoker ferry up through Drumchapel to the start of Baljaffray, as there are only 3 turns involved. The first we've already done when we went onto Dunreath Avenue from Kelso Street, and after crossing the canal we then enter Drumchapel itself when we go under the next rail bridge.

The massive Edrington Group whisky plant is on the left now, fronted by its blue board, and once we pass through the next roundabout we are into the main part of the 'Drum' scheme itself, as the locals call it. The Drumchapel shopping centre, also blue-fronted sits just ahead on the left, and we pass this and continue on round, still staying on the one road. This road, or rather drive, will take us all the way up, through its white-fronted tenement blocks, till we come to the police station, where we turn left onto Peel Glen Road. Drumchapel itself is a massive scheme, one of the largest if not the largest in Europe, I believe. It was one of several built in the 50s and 60s to solve Glasgow's chronic housing problems.

The Drum alone was constructed to house 34000 people, which resulted in a lot of houses being built but not much else. These schemes were so devoid of facilities that it led to the Big Yin, comedian Billy Connolly, calling them 'deserts with windows'. He, for one, should know, because for a time he actually stayed on the very street you are riding on at this point, Kinfauns Drive. That was before he moved back to White Street in his beloved Partick.

One of the ploys which the builders of such schemes used was to give them very pleasant names such as Drumchapel, Easterhouse, or Castlemilk. Hardly surprisingly, most suffered from social problems, with antisocial behaviour being top of the list.

Still, there are plenty of good people in there, too, and it is with this optimistic thought we draw level with the local nick, just across from Saint Claire's Primary School. And with that it's onto the Peel Glen we go. We're almost out of the scheme now, and just have the last few houses to pass. As we do so, we swerve through the chicanes and bollards of what they now call traffic calming. It isn't only the old scheme designers who went in for flannel; obviously, the road designers nowadays do it, too.

We now enter the country road stretch of the Peel Glen. Get ready to climb, and fairly hard at that. From a built-up area, you're suddenly hemmed in by the trees and greenery, along with the necessary crash barriers either side, because this is a slightly twisty steep climb you find yourself on suddenly and ouch!! It's the first of the day for me.

It's quite an interesting wee climb, though, what with the sudden contrast from the massive housing complex and the way it just turns up ahead and keeps you guessing as to what is coming next. It's a case of riding out the bends and then flatten out green and straight through the higher fields. Fields, I suspect, belonging to Langfaulds Farm, which isn't far away now, as you near the main road above, the A-810 Duntocher Road. On getting there, turn left and drop shortly down to the start of the Baljaffray.

On the last run (Rowardennan), we covered the next stage of this run blow-by- blow, so only as a quick recap: it's over the Baljaffray Road (the B-8050) and turn left onto the Stockiemuir (the A-809).

Shortly, you will pass through tiny Craigton, and note as you do that one of the houses there, an old white farmhouse, is known as Tam Bowie Smithy. I assumed at first this was a working smithy, at one time belonging to one Mr Thomas Bowie. Old smithys and their name places seem fairly prevalent in this neck of the woods, and it's easy to forget just how essential this line of business was in the days before motorised transport took

over. However, as a lot of property around Craigton is called Tam Bowie, it might be an anglicised version of what was there before.

As always with the Stockiemuir, take your time on the several tough rises you'll meet, and conserve your energy as best you can when going up past the Hilton Park golfie. And especially so after the Carbeth Inn, till you clear that long climb at the Auchengillan campsite. A plaque on the side of the Carbeth tells you it was once known as the Halfway House, and also that Sir Walter Scott gave the place a mention in his 1817 novel *Rob Roy*. Enjoy, as always, the long wonderful drop from the Whangie carpark, which will carry you speedily down almost all the way till you meet the B-834 and follow it, signed for Killearn.

You can't help but enjoy the beautiful swift road through and under the canopy of trees that you encounter here; it's just so delightful the way the light comes through the leaves and branches. This only stops when you cross the Blane Water by a stone bridge and become enchanted by the scene here, too. The meanders

Just starting the long drop down onto the flat fields around the Kelty Water at the very edge of the Flanders Moss. If you think the road has been good up until now, just wait till you start on this descent. Mind your speed now!

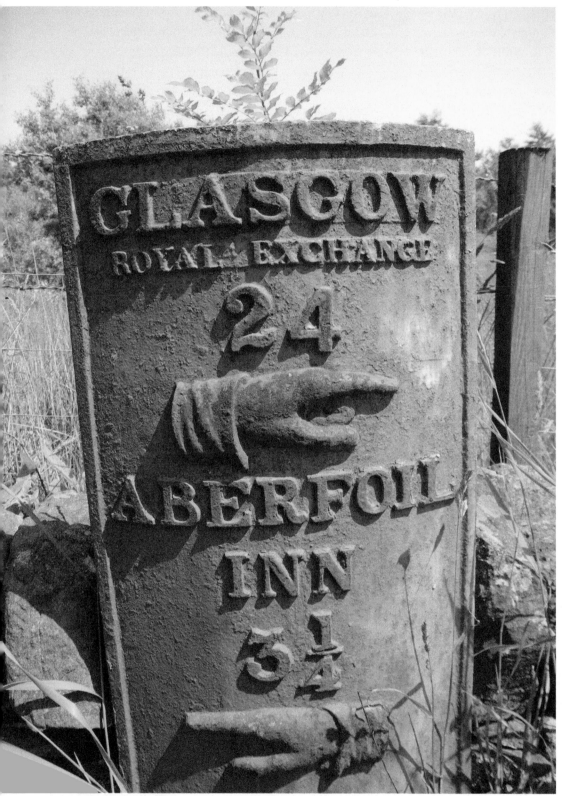

One of the many great old mile post signs you will meet in the area; their accuracy is very impressive, right down to a ¼ of a mile in this instance. Please note ye olde spelling of Aberfoyle.

its cluster of buildings waiting just round the corner.

This is where it gets good, seriously good. For when you turn left you are on the A-81 and it is one helluva road to ride. I repeat! It is one helluva road to ride. So much so that if you are coming the other way, and have to leave it for the Stockiemuir Road, then you will be one unhappy bunny to have left it behind. It really is that good. Now, before I ever rode the Inversnaid run, I was coming down the Stockiemuir one day when the idea of this run came into my mind. Giving it thought after, I looked at it on the mapand – as can so often happen –was under the impression that it would be a lot tougher and a lot harder to ride than it really was, and especially the A-81. How wrong can you be?

Just to be on the safe side with the ferry from Tarbet, I did the run initially the other way and, boy, did I enjoy the stretch from Aberfoyle to Blane Smithy. This, of course, was followed by all the climbing back from there over the Stockiemuir first, then the Baljaffray Road, and that is how I know how much you will miss it.

of the Blane, curving through the sheep fields and round tree-lined banks, couldn't be more pastoral. It's all still and calm here and gives you a little lift, which comes in handy to see you up the small rise that takes you off the river bank and up to the Blane Smithy roundabout, with

So, away we go then, heading north on as good a bit of road as you are likely to find and enjoy just about anywhere. It starts as it means to go on, with a long, low, sweeping bend through the fields of this flat plane. Ahead now lies long straight after long straight, with a curve and a gentle rise thrown in from time to time. Keep your eyes open for West Highland Wayers in a short time, as it actually crosses the road here, though it isn't too easy to see it as passes through the fields at this point.

Shortly after crossing the Endrick Water on its great old bridge, which was built in 1844 – according to the plaque – you pass an isolated enclave of houses. You then go under the rail bridge that once carried the line to the former Balfron station, which was situated nearby. The bridge still retains its yellow and black warning stripes for high vehicles and, most noticeably just before it, there is a sign saying 8 miles to Aberfoyle. So you are left in no doubt as to the distance to today's main town. So far so good, and so good it will continue to the next point of interest, which isn't long in coming. And that is the Ballat junction. This is a large, straggly crossroads that allows vehicles to break off east or west from the north/south running A-81. The road from the left is coming in from Drymen, and the road shortly leaving right is heading for Stirling – they are one and the same, both being the A-811. We want neither of these, of course, so charge straight through.

And charge is the operative word here, for the 81 is just made for charging along. No real hills or rises to test us here, as the road skirts along the extreme edge of the flat expanse that is Flanders Moss. This is the largest expanse of upland bog in the whole of the UK to remain in a near natural state, and that is despite the best efforts of Lord Kames (Henry Homes), the lawyer, historian and improver, who encouraged drainage of the land in the 18th century. Today it is a protected site, I'm glad to say, as a Site of Special Scientific Interest looked after by Scottish Natural Heritage. What this means to the bike rider is that this sort of terrain feeds fast passage over its gentle undulations, as onward we travel towards Aberfoyle.

There is a noticeable improvement in the land, as regards to agriculture, once you pass through the Ballat, as before it very rough meadows prevailed. Now farming seems to be more prevalent this side, possibly to do with Lord Kame's handiwork from way back. Only a slight shimmy in the road at the old Garraud Farm breaks the pattern of the long straights in this stretch, but only briefly, as they resume long before you even reach Hoish Farm. This is the point at which the high ground is starting to make an appearance as the gateway to the Trossachs – as Aberfoyle likes to call itself – is neared.

Another straight, this one descending through trees, brings you out near the first of the side roads that lead to Gartmore Village, which sits away to the left. And then it all opens up.

Quite a broad striking spectacular vista hits you full in the face when you emerge from the trees, and you appreciate it even more by the fact that the A-81 is at her best here. She takes you speedily forth on a long angled descent, which allows 25 mph to be attained without too much effort. The feelgood factor is off the scale here, and why not? For all the real good stuff is still to come, and you're almost there.

Gartmore sits fairly openly on a hillside away to the left, and beyond that the shapely Ben Lomond shows another side to its character, and most impressively at that; a long elegant whale back, from this point. Now just when the road levels out after crossing the Kelty Water, another side road to Gartmore is passed, at which point you should keep your eye open for a real old tablet of a mile post down low on the right.

All its white paint has gone but none of its quaintness, as it points the way to Royal Exchange in Glasgow 24 miles one way and (note the spelling), the Aberfoil Inn 3¼ miles the other. I'm impressed with the accuracy, I must say. There is another mile post, painted white this time, showing similar accuracy just up the road as you pass Gartartan Farm, and then you drop down slightly out of the trees to cross the infant Forth on a modern uninspiring bridge. This is followed by a short series of bends and undulations that won't stall your progress any, as you finally close in on the roundabout ahead which will lead you into Aberfoyle.

The Menteith hills always show well, with their steep, colourful, purple heathery slopes, as you approach the cut-off for Aberfoyle. It lets you know what is to come and puts you in the mood for more.

The first time you ride down Aberfoyle Main Street, you will be blown away by the sight of Ben Lomond. Although far in the distance, it seems to totally overlook and dominate the street. It is a most impressive sight.

The Menteith Hills have a great rugged-looking south profile, and the rocky outcrops on their plunging green grass and purple heathery slopes gives an impression of a much higher and more serious mountain. Rolling up the flat, straight stretch to the roundabout, beside the low, sprawling Rob Roy Motel, means you're going to break left off the A-81 – possibly for the moment at least – and head due west on the A-821 into Aberfoyle. This is all done in overgrown lush greenery, where to prove the point the first field on the left has grass and reeds so high that the one or two cows usually in there can hardly see over the foliage. A well-hidden road sign tells you, if you look hard enough, that it is 16 miles to Inversnaid and 12 to Stronachlachar.

No problem, says you, as you burl forward, at the same time being impressed by another early Trossachs hillside, this time Craigmore. It sits right above the village itself, and shows as impressive a flank as its near neighbours in the Menteith Hills. After about a ¼ of a mile in fairly flat open country, you enter a tight wooded section of road, from which you emerge out of the other side and follow the double yellow lines round the bend and into Aberfoyle itself.

Now, the first thing that hits you is the red trim of the local garage/filling station roof, and also the empty former upholstery store right next door. These two give the early impression of a rather run-down backwater village, but this is a most misleading persona. It is very well to do in places, the old Aberfoyle lady.

But as you swing onto its long, straight main drag, the thing that totally catches your eye isn't its other buildings, but the grand bulk of Ben Lomond, seen far in the distance dead ahead. It has such a presence, especially the way that such an untameable wild thing is seen through an urban environment, that you can't help but remain transfixed by the strange contrast in front of your eyes. I'm sure the locals are used to it, of course, and never give it a second thought, but when confronted with this scene for the first time, or the first time in a long time, it really hits you between the eyes.

Wow! you wonder, as you roll gently in, taking as much in about the place as you can. That's quite a hard thing to do, as there is a lot crammed in to this one road, what with solid stone B & B's, butchers' shops, Tudor-style rows of houses, the fire station, pubs, and just about anything else you can think of. Aberfoyle Main Street has it all. However, for us the most important building coming up on the right hand side will be a grey stone, red-painted Bank of Scotland, which signals our arrival at the bottom of the Duke's Pass. This is a continuation of the A-821. The bank comes after Liz McGregor's coffee shop, always good to know, and it means we have the main decision of the day in front of us now.

We can either continue straight ahead on the quieter B-829 towards Kinlochard and make directly towards the Inversnaid Hotel, or take the road over the Duke's Pass and make a loop round. For the record, once the Duke's Pass has been climbed and descended, you are in a position to make a loop round in either direction. One is left round Loch Katrine, and the other is right for Callander. All the options will be covered in good time, going from left to right, to keep it nice and simple.

INVERSNAID HOTEL-TARBET

SAILING TIMES: 12.00, 2.15pm, 4.30pm.
SPRING TO AUTUMN ONLY
£8.00 adult, £5.00 child, £1.00 bike. (2014)

On leaving Aberfoyle, the scenery just gets better and better, as this scene shows at Milton. This is just before the rise and fall ahead carries you onto the shores of Loch Ard. You're now on the B-829.

So from the junction at the bottom of the Duke's Pass, across the road from the bank, we trundle forward with great expectation. And rightly so, as there is some real quality scenery to come. It starts right away, just the way that the initial striking stone villas sit below the towering presence of Craigmore behind. Now the Craigmore fellow is not only a beautiful hill, but was also one of the town's main employers. From its steep slopes, slate was quarried for a long, long time, from the 1820s to the 1950s. The 1950s was also when the Strathendrick and Aberfoyle railway pulled out, and the place has since been left to fend for itself ever since, mostly with forestry and tourism.

The rough meadow to your left hides the newly-born River Forth from your view, and soon you pass the first of a series of oddly-shaped mile posts that announce you are now 1 mile from Aberfoyle and 10¼ from Stronachlachar. The Trossachs mile posts definitely like their accuracy, often coming in ¼ or ½ mile increments, and these ones stand about 2½ feet tall, are white and oddly diamond-shaped at the head.

It is now going to get chocolate box pretty, as you head round through Milton. Its curving tree and crag-lined road shortly meets the first small lake, the first of two between here and the larger Loch Ard, and you may have seen this scene before in a calendar or on the front of a shortbread tin; it's so quintessentially Highland.

An upturned rowing boat sits on the grass beside an old wooden pier, with the top of Ben Lomond appearing above the water between the trees in the distance. We are talking 'Grannie's ain heilan hame' here, big time. But what a sight indeed; it's very, very beautiful I must say.

The ride along the side of Loch Ard will please every inch of the way, and lacks nothing in scenery situation and style. A stone wall guides you round the Lochside, and lets you curve flatly beside the bays in effortless silence.

Go round the corner, and the second slightly larger lake is passed, containing old rusty iron boat sheds, which helps it to rival its smaller counterpart for charm. The road, too, at this point does its bit. It rolls along the side of the water, running with a quaint old iron railing on the water side, before it takes its leave of the lochan and heads in through the woods, twisting and turning as it goes.

At this point, just before you rejoin the waterside at Loch Ard, you pass at least three – if my memory serves me right – driveways to large houses and even a farm, which uncharacteristically for Scotland have locked electric gates guarding the entrance. Just who lurks behind them? Could there be Nazi war criminals fed up of Argentina and eating corned beef perhaps, or former members of the Costa del Crooks clan, sick of the Spanish sun? It's difficult to say, of course.

So, down out of the woods and onto the shores and stone walls of pretty Loch Ard we go, only briefly at first,

as there is a wee lift off through the rhododendrons and then back down to the water's edge, and now we can fully enjoy this great stretch of lochside riding.

Loch Ard doesn't disappoint as you contour its 3 mile length, always flat and pleasant, and always with Ben Lomond rising above the far bank, making a most striking sentinel. I've said it before, it's no wonder the Norsemen called it the 'Beacon Hill'. There are some very impressive houses and even hotels on the banks of the Ard, with Altskeith House being about the finest, but not the only one you meet, with its exquisite wee boathouse down on the shore. Some stunning big Yankee pine trees adorn gardens along here, and I always like to see them. The early stretch of the loch is lined with a low stone wall, and that always adds to any lochside setting.

The low hills across the loch are having their forestry cut in many places, quite noticeable even from this side, as you ride past the large Forest Hills Hotel with its water sports complex, and finally clear the loch. It's then through the buttercup meadows into Kinlochard. You now, for the most part, enter the woodlands and start to – just gently at first – begin climbing upwards, taking you into the high hills and reservoirs that sit in the distance above. You are tight in the trees for some time, where some great old specimens are passed, but a lot of it is rather scrubby and scatty in places; certainly dense, for sure. Little Loch Dubh, which sits on the left, breaks the pattern for a bit and then it's on towards the larger and finer Loch Chon.

Turning and undulating, quite markedly at times, the Forestry Commission sign for the loch also heralds the start of better quality woodland, with more grander trees and ferns to delight below. Keep your eye open for feral goats in this area, sporting magnificent long, curving horns, as they make a most entertaining sight. The road sits above the Chon at first, which is hard to spot through the dense woodland, but then it drops down to the water's edge just before the long straight pull up onto the high ground begins. This climb is nothing to fear for two reasons. First, it is only about 5%; and second, the road here is brand new tarmac.

Smoothly you ascend, purring enjoyment as you sit high on the bars or the hoods, whichever is your preference, and continue bolt straight up through the big trees, the passing places all having their own personal black and white marker poles. This will continue for a time till you cross a dreaded deer grid, and then you're out on the flat and on the barren magnificent moorland. What a sight greets you up here, as you join the gods and the real high mountains. The last of the diamond-shaped mile posts is now passed, showing 10 miles to Aberfoyle and 1¼ to Stronachlachar. A bend taken in the road allows Loch Arklet to open up, and it's the view across it that holds your gaze from now on in.

The big Arrochar Munros really show a stunning broadside of Narnain, Ime, and Vane, with wee tough A'Chrois out in front. What a sight the four of them make, as does the rugged ridge of Maol Mor which sits dead ahead as you swing round and drop down to the T-junction. It has been Maol Mor which has been showing for some time as you made the long climb up from Loch Chon. The feeling you get is very rewarding as you can freewheel all the way down towards the two old grey houses that sit beside the road at the junction. The B-829 is coming to an end now, as you hit the single track unclassified ahead.

Delightfully enclosed woodland and gentle rising road will greet you on the way up to the side of Loch Chon. The road surface lets the side down somewhat here; so much so, it's better and safer to climb on this stretch than descend on it.

The sign says it's ½ a mile to Stronachlachar on the right and 4 miles to Inversnaid left. We want left this time, and away we go fast on the flat, passing the iron railings of the two houses that sit isolated there. I assume they must have been water workers' homes at one time; the last couple of times I passed, a wet paint sign on the railings looked like it had been there for years[3].

A long, straight and barren-looking beginning starts us off down the side of the Arklet. The far side of the dam, ½ a mile across, looks even more desolate than this side, if that is possible. Just over a mile later, the farmhouse of Corriearklet is passed, which was the wedding place, in January 1693, of one Rob Roy McGregor. That is some claim to fame.

Now, this being flat and fast, it is a good bit of road to approach on if you feel you are running late for the ferry; bear in mind that there is over two hours between them, and the last one leaves at 4.30pm. Two bits of good news again – the last mile down to the hotel is a very steep

3 - It appears to finally have gone now.

195

descent, probably too steep in places, descent; and the ferries tend to run late here fairly regularly, by about 10 to 15 minutes in my experience. So, don't throw in the towel if you are cutting it tight. Chances are you'll make it comfortably.

As the western end of the Arklet is approached, the dam wall is preceded by a small gathering of pines – some of them Scots pine, I'm glad to say – which will be the first time you will have taken your eyes off the Arrochar Hills for a while. This is because the trees obscure them for a bit, and that would be the only reason you would stop admiring them.

A rather splendid large plaque on the dam wall itself tells you it was completed in June 1914, after taking exactly 5 years to complete the whole project. There isn't

Approaching Loch Chon from Loch Arklet on one of the few occasions when I headed for Tarbet Loch Lomond first. I had been greeted by rain on my arrival in the Trossachs this day, and also by some stunning long-horned goats when I got to the Chon. One of these can just about be seen in a bush in the centre of the photo. The brilliant long straight descent down from the Arklet has just been done, on very smooth new tar, I'm glad to say.

much further to go now as you first pass a fine-looking black and white house sitting right beside the dam, before swinging through a few dwellings belonging to Upper Inversnaid. Now, the final approach to the hotel is a real helter-skelter job, just the way that the road drops and turns down fast and is hemmed in by big bad rhodies4. As always, the tightest steepest corner is the one with the crappiest road surface, so take care at that point.

A more open final big sweeping left hander (only slightly less steep) fires you down to the hotel and into more tartan than a Bay City Rollers' gig of yesteryear. On

---

4 - Rhododendrons.

A picturesque wee passing place on the side of the B-829 on the long climb up to Loch Arklet. These old black and white marker poles really do add so much charm along the way, and the new road surface makes this a dream of a pull up, too. Then you top out into some stunning countryside once you get up.

a decent day, there will be numerous backpackers (mostly foreign West Highland Wayers) sitting outside eating grub that is carried out to them by a member of the hotel staff. It goes without saying that I don't eat out here, as I usually won't have time and it looks a bit too expensive for me anyway. I could be wrong on that score, of course.

With a bit of luck, any minute now you should spy your faithful wee tug making its way across the loch to ferry you back to the west side. I only go into the hotel to use the cludgie if needed, and fill the old water bottles free gratis. I want you to bear in mind that the hotel is actually owned by Lochs and Glens, whose buses you would no doubt have seen from time to time as

The most welcome site of Loch Arklet greets your arrival when you level off after the big pull up from Loch Chon, and the Arrochar Alps behind it always make for a dramatic backdrop. If you intend to make for Inversnaid and the ferry, then all the climbing is just about over for the day. The next stretch is top-drawer easy-street.

Another view of Loch Arklet and the Arrochar hills, this time in changing light. This photo, like the last, was taken from the B-829 on the way down the easy-angled stretch to the Stronachlachar T-junction. Expect conditions to change very rapidly in the Trossachs, and it's usually a good idea to carry a lightweight rain jacket in the old back pocket, just in case.

they plooter about the Highlands. An older clientele is, therefore, catered for here, and the first ever time I went through and into the hotel bar, they were playing Andy Stewart singing Donald, Where's Your Troosers. So don't say I didn't warn you.

Sitting outside waiting for the boat is no hardship if it's dry, though, as it is a really beautiful spot, with the loch, the mountains, and the falls of Arklet right next to you. Most delightful.

And a delightful sail across the water is also in store when the Lomond Cruiser arrives. There are several different models in the quite extensive fleet; however, they all follow a similar style of being long, low-sitting, and white, with a closed cabin downstairs and an open deck on top. The often busy wee boat is well staffed and

friendly with it, as on you go with the bike. Tea and coffee, along with snacks, are served on board, which also has a wee bar to boot.

It makes a great sight looking back to it, the old Inversnaid. It's a fairly sprawling large white affair nowadays, but I'm sure it was a different animal totally when it was built as a hunting lodge for the Duke of Montrose (William the 2nd, I think) in 1790.

If you do find yourself ever stranded there overnight (God forbid), the going rate is about £90 a night, though you will be following in the footsteps of some very prestigious company, as Queen Victoria once stayed there. This was because when she came up to officially open the Katrine Reservoir, the 21-gun salute that followed blew out all the windows in the cottage she was supposed to be staying in, and as a quick plan B, they shoved the old doll into the Inversnaid Hotel instead. 'We are not amused!'. So there you have the reason for her stay.

In the meantime, we are sailing across the water and it's a most unusual feeling you get as you cross the mighty Loch Lomond and get a duck's eye view of all around. You won't be used to that, unless you are a keen kayaker or the likes.

The Sloy Dam power station and its pipes are directly across from you, and show themselves fully from where you are now. It's a good wee chance to recover on the half hour crossing. The coffee isn't the best, being a prepared job in a polystyrene cup, but that and a bit of shortbread does the job. The only possible drawback when using

The Author and Eddy Merckx outside the Inversnaid Hotel, awaiting the boat. This picture was taken by an obliging German tourist, who actually volunteered to take it and wasn't asked or cajoled in any manner.

Now, first of all, the reason I mention the cost of a return ticket on the ferry here is because it is an option to either ride or drive to Tarbet and then access the Trossachs via the ferry, and after what would be most likely a circuit of Loch Katrine, return by the ferry again. I don't tend to do it that way, but it would make a great day out and is a good card to have up your sleeve, especially as a family option. The steep initial pull up out of Inversnaid would rule this one out for young children, though.

At Tarbet there is a good toilet and a great wee snack bar in the same block, which is especially useful if going clockwise. Mind what I said about doing the Inversnaid run clockwise first of all, as it lets you know what's what, with the ferry times and distances from Inversnaid back to your home, and all.

Heading west from the Stronachlachar T-junction, and making direct for Inversnaid. This road runs right beside Loch Arklet before a steep drop takes you right onto the banks of Loch Lomond itself, right at the Inversnaid Hotel. Although you can reach this junction by coming directly from Aberfoyle on the B-829, it can also be reached by ascending the Duke's Pass which starts in Aberfoyle, too, and then contouring round Loch Katrine to Stronachlachar that way.

the Lomond Cruises is that from time to time the guy steering the boat will give you a bit of a local history and a running commentary as you make your way over, which is fine in itself and interesting, too, as far as goes. However, the last time I crossed, it was an Irish bloke piloting. He could have talked for Dublin, if not Eire, and by the time we made it to Tarbet I was just glad to get off.

TARBET-INVERSNAID

SAILING TIMES: 11.30am, 1.45pm, 3.00pm.
£8.00 adult single £11.50 return
£5.00 child single £7.00 return
£1.00 bike each way
(Note: the 3pm sailing does a tour before docking at Inversnaid at 4.30pm)

Inversnaid's bonnie wee pier, right beside the hotel, is where you await the ferry to carry you over the loch. Grub can be ordered from the hotel, if you so wish, but I usually don't have time and rely on the onboard snacks, usually tea and shortbread, to get me ready for the next leg down the other side of the loch.

The welcome sight of the Loch Lomond Cruise boat approaching the pier at Inversnaid. There's a long wait between ferries, so it's a relief to be on time and not miss it. That thought is always at the back of your mind as you near the Trossachs on the A-81.

So now back to our original anticlockwise run, where the return leg begins down the new-look Loch Lomond road, the busy A-82. More suited to vehicles than cycles, I have to admit, but it is slick and fast for us as well. I already mentioned the long cycle lane it has running beside it, on the Dunoon run, and that there is also an unofficial cycle lane by the side of the main road. This is the one which I, and most other road bikers, use. It does the job just as well, only faster.

So, it's out of Tarbet you come, all a bit tight in the early stages as you are still on a bit of the older road and are inside the white line, rubbing shoulders with the traffic. But then the newer road soon appears at the clearway signs, and into the side you go, where you can take shelter and keep up a good cadence and rhythm. All the time you are cutting along fairly flat, or rising and dipping slightly between long bends, through thick greenery on the lower slopes of gentler hills.

A big, bad, broad bend sweeps you round a cutaway rock face, as down onto the long straight you swoop just before Inverbeg, getting into time trial position if you fancy it, to take you dead flat along the lochside. Great views from here, all across the water's broad greyness, give you a real appreciation of just how big an expanse of water the Lomond really is, as you head down towards its wider southern shores.

This view and style will continue for some time, till the cut-off to Luss is reached and you are presented with the option of sticking to the faster, newer road or taking the older road through the village. If I'm running late or not hungry, I stick to the A-82 and batter straight on. However, I do like to take the Luss road every now and

The impressive bulk of Ben Vane from the Inversnaid ferry, and a bloody tough wee hill she is. There was nigh on about 25 years between my first and second ascent of this hill, and I was totally shocked when I saw the erosion second time around. She is as steep as she looks, and will test you well any time you fancy climbing her.

then, for old time's sake, as it is quieter and very pretty in places, particularly – as stated before – around the bay at Aldochlay. The toilet and snack bar in Luss are also both handy to have at times.

Anyway, both roads rejoin again not far further south, just at the start of the prestigious Loch Lomond golfie, and it's more of the same again from the 82.

The plan will be to follow the same return route back home that we took in the very last outing, the Rowardennan run, so obviously I won't go into great detail about it this time again. But if you didn't read that one yet, or need a quick recap, here goes. Continue down the A-82 till you are through the big Arden roundabout, and then it is recommended you take the old road section past the Duck Bay Marina. At the entrance to Cameron House, again I recommend joining the official cycle path which leads via the pavement onto the Old Luss Road, which drops you long and leafy into Balloch.

Carry straight on, going directly through the next two roundabouts, leaving Balloch and entering Alexandria, and don't forget to turn left at the traffic lights – you know the ones: the ones with the big ornate and eternally dry fountain. This will take you down and then over the dazzling Bonhill Bridge, where you turn right for Dumbarton. After turning right onto the A-813, which soon becomes Stirling Road, Bonhill, roll under all the greyness of its schemes till you're into the roads and roundabouts of the industrial estate, and then find yourself at the A-82's roundabouts just outside Dumbarton.

Looking back at the big sprawling Inversnaid Hotel from the ferry as she cruises back across the loch. It makes for a very impressive sight.

DUKE'S PASS

Docking at Tarbet and now it's down the A-82 we must trundle, heart set on the Erskine Bridge. The pointed peak across the loch is Ben Lomond, showing a different face from this direction.

For another treat, stay on the A-821 by banking hard right at the Bank of Scotland on Aberfoyle Main Street, and get ready to climb. It's nothing too brutal, let me assure you, and after an initial wee ramp, the road doubles back and lies back, as it now winds its way round what is left of the houses of upper Aberfoyle, if that's what you call it. Nice and easy does it, as you sit down and get into a rhythm for this great classic climb, which is known and loved by many, myself included. The road doubles back again, straightens out, passes a cycle track on the right, and then leads into some fine foliage in the shape of ferns and silver birches.

Nothing too steep here, as promised, and the road now bends and snakes further up into the hillside. With hands on top of the bars, you won't be under any pressure to keep up a good speed and cadence. Great views are to be had away to the right towards Stirling, just as the road adjusts left and steepens to around 10%, and a little bit

The two options which present themselves to you now are following the A-82, if it's not too busy, for speed and expediency; or diving down into Dumbarton on the Bonhill Road and picking up the cycle lane on Glasgow Road, just before it rejoins the A-82 at the Dumbuck lights.

Now, for years – and I do mean years – I never touched the 82, even the part round here which is either a 30 or 40 mph limit. But now I do from time to time, if it is a quiet part of the day, because it can save a fair bit of time. It makes for a quick dash from Dumbarton to Bowling. However, it is a lot quieter to run into central Dumbarton, and also straightforward to turn left and head out the Glasgow Road, where you keep an eye open for the unofficial entry to the cycle track, through the hedge on the left, very near the road's end. The pleasant hurl along beside the railway on the cycle lane and the A-82 route both meet each other at the big Dunglass roundabout, and then it's into brilliant Bowling itself.

After following the road into Old Kilpatrick, take the signs up onto the Erskine Bridge to gain its cycle paths via Station Road, and then cross the mighty one to Renfrewshire. Ever-evolving Erskine, courtesy of the A-726, leads to the alleged mean streets of Paisley, and home *pour moi*.

So, that is the Inversnaid ferry route covered, and trust me when I say it will be to your liking. But from Aberfoyle, it isn't the only route available to you, and the wonderful Duke's Pass provides a couple of others that won't disappoint either.

The cut-away face of the rock, which made way for the newer faster A-82, is seen just south of Tarbet as we head southbound for Arden and the Vale of Leven. The modern road is nowhere near the charmer of the old one but it still has its moments, like the one above.

more effort is required to propel yourself forward, but not for long. This will more or less take you up high enough into the Duke's Pass itself, and you can rest up a fair bit when up amongst the high rough meadows.

You're not at the top of the climb entirely yet, but the bulk of it is over. A Forestry Commission sign lets you know officially that the pass has been reached. It's named after Douglas Graham, 5th Duke of Montrose, who had the road built in 1885 to allow him access to his land, and was opened to Joe Public when the forestry got its hands on the land in 1925.

Coming down the A-82 round about Luss, and don't forget to use the space inside the white line as the unofficial cycle lane. You won't be long in battering down it.

So, it's flat for a curve and a bend now, and then some gentle rising long and flowing round more of the same, passing a small white cottage across from a striking roadside crag. The road turns right here and starts to make a bit more directly for the top of the pass. This is reached quite easily, just after you pass another forestry sign for the 'Three lochs forest drive'.

Now, the point where you start to descend has a very personal memory for me, because down the hillside in front of you is where I once crashed my wee black Fiat

van (known to one and all as the Pope-mobile), into a thick bank of snow back in 1997. As I went over the edge, I thought my number was up, honestly!

Down you go, and the way down will delight as much as the way up did, only with a lot less effort. Although large swathes of the land here are dominated by sitka spruce, a lot of the roadside is lined by more traditional trees, which keeps the natural look of the Trossachs, and I dare say this was good planning by the forestry boys. It certainly gives a more pleasant feel to the place.

Away to your right, the unfortunately-named Loch Drunkie very quickly comes into view. A fine-looking fellow he is, though, despite the name, nestling snuggly in among all those pine trees. It appears as a semi-hidden dramatic watery wedge from this angle, and I always stop to admire it.

After that brief stop, away we go again and from here on down it gets seriously good, wild, and dramatic. It starts off with a tight swing over a stone bridge and then a steepish short drop into the first of many magnificent bends. Each one opens up a real highland show as you skirt round. Going so fast down and everything changing so dramatically and quickly, it feels like you're in the middle of a highland reel at a ceilidh.

Binnein, AKA wee Ben A'n, shows off its dramatic shape across the glen, as Ben Ledi's bulk shows away to the east. Next, it's the turn of Ben Venue lying to the west, as one after another, more twisting bends come slalom-like at you to test your descending skills, as the lower road snakes even more than the upper does. Tree-clad ridges cut in front and behind Ben An, and now it's close enough to show off its rocky flank. Its pointed shape is most dramatic and gives this little hill a distinction and status usually afforded to its higher neighbours. They, too, are in the scene, coming at the speeding biker faster than he can contemplate, and finally there is a soft falling onto the banks of the still Loch Achray.

Before this is reached, the striking grey turrets of the old Trossachs Hotel can be seen from across the loch, and with that it means that the Duke's Pass in all its glory has been climbed. And what a climb it is… in either direction, I might add.

As you go along the flat lochside, you can't help but notice the massive white walls of the Loch Achray Hotel, sitting below Ben Venue's east face. Both the Achray and Trossachs hotels were built to cater for the onslaught of

Nearing the top of the Duke's Pass on the A-821 heading north, after enjoying the very beautiful pull up through all the birch trees on a climb that is never too steep nor too taxing in any place. It is a long slender climb up into the pass, and the whole route will be thoroughly enjoyed the entire way.

tourists that arrived here to view Loch Katrine and the surrounding area, spurned on to a great extent by Scott's poem *Lady of the Lake* from 1810. The Achray started off as a lodge house in 1870 and grew from there.

After passing it, you go swiftly along the top of the loch, under a canopy of trees, till you arrive at a T-junction, and no matter which way you turn, you will stay on the A-821. This is an important point for us, because we now have a choice of which circuit to take, and two options. Both are good, both popular, and both should be tried at different times.

It's left for a loop round the Katrine and a return back down to Aberfoyle via Stronachlachar; or right for Callander and a return back to the Rob Roy Motel on the A-81. The Loch Katrine loop also gives you the option of heading for the Inversnaid ferry; if you want to or have planned that.

LOCH KATRINE

So; heading for the Katrine first. Turn left at the junction and follow a great helter-skelter bit of road for a mile, through the woodland, to take you up to the Trossachs pier. It's quite a surprise to suddenly come across all this concrete and cars after the wild greenery you've just ridden through, and there is quite a collection of tourist traps here, too. Yes, the carpark is a fair size and has to be, what with all the coach trips coming in along with all the day-trippers. And on top of that, there is a good toilet block, gift shop, and ice cream parlour, as well as the boats and pier. Not forgetting a well-run cycle hire shed called Katrine Wheelz.

Don't become despondent, however, for the sheer beauty of the loch itself will immediately over-ride all of this as you go past the barrier and start to make your way round the waterside. No hanging around here, if you

Looking north from the highest point of the Duke's Pass to lovely Loch Drunkie, and it always looks so cute as it nestles in among its firs. I wonder how it got its name, though.

know what's good for you, or you could end up with a large cone in your hand.

It is an absolutely stunning spot at the beginning of the Katrine road; it's got the lot and more. There are numerous striking wooded headlands, making for a very narrow dramatic inlet and a rock-blasted road on the right to suddenly grab your attention. The loch's famous boat, the *SS Sir Walter Scott*, sits berthed alongside the left bank, if it's not out on a jaunt. In its resplendent white, with its funnel and bunting draped above its red and white striped canopy, it cuts a fine dash.

Big Ben Venue, sitting across the water, looks down from above, no doubt enjoying the view as well, and the road pleases as it follows its iron railing round between the drop to the water and the rock face inside. Soon the first of numerous white painted, iron-railed bridges is crossed, to give you some idea of the charm ahead. This is no ordinary road you're on, but one used and kept by the water company, and is therefore something quite different from what you are used to riding. You also soon pass the first of many information plaques, which either contain information that is fact or fiction. Some inform

you of settlements and villages once found here, while others tell of folklore and fairies, if you believe in such things.

The initial curving dam wall section leads into a beautiful aged woodland stretch, as the road takes you off towards Stronachlachar 12½ miles away. Now, being a tight, narrow, twisting wee road, the Katrine can eat up a lot of time, much more so than doing the loop round the Callander way. And from the start of Loch Katrine, please note that you are 17½ miles from Inversnaid, if you are watching your time for a ferry. It is, however, much more wild and scenic doing the Katrine loop, I think you'll agree. From time to time you will hit one of the six cattle or deer grids on the way round, but they all have gates at the side to help you avoid getting that bone-shaking feeling.

Now a general pattern starts to emerge, where you go from woodland to open ground, mostly bracken and fern, and the first open stretch comes just before you reach the isolated dwellings at Letter and Edra. It's when covering the road on the open heath that you get great views up and back down the loch, and both her and her surrounds are very wild and pretty, all at the one time.

On the bridge that crosses the Strone Burn, a small attached signpost tells you you've travelled 5½ miles from Trossachs pier, with 7 miles to go to the Stron (Stronachlachar). These wee mile posts pop up from time to time and are handy to have. The quaint information plaque here also tells of a village that once stood on this spot, but was deserted and demolished by the 50s.

Now begins a fairly long arduous pull up after the Strone Burn – the main climb when going this way – and what this does is to open up a brilliant view west when you level out. Those big Arrochar Munros show themselves off for the first time, with the highest of them all, Ben Ime, by far and away the most imposing. Also, you look across the loch and see Stron sitting opposite and you think that you are almost there, but that's because the true top of the loch is hidden away from view. In fact, you are roughly only halfway round at this point and there is still a lot more remote road riding to go. Again, it follows a similar open heath then enclosed wooded pattern, all this change and variety keeping it interesting.

The next couple of miles are magic, because they're mostly stable and mostly open, and sitting above and off the loch, it's a continuous panorama all the way along.

Descending the Duke's Pass, when going north, is always a bit of a diving, dancing, bobbing, and banking thrill-a-second, with the bends and twists presenting a new view and scenery at every turn. You think you're doing a reel at a Highland ceilidh. Here, wee Ben A'n shows itself for the first time today.

The ferns don't half swish by as on you go, always on good tarmac – unsurprising, as it doesn't get a lot of usage. Then appears the rocky Meall na Boineide, the steep nose of the rugged local hill, An Garadh. As it does, a warning triangle lets you know a 12% drop in the road is imminent, so get ready with those anchors, for you're gonna need them here. The road plummets down hard and twisty, very tightly indeed, and only starts to behave itself when another bridge is crossed and you're back out into the flat and open.

It's at this point that another plaque is reached, which tells you the manmade peninsula jutting out into the loch is the burial ground of the Clan McGregor – the Trossachs was their former stronghold. A grander resting spot would be difficult to find. Missing from it, however, is the clan's most famous son, Rob Roy, who is buried in the graveyard at Balquidder. This is despite the fact that

he was born only a short distance away at the head of the loch, in a cottage at Glengyle.

And it's towards Glengyle we speed, through open ferns at first, then into some great big trees as the woods are reached. A lovely descent down to Glengyle House, beside an impressive large stone wall, brings the large white modern house to your side.

Red Rob[5] was not born in this sizeable house, but in a small stone cottage that stood in its place beforehand. One of the country's best known characters, which again to a great extent is down to Sir Walter, Rob was always at loggerheads with his great adversary, James Graham, the 1st Duke of Montrose. He was the man who had him outlawed when a loan went unpaid, through no fault of

5 - Rob Roy McGregor was also known as Red Rob, due to his red hair.

Next it's the turn of bold Ben Venue to steal the show on the fly down to Loch Achray.

Rob's. The stories of his and his clansmen's exploits are legendary. In fact, the loch itself got the name Katrine from the Gaelic 'cateran' meaning highland robber, after the McGregors who resided here.

Not far now to that great wee spin of road that takes you finally round the head of the loch. And as you ride it, look up the glen to your right and you'll see some real wild country in the shape of the Loch Lomond Munros. An Caisteal (The Castle) and the like sit up there, and a tough climb they are. But our attention is now focused on the shorter return leg back down the loch to Stronachlachar. It's only 2½ miles away, with more ferns and crags to come, all the woods absent from this stretch. But that means there are uninterrupted view across and down the loch, so no complaints.

We pass another information plaque telling us a bit about old Glengyle and this area known as Dhu. It shows some old photographs of the more modern house before the place was dammed. The original road, running from where you are standing to the house, is partly submerged, though still visible even today. The plaque also lets you know that more McGregor chiefs are said to be buried behind the house, including Black Knee, who led the boys during the '45. Most fighting McGregors weren't at Culloden, but further north in Sutherland at the time, pursuing Hanoverians.

So, enough of the old history, it's on with the show. And what a show it is. Such is the ruggedness and beauty all around you that, for a keen mountain man like myself used to seeing this sort of terrain only in very remote settings, it's hard to believe I'm actually on a tarmacked road here.

Talking of which, it now leads you down through the ferns, fairly flat and level at first, before it starts to rise gradually for quite a distance. What this does is to give you enough height to eventually make an exciting dive round the crags, ferns, and deep-looking bays of the loch, till you eventually drop dramatically down to Stronachlachar. Not so much a village, this place; more a collection of houses owned at one time by the water works. This is borne out by all the railings and dam walls associated with such places. What a stunning setting it is, all the same. It's got the lot, from the view down the loch, to the striking fir-lined headlands and islands, and houses in a situation to die for.

You can actually bypass most of it, if you want, as the road skirts the edge of the headland. Stronachlachar actually means headland of the stone mason. But there is no need for a diversion, as the direct route actually carries straight on past the place and up to a green gate

On the final bend of the Duke's Pass, and just about to drop most delightfully onto the banks of Loch Achray. Above, Ben A'n shows well, and the bit of road you've just ridden will have put you on a real high. The descent of the Duke's Pass is one of the highlights of the whole run.

Looking down the Achray as you make your way wooded and wonderful to the T-junction ahead. That is the major make-your-mind-up time when taking the Duke's Pass route. Is it left for Loch Katrine, or right for Callander?

that is easily passed. Then another ½ mile of climbing up through rough ground leads you to the junction at the east end of Loch Arklet. However, there is the Katrine Café right on the pier and, although I don't actually use it except the cludge for water and all, I know a lot of riders do like to stop for a bite to eat, especially if they ride in a group. It is a most splendid structure, and resembles a Victorian railway station.

If you require the support of the aforementioned café, turn left when you see the sign and run through the courtyard of a large tired-looking farmhouse, and reach the pier that way. Nearby, but out of sight, is the Royal Cottage, built in October 1889 to house Queen Vic when she came to officially open the reservoir. She never actually stayed in the cottage, as previously mentioned, because the 21-gun salute shattered all the windows. Still, the reservoir is quite an engineering feat, I must say, just the way that the aqueducts and tunnels feed water all the way down to Milngavie.

Katrine is Glasgow's main water supply. For a loch

that's only 8 miles long, that is very impressive indeed; its depth helps, of course. Only a slight drop in height all the way from here to the top end of Glasgow ensures that no pumping is required to get the water down there.

Regardless of whether you stop or not, the arrival at the Loch Arklet junction will follow shortly, and with it that stunning view of the loch and the Munros beyond which will stun you into silence again. By all means, if you've planned it, it is possible after going round Loch Katrine to make the 2.15pm sailing at Inversnaid, even when coming from Paisley. I have done it on occasion. But as we've already covered that option, we will do the full loop back to Aberfoyle by turning left and heading back down the B-829.

We came up this road when heading for Inversnaid direct, so it is simply a case of retracing our tracks on the way back down. It begins with a slight climb up through the rough and open ground, always finding ourselves looking right and admiring that great vista away to the west.

The first white mile post tells us it's 10 miles exactly to Aberfoyle, and what a 10 miles it is. Soon we pass over the deer grid and begin the long straight descent through the pine trees till we hit the shore of Loch Chon. It's here I'll give you a tip about riding in the Trossachs, because whoever decided to build Glasgow's reservoirs in this place, knew exactly what he was doing. I am talking wet, wet, wet, here – and I don't mean big Marty Pellow and the boys. What I'm trying to say is that it is always prudent to carry at least a light waterproof jacket with you if you intend to ride this neck of the woods, unless it's the middle of a heatwave.

The beginning of Loch Katrine from the carpark at its east end which, although very busy and touristy, will soon become all quiet and quaint again in no time. Remember, cars are not allowed for the most part on the road round the loch.

Looking back soon after starting round the Loch Katrine road, and even at the very beginning it is stunningly beautiful. Doing the loop by the Katrine way is undoubtedly harder than going via Callander, but it is the more scenic route by quite some margin.

From here to Kinlochard, you will descend through the trees for the best part of 6 miles and have great fun in doing it. You can see a bit more of Little Loch Dubh when going in this direction, and you will also notice just how poor the road surface is in places, much more than you would if you had climbed the road. The extra speed you attain on a descent will highlight all the slight and not-so-slight imperfections in any road surface, and the one you're on now is anything but perfect in places. But with the levelling out at Kinlochard comes respite from all the mayhem, and you purr contentedly past its fields and onto Loch Ard's shoreline.

Enjoy the peace and soft twisting tranquillity of the road here, calmness surrounding you in both the water and the rich homes either side. That most delightful of guides, a lochside stone wall, escorts you round what's left of the Ard before you lift off back through the woods and on down towards Milton's gardens, then back below Craigmore's steep slopes. And with that, it's welcome back to Aberfoyle.

As you pass the start of the Duke's Pass, the loop itself has been looped. A lot of people will drive up and park around here, before getting the bikes off the back of the car and doing the loop itself. That is fine if you only want to do that. No problem there, of course[6].

For me, well… no rest for the wicked. I've still got 32 miles to go till I'm back home, if I return via the Renfrew

---

6 - There's a large carpark conveniently placed right across the road for such purposes. It also contains a snack bar, and I can recommend the hot dogs.

CALLANDER

We know that by turning left at this junction it will lead to Trossachs pier on the Katrine, but we want right this time and will head east towards Callander. Now, we have barely started when we encounter the now massive and impressive grey walls and turrets of the Tigh Mor Trossachs Hotel. It is the one you saw so clearly as you descended the pass. It initially grew from an inn which stood here from 1877, then it started to grow arms and legs to accommodate all the flocking tourists. It is in such good condition now that it is hard to believe that it was actually derelict as recently as 1991. Since the 1950s, downturn in business meant that many hotels like this were struggling for survival, but things have turned around since.

So, off down the side of the Achray we go, which is an absolutely brilliant road. A dainty delightful dance it is, disappearing through wooded twists and turns as you follow it down. Its iron railing and aged trees line the waterside, as rocky wooded slopes line the other. Great views across the Achray are glimpsed from time to time through the trees, and bold Ben Venue shows himself as the big baby on the block across the loch. The east end of the loch is even quainter, when a stone wall replaces the railing, and the narrowing of the water makes it feel more pond-like and perfect. The mile post tells you it's only 7 miles to Callander.

This is typical Loch Katrine-side riding, pretty wooded and pleasant. The white-railed bridges are commonplace, and often attached to them are distance plates telling you the mileage to Stronachlachar and how far you've come from the start of the loch.

Ferry, and 36 if it's via the Erskine Bridge. Just as you pass Liz McGregor's café, you will pick up the smell of chips, as the chippy is just a little further along on the left. So stop there and stock up on the carbs, if you need some. After this, continue along the very varied Main Street and out towards the roundabout at the Rob Roy Motel, in a mile or so's time.

When you reach the roundabout, you'll want to turn right to come back down the A-81, but if you look straight ahead, you will see a road running downhill towards you. This would be the way you would arrive back if you had chosen the Callander loop, as opposed to the Loch Katrine one.

The Callander loop is somewhat faster, as it sticks for the most part to A-roads and is also a popular choice with many riders. Being a loop, it can be done in any direction, but just to keep it simple we will do it clockwise, which entails turning right instead of left when you clear the Duke's Pass and come to the T-junction on the A-821, at the head of Loch Achray.

A fantastic look across the Katrine can be had once the road starts to climb at the far end, and this view looks right across to Stronachlachar with a glimpse of Loch Arklet beyond. The big flat top mountain in the distance is Beinn Narnain. Just before you reach here, the length of the loch can be very deceptive because the top half can be hidden from view. It's only when you gain some height that the full distance to go becomes apparent.

This is the burial ground of the Clan McGregor, who of course held sway in this area for such a long time. Their most famous son, Rob Roy, is not buried here, however, as he was laid to rest in a churchyard in Balquidder. It is a most beautiful spot for a final resting place, I must admit.

Looking right back down the full length of Loch Katrine from Stronachlachar. There is a great wee cafe on the pier here which sells ice cream, ideal for a hot day, and is a picturesque spot to linger for a while. You are only a short hop up to the T-junction with the B-829 coming up from Aberfoyle, so you have a couple of options open to you as regards which way to return home. You can either make for Aberfoyle and the A-81, or the Inversnaid ferry and the A-82.

All is flat and fair till the end of Loch Achray, which isn't long in coming as it's only about a mile long. Then you quickly reach a beautiful broad curving stone bridge that carries you over the River Turk, just before it joins the Black Water, which has been your companion ever since the loch stopped. Once over the brig, the road climbs for the first time, and this will mean your imminent arrival in the village of Brig o' Turk. Turk is the old Scots word for a wild boar. The brightly-coloured green and yellow village name sign shows such an animal, to inform you of this fact.

On the left is their classic old wooden hut of a tearoom, one even I've stopped at recently and recommend it to you. It looks more like an old scout hall in its green/grey colours. The brig and its tearoom seem to have some connection to the film *The 39 Steps*, but I'm not a movie man so have never seen it.

It is only a tiny place, at any rate, and once you pass the teashop, continue to the top of the brae and spin out in a

There is much upping and downing like this at the top end of Loch Katrine, and a fast road it ain't. It's one to take your time on, to be honest, and if you plan to return by the Inversnaid ferry then leave plenty of time to catch it.

and brings you to a side road running off to the right. This is the Invertrossachs Road, and we are going to take it[7]. It's another delight to ride, is the Invertrossachs, and starts as it means to go on by taking us gently down and over as quaint a hump bridge as you could wish for.

This enables us to cross the Eas Gobhain with dry feet, and also to get a view of its gentle murmur below. You have now joined the official cycle lane at this point, and on the other side of the bridge a cycle route sign says turn right for Aberfoyle 12 miles away. We will ignore that direction and turn left for Callander, because going right, I believe, will use an off-road track – the one we passed at the start of the Duke's Pass. The old Invertrossachs is a great wee single track road to ride, and I assume it was the main road at one time leading over from Callander, where we are heading now.

We get the pleasure of the Eas Gobhain running beside from time-to-time, as we make our way down what is

7 - Taking this road avoids the village of Callander. If you prefer to include it, continue straight ahead.

high gear to help you recover as you re-enter the woods. The road undulates a bit more between here and the start of Loch Venachar, as it goes through newer woodland than we found on the Achray. It's just a little bit more taxing, yes, but enjoyable all the same.

A drop down takes us onto the banks of our next loch and, what with the deep ferns and low-lying Menteith Hills beyond, she is another pretty affair. The Venachar is another pleasure to ride, which is just as well, as she is our last Trossachs water and always seems somewhat longer than she really is. This is also just as well, as she doesn't stretch as far as 4 miles.

The western half of the loch sees us on a splendid slalom of curving dips and rises, all gentle and back in amongst the older sturdier oaks and the likes. However, the second half – the eastern end of the Venachar – is a different affair entirely. Here, the road straightens and departs the loch shore, and runs over the moorland and pastures in a long elegant line, and things open up very broadly in front of you. This continues till the road makes a snaking, slender, and pretty chicane below the hillside of Dunmore Fort,

Glengyle House, at the very top end of Loch Katrine, sits in a most idyllic situation. Rob Roy McGregor was born there, though not in the house you see today but one that stood on the exact same spot much earlier. There you go, how's that for a claim to fame

If you turn right at the bottom of the Duke's Pass and head for Callander, you immediately run into beautiful old wooded stretches of road that help you skip eastwards and daintily dance beside the Achray. No other way to put it.

in essence a leafy lane. Not one without some major development, because apart from a few houses, we soon pass Wheelz, a rather large cycle centre, and then a fairly well-hidden caravan park, the Callander Holiday Park. Most of the way, however, is old leafy green, and with little or no climbing, it's a good recovery stretch. This will be needed soon, because the long road back to Paisley is about to begin for me, and to Glasgow for a lot of others. When we regrettably emerge from the Invertrossachs, we only just touch the edge of Callander, as we swing right onto the A-81 at a small mini roundabout.

We only catch a glimpse of this well-to-do village's homes, all strong and neat, as we begin the long haul home. It more or less begins with a long, flat, straight mile or so of road (very rare in Scotland), which runs past a fairly lengthy procession of white bungalows lining the right hand side, before heading for the distant conifer plantations. These are seen way ahead and are reached by running flat through a real mixed bag of different fields to get to them. The conifers are finally reached by a slight climb, which ends at a hard right swing in the road. The

minor road here going straight on to Thornhill (the B-822), can be used as a return route and is useful as it misses out the climb that we are about to undertake on the A-81.

On this occasion, we will stick to the main road, not only for information purposes, but also because it is shorter and the climb isn't too bad, either. On top of that, it is a very good curvy piece of tar to ride once you are up and around Loch Rusky. So, down the gears a bit and dig in a little, for we've a lot of miles in our legs now and any climb feels a little bit of a challenge. This area is very heavily forested, and this is apparent right from the word go. All the trees are still standing[8] at the beginning, as you sit in the saddle and rhythm your way up past Cockhill Cottage. But higher up, you'll find a lot of cutting has taken place, as this crop's time is near an end. Despite the destroyed landscape, the riding on the road is good now that you are well up at around 170 metres high.

The road lends itself to easy and enjoyable going, dipping a bit, bending a bit, with a more natural roadside foliage helping the cause. Soon we pass little Loch Rusky, always seemingly still and a little forgotten, perhaps because you only glimpse it when travelling past. The road lifts slightly as it leads on to the entrance to Letter Farm, and at that point the shimmering sheet of the Lake of Menteith shines below for the first time. The descent down will begin shortly, and is very fast and a bit brutal. I say brutal because of the road surface,

---

8 - They've now started cutting them down.

Loch Achray matches all the other Trossachs' lochs for enjoyment, charm, and beauty, as this shot shows with a great look across the loch to Ben Venue. Old iron railings and aged woodlands go hand-in-hand, and give you that time-stood-still feeling as you mosey along.

which isn't so much pot-holed, just not in the slightest bit smooth overall.

This is a pity, and ruins what would otherwise be a great bending descent. The bending is at the top half only, as the road straightens out when it drops through the fields at the bottom, just as it approaches and abuts with the A-873.

Turn right to stay on the A-81, where the road sign says 5 to Aberfoyle and 30 to Glasgow. And it won't be too much trouble to head slightly downhill through the walls and big trees that line this exquisite stretch of road which takes you into the tiny Port of Menteith. If you sneeze, you'll miss it; only the right hand side of the road contains just about all of it, with the exception of the wee brown wooden bus stop, servicing both ways, that sits on the left.

You will notice numerous mileage posts like these as you tour the Trossachs, as they are totally unmissable due to their distinctive shape. I know of nowhere else that has anything similar. They give very precise and accurate distances, in my experience, so if you don't ride with a computer you can trust their information.

The lake itself lies a good couple of fields' width away, and contains the Inchmahome Priory on one of its islands, the one so beloved by Mary Queen of Scots as a child. The road now runs below the very striking flank of Beinn Dearg, and you wonder just how those high trees cling to that steep upper slope. The road that carries you west towards the Rob Roy roundabout is fairly friendly, save for one short and taxing wee rise. After this, the Queen Elizabeth Forest is entered, and as you emerge out the trees and round a bend, mighty Ben Lomond welcomes you back to this neck of the woods. The finish is a fitting one, as the road descends and allows you a freewheel down past the Aberfoyle golf course, before a cluster of white houses at Braeval Farm – and, of

Although taking the Callander option is perhaps not as scenic or dramatic as the Katrine, it still has very pleasant views (like the one above) of the road as it passes Loch Venachar. Being an easier road to ride also gives it appeal, and as Callander is approached you have the choice of going through the village via Kilmahog or by skirting the edge of it on the Invertrossachs Road. I usually choose the latter.

course, the large road sign – announce your return to the roundabout.

And so the Callander loop is completed, thus far anyway. Because now it's to a southerly direction we turn, and start to make our way back down the long straight of the A-81, which for me will only end when I get to Blane Smithy. This is merely a retracing of the tyre tracks back the way we came, and so it will just be a quick recap. But, as mentioned before in other runs, doing a road in the opposite direction and much later on the same run, can make it feel like a whole different animal.

Reaching Callander by the Invertrossachs Road, which is a lovely old moss-covered wall-lined way. If using it, it means you actually miss the village centre and just touch the edge. If you want to go through Callander, it's best to stay on the A-821 and head for Kilmahog first, which will let you run right down its Main Street. But be warned, if you like it quiet then it's not for you.

A great view down and across towards the Lake of Menteith can be had from the A-81 after it climbs high up past Loch Rusky on the return from Callander. On a lovely summer's eve, the lake will glint and twinkle in the distance and makes for a most pleasing sight. The fact that you know you have a lot of height in your favour which is just about to get cashed in doesn't do the setting any harm, that's for sure.

On descending down from Loch Rusky on the A-81, it meets with the A-873 at a prominent bend. A right turn here will run you downhill, in rather some style I might add, into the Port of Menteith. Having the gradient in your favour with a beautiful old mossy wall and very mature deciduous trees for company, I cannot begin to describe just how delightful this stretch of road is to ride.

Certainly, the views will be different, and this is quite noticeable early on returning down this road, when the Campsies show a tremendous flank in the evening sun, away to the left in the distance. Rising off the flat early plain will take a bit of oomph, as you lift long and gently up into the woods that are guarded by the white sentinel of the Ward Toll Cottage. Easy does it, as it goes on a fair bit and it's late in the day, and all that. But once up, it's now purr along merrily time, and when passing through the chink in the road at Garraud Farm, you will notice cars opposite, across the fields on the left. This means that the Ballat junction is approaching. Fire straight through, stopping for nought, and continue the charge south.

Yes, we charged through on the way up and we charge through on the way down, as you will have the bit between your teeth now, if you have enough fuel left in the tank. This can take a bit of practice to get right, but

As you make your way down the A-81, heading from the Port of Menteith towards Aberfoyle, that great sentinel of the Lowlands, Ben Lomond, appears rather magnificently again right in the centre of your view. It is amazing how the sight of it can have such an effect on you and lift your spirits even this late in the day, with so many miles in your legs and a lot of tough miles still to come.

with more experience at doing the long stuff, you will get better and better at judging just how hard to go early on. On top of that, the more long runs you do, the more efficient the body will become at burning fat for fuel, and you will find yourself eating less and losing more weight.

So down and up over the Endrick Water, and finish off on the great sweeping dip and rise that precedes the roundabout at Blane Smithy itself. Ok, so far so good, but now it will get a little bit tougher, as there is a fair bit of climbing to come for us once we make our way down the B-834 and cross the Blane Water.

The late evening sun will enhance the tree-lined avenue that pulls you back up to the Stockiemuir Road. The same sun has delighted all the way down the 81, and it is amazing how it can light up even the roughest meadow and bring forth lighter hues you never noticed before.

After just a little huff and puff, you're on the A-809 and turning left for home. Shortly, the long pull up back up to the Queen's View/Whangie carpark will begin, and it is one I have made much of before. How tough you find

Returning back down the glorious A-81 and just approaching the disused rail bridge near Balfron Station. This bridge sits approximately 8 miles south of Aberfoyle and is a good time-marker if you're heading for the Inversnaid ferry on the way out. However, the 81 is as good to go south on as it is to go north on, and you will be enjoying this a lot, let me tell you. For me, it means that I must depart the A-81 at Blane Smithy roundabout and make the long tough climb up on the Stockiemuir Road. That's when you realise just how good the A-81 really is.

A great moment of joy is had on the Trossachs run when you clear the long hard pull up on the A-809 Stockiemuir Road just at the Whangie carpark. Here the photo is looking back towards the Loch Lomond hills in the late evening sunshine. All the climbing isn't over, by any means; that won't be the case till we reach the Langfaulds roundabout on the other side of Baljaffray Road, but then it's nice and easy through the Drum and gently to the Renfrew ferry.

it is down to what nick you're in, the weather, what bike you're on, the time of year, and all. Even with a lot of hard Trossachs' miles in you, if you've trained well enough, you won't be going into the red zone when ascending it. Though, as always, you're glad when the job is done.

Still much huff and puff to go, for me at least, though that doesn't ever stop me enjoying the dive down past the Carbeth Inn. It's a bit rollercoaster to the Baljaffray roundabout, and then a right turn to start climbing over Baljaffray itself. It looks a lot worse than it is. Once Baljaffray is cleared, it is a most rewarding moment as I drop down to the Langfaulds roundabout, because that is all the hard work just about over. A left and right turn brings the Peel Glen descent into play, and this is followed by a gentle wind down and doodle round

Kinfauns Drive. If it's a glorious evening, the late summer sunshine can even make the Drum look good.

The way back to the Yoker ferry only requires a right turn at the next roundabout to run you up and over the rail bridge on Kelso Street, before a final turn on the cranks on Yoker Ferry Road leads to the cobbles of the slipway. Standing on the banks of the mighty Clyde on a nice summer's eve, after putting in so many miles, can be quite a moment of reflection. Only then does it hit you, just what you've done.

Nice and easy is the feeling as you walk onto the Silver Swan and pay your £1.70 to take you across. The old Clyde never looked so good when viewed on the return journey, then off the boat we go again. Bugger! It's one last time onto the saddle, 5 miles, and about 30 minutes for me.

The road back home is as straight as a die all the way through Renfrew and then the Renfrew Road, Paisley. It's a lot quieter in the evening than it was in the way out, I guarantee. So, too, is Paisley Cross and Causeyside Street, and then the tough wee twist of the Munt is mounted and, with it, the last mile before home. Now, if the Trossachs doesn't put the Ross back in your Cromarty's, I don't know what will…

Liam Boy

N.B. A full loop, incorporating both Callander and Loch Katrine, is possible. It's a slightly longer day, it has to be said, but a great one, coming in at just over the 100-mile mark if you return back down the A-81. The details are at the beginning of the run.

APPENDICES

Below are a number of training runs, and the local testing run that I and many other riders from this area use. If they are handy, you may wish to use them yourself or, if not, you can devise your own. These are useful to build up stamina for the longer runs, and can also be used when time is tight or you are just in the mood for a shorter jaunt.

I describe them, very briefly, in the direction I normally do them in. But as they are all loops, they can be just as easily done in the opposite direction. They all, apart from the test run, have at least one good climb in them, to maximise the benefit. All runs are contained within the O'S Landranger 64 map, unless otherwise stated.

ROWBANK RESERVOIR

16.7 MILES

1.07 HOURS

ASCENT 980 FT

713 CALS

This is a great short and very picturesque training run that packs a fair climb in its armour, and one I like to do often. After gaining Howwood on the Beith Road (the A-737), turn left up the Bowfield Road (the B-776) and, after a fantastic long climb, run past the beautiful Rowbank Reservoir. Continue on up to the crossroads at Hall Farm, where a left turn onto the B-775 will run you back to Paisley along the top of the Gleniffer Braes.

FERENEZE HILLS

10.9 MILES

0.50 MINS

ASCENT 860 FT

574 CALS

This is a great quick but hard wee run I like to do, especially if I'm short for time. It involves heading into Barrhead and along Paisley Road, then turning right before the rail bridge and running up to Gateside. Continue up onto the steep side of the Fereneze Hills, which are similar and therefore good training for Arran's roads. The gradient gets up to about 15%. The height gained actually allows views of Ailsa Craig. Continue right to the end of Fereneze Road, til you meet Shilford Road. Turn right and come back over by Middleton Farm, where you descend to the B-775, where a right turn will return you back down Gleniffer Braes.

LOCHLIBO ROAD

15.2 MILES

1.03 HOUR

ASCENT 840 FT

608 CALS

This run also involves running up Paisley Road, Barrhead, but this time continue on to the end til Allan's Corner roundabout. Turn right onto Kelburn Street and climb out of town onto the great Lochlibo (Irvine) Road, the A-736. The Fereneze Hills look awesome, as does the big white Nielson Mill, which is where the road starts to climb up to Shilford Hamlet. When you reach Uplawmoor, turn right at Caldwell Golf Club onto the B-776, and again climb hard to Hall Farm on the B-775. From there, turn right and return back over the Gleniffer Road and Braes to Paisley.

DUNLOP

21.7 MILES

1.29 HOURS

1320 FT/ASC

929 CALS

The Dunlop run is another good climbing one, which follows the same start as the Lochlibo Road run all the way to the top of Kelburn Street, Barrhead. This time take the left fork for Nielson and not the Irvine Road, and climb long and great up into Nielson Village itself. From there, turn left onto the Kingston Road and undulate wildly and upward into the wild country leading to Dunlop. You can either go right to the end of this road and turn right on the A-735 and enter Dunlop that way, or take the right turn before the end, which will lead to the village centre by a slightly shorter route. Return back through Lugton and then the B-775 over glorious Gleniffer.

STEWARTON

28 MILES
2.11 HOURS
ASCENT 1680 FT
1320 CALS

The Stewarton run entails heading up through the Barrhead Dams on the Aurs Road, til you meet with the lights at the bottom of the Stewarton Road (the B-769) and then turning right. This will carry you straight to the Ayrshire village with a real tough climb along the way, but a great descent down to finish. This is another high moor road and, when going clockwise, allows another long distance view of Ailsa Craig. On reaching Stewarton, turn right at the centre crossroads and return back through Dunlop and Lugton on the A-735, before that old stalwart the B-775, carries you back to Paisley via bonnie Gleniffer.

EAGLESHAM MOOR ROAD

29.8 MILES
2.15 HOURS
ASCENT 1380 FT
1231 CALS

Without doubt, this is a superb run. One that's long enough to be a run in its own right and was denied to us for years because of heavy traffic on the A-77, until the new M-77 and A-726 Eaglesham bypass were opened. It is enjoyed by many south side riders and why not? Not only is it A-1, but it just falls in handy for good measure. It entails heading for Eaglesham through Barrhead and then along the Humbie Road, or by using Clarkston Toll. Turn right at the Gilmour Street crossroads in Eaglesham centre and climb initially up Montgomery Street (the

B-764), running you up and onto Eaglesham Moor. All's quiet nowadays, with no more thundering dumper trucks; in fact, there is a cycle lane marked out on the road and you may even enjoy the call of the curlew in summer.

Wonderful rise follows wonderful rise until, at the crest of the road, you can see the sea. When you hit the old A-77 (which has a superb cycle lane, too), turn right and return down to Mearns Cross and back by the Barrhead Dams, if it suits. I personally prefer to turn left earlier than that, using the Malletsheugh Road and then come back in down the Springhill Road, Barrhead.

CLUNE BRAE

29.8 MILES
2.08 HOURS
1120 FT/ASC
1165 CALS
O'S MAPS 64, 63.

This run is probably the most famous training run in the whole area, and used by local groups as well as individual riders. It entails heading for Bishopton and then dropping down onto the busy A-8 which takes you to the big Woodhall roundabout. You can either stay on the A-8 or head through Woodhall to take you to the bottom of the Clune Brae. There is a bit of a shortcut when using the Woodhall route, which entails taking a left turn at Woodhall station and climbing steeply up to the middle of the Clune on Heggies Avenue.

If you don't take the shortcut, expect to meet the Clune at its steepest early doors. From the roundabout at the top of the brae, continue to climb, though much more gently, till you are on the road to Kilmacolm. Continue to run right through millionaire's row on the A-761, which allows you a fantastic flier of a fall towards Bridge of Weir. Personally, I prefer to return from Bridge of Weir by Kilbarchan, which requires another short sharp shock of a climb, but gives a great descent into that old weaving village on the other side as compensation. From Kilbarchan, I return along the Beith Road, Johnstone, before taking the Glenpatrick Road, Elderslie, up to Foxbar Road and into Paisley that way.

LOCHER BRIDGE

27.1 MILES
1.52 HOURS
1300 FT/ASC
1181 CALS

This is about the best way to see rural Renfrewshire wearing its prettiest petticoat. This one involves heading for Kilmacolm on the A-761 and then, at the crossroads in the centre, turn left onto the Lochwinnoch Road, the B-786, and climb very highly on that road. It carries you over the Locher Burn, before the road drops splendidly and dramatically down towards Lochwinnoch. Before you reach the top end of that village, however, turn left onto the Howwood (Bridesmill) Road and, after a double whammy climb, descend like a banshee into the centre of

that village. A run back to Johnstone then follows on the Beith Road, before the Abbey Road and then Glenpatrick Road, Elderslie, are used to return to south Paisley.

HOUSTON ROAD: TEST RUN

7.3 MILES
60 FT/ASC

Now this is not a training run per se. Rather, this road, the Houston Road (also known as the Georgetown) is used by many riders as a test run. Principally this is because it is one of the few flat roads in the whole area. It is also used by local clubs as a short time trial route. On occasion you may need a flat stretch of road, several miles long, to let you work out your average heart rate and help you set certain training zones on your computer. If you are not attempting to do this, then you need not bother with the Houston Road.

Some guys will actually trip out a certain distance on this road and leave a marker by the side of the road, such as a traffic cone, to let them know exactly where it is for future reference. Others just use their computer trip distance. The road runs off the Barnsford Road, which is the A-726 behind Glasgow Airport, up the roundabout at Crosslee and back down again. On the whole seven mile stretch, there is really only a dip and rise as you pass Loanhead Cottages.

THE BIKE

As I mentioned in the opening run, it can be difficult to know which bike to go for early on, as you simply don't know what you're about yet. If you already have a machine in the garage or one that you haven't used in a while, then simply dust it down, oil it up, and use it to get you going. The price of bikes has shot up in recent years, and unjustifiably so. There is no need to go high-end, top dollar unless you intend to race. Just remember that the difference between a top machine costing thousands and a level-entry one costing hundreds is two miles an hour on a hilly course, with the difference being reduced to negligible on a flat course.

A level-entry machine is more than adequate for non-racing recreational riders, and a lot of the runs in the book can be easily ridden on the modern, lightweight, slick hybrid bikes, but my preference is for the racer. I actually did the Clyde coast run many times on a GT Talera mountain bike before I bought my first roadie, which was a Greg Lemond Reno. So a level-entry machine is a good way to start. And if you do decide to buy one that is a lot higher spec in the future, the level-entry one will make a good winter training bike, which is a good thing to have, as you will find out in time.

Despite what I have already said, I will finish this brief piece of advice by saying that when doing a long run on a top-end, high spec bike, the difference it can make – even from a mid-range descent machine – is quite noticeable. And although it will come down to personal circumstances, such as justification and cost, I would say that if you do decide to splash out and treat yourself to a really good machine, it will be money well spent, especially in the long run. I thoroughly recommend you do.

My two machines, which were used when writing the book, are pictured below. On the left is the trusted trainer, the Dolan, which is pictured at Wemyss Bay station, just before a jaunt over to the Isle of Bute. It is carbon fibre with a Shimano gruppo made up mostly of an ultegra/105 mix. It sports the essential mudguards, of course.

To the right is the pride of the fleet Eddy Merckx Cima, sporting wall-to-wall dura ace. On this occasion she is on Largs pier.

SADDLE BAGS

The photograph shows the two saddle bags which I use, along with their contents and the pumps that I carry on a ride, the lights, and also the home-based track pump I use. Both my bags are Top Peak, though there are numerous other good brands on the market, mostly about a similar price of between £15 to £20. I just like the internal pockets or attachments that come with the Top Peak for keeping money and keys in, etc. The difference between the one on my training bike and my best bike is size. The training bike one is slightly larger to accommodate a beanie hat and thin pair of gloves during the winter time.

The contents are, for the most part, identical, though the multi-tool and patch kits in the smaller bag are more compact. In fact, the only additional thing I carry in the training bag a lot of the time is a couple of cable ties in case my mudguards start giving me gip. Other than that, they are as near as dammit the same.

I did try out some very lightweight expensive compact tubes from Continental in the small bag at one point (they cost £11 each), but they proved to be far too susceptible to punctures, even when you only rode over a small stone, so I don't use them now and don't recommend you do either. Stick to the standard tubes and you'll be fine. The list that I carry is as follows:

- Spare tube
- Tyre levers
- Multi-tool (with chain splitter)
- Two pre-glued patch kits (winter ones in a more waterproof cover)
- Two cable ties (training bike only)
- House keys
- Money bag (I always carry 7 tenners & 7 fivers)

NB. I only use the pre-glued patches to get me home. If I intend to continue to use a tube that has punctured, I have a more traditional puncture repair kit at home, which I will use on occasion to provide a more dependable, solid, and lasting repair.

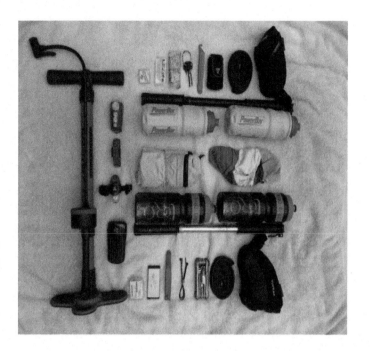

PUMPS

Both on-bike pumps are Mt Zefals, which are the big babies on the block. I take them instead of the more lightweight pumps, because when push comes to shove they do the business without the strain and effort required when using a mini-pump; therefore, they are my preference. Park Tool do a similar model to Zefal which, although it has a better frame-fitting set-up, the pump action isn't to my liking and therefore I prefer the Mt Zefal.

I also recommend buying a track pump for the house, as it is good practice to check your tyre inflation before every run, and a bike-mounted pump is not adequate for this regular operation. Buying a good track pump, costing between £30 to £40, will save you a lot of time and elbow grease in the short run, never mind the long run. Get one pronto.

LIGHTS

Nowadays you may see some road riders using a flashing rear light even when they are out for a daytime jaunt. I personally don't use them all the time, but do so when the weather turns bad or if I am riding on a busy road. I will, of course, carry lights on a run that I know will end after dark.

My front light is a re-chargeable Cat Eye Nano Shot + and I have two rear lights. Both are Top Peak, as I tend to find their mounting system safe and secure. The larger of the two lights can either be mounted on the frame or clipped into the rear of the saddle bag, but the smaller one can only be mounted on the frame. It weighs nothing, and is ideal to carry on a long run on a day when you suspect the weather might turn bad and you might want to become more visible in the rain.

On top of that, for the winter I also bought a small flashing light that you fit to the top of your helmet. The idea here is the higher the light sits, the better. However, just to prove that nothing can guarantee your safety, the only time I have ever been brushed by a car was very recently when I was wearing a yellow hi-vis rain jacket and using a flashing rear light. It happened just as I neared the top of the Rest and Be Thankful. In this instance, though, I have a sneaky suspicion the driver was either stoned or drunk, just by the way he drove (he never stopped) after the incident. So it's better to carry a lot of luck as opposed to anything else.

NB. Also please note the rolled-up hi-vis rain jacket and cotton cap that I carry on many long runs, if there is even a hint of bad weather in the forecast. It's a good insurance policy to do so.

SADDLE HEIGHT

I am of the opinion that the most important thing to get right if you are bike riding for any distance at all is your saddle height. Once you get that right then the rest can follow on. That is how I work it. Not only that, but the type of saddle you have can be the real make-or-break component on your bike; if it is uncomfortable even after quite a distance, then it can put you off riding the bike altogether. Simply put, if your saddle is uncomfortable, it doesn't matter how good the rest of the bike components are as they won't even enter into it. Most serious bike commentators will tell you that the frame is the most important part of the bike, which is true in many respects, but you could also put up an argument for the saddle.

There is a chance that the saddle which comes with your bike may suit you, especially if you ride only fairly short distances. However, there is also a high chance that it will not, especially if riding long distances. That's when you have a problem. You have to find a replacement, and this can be a long expensive search for some.

Seeking advice from fellow riders with a lot of experience can help, as can going online and reading reviews of saddles, and such like. One guy whose advice I like to take is Aussie bike-fitting guru, Steve Hogg, who is a man I will refer to several times with regards to fitting of bikes and components. But for the moment let's deal with getting the saddle height correct first, because without that it won't matter if you do have one that is suitable, as you won't be getting the best out of it.

If you ever have to get on a strange bike at short notice (such as a hired machine), or for any other reason you don't have time to do a proper job of setting your saddle height, then a good quick fix is to sit on the bike and – with your heel on one of the pedals – put the pedal in the furthest positon from you (i.e. not straight down but slightly forward). Adjust the saddle height til your leg is bolt straight, and when you move the ball of your foot onto the pedal, there will be as near as dammit the correct amount of bend at the knee to ensure a reasonable fit. That, as stated, is fine as a quick fix. However we want something much more exact and accurate for our purposes, and for that I use and recommend the Greg Lemond method.

GREG LEMOND SADDLE HEIGHT METHOD

This simple but accurate way of getting the correct saddle height was devised by the great man himself, way back when they still used pedals with straps and clips and people still listened to LP records. I mention this because I will, as far as possible, give you the method he used as he described it then, along with some modern substitutes where necessary for you to get the correct height. So here goes.

Greg says stand with your back to a wall, wearing only socks and your riding shorts. Take an LP (long playing) record and, with the side of it placed right along the back wall, jam it as hard as you can into your crotch just the way the saddle would do if you were sitting on your bike.

Measure the distance from the floor to the top of the LP and record this in millimetres. Now get out the old calculator and multiply this number by 0.883. With the number which the calculator gives you (also in millimetres), measure from the centre of the crank bolt to the top of your saddle in line with the seat post – and this is your saddle height (Photo).

I use a flat blade screwdriver to ensure the ruler is in the centre of the crank bolt. Greg also says to subtract 2 millimetres if you are using clipless pedals. Don't forget that this was back in the days when a lot of guys weren't using clipless, even top pros like Shaun Kelly. As just about everyone uses clipless now, remember to subtract the 2 millimetres before setting the saddle height.

Also back in those days just about every household had a stack of LP records, nowadays I doubt if few households even have one. So we need a replacement for the LP. You can go into a second hand record store and get an old LP to do the job, or you can use a square or rectangular piece of very thin wood measuring 10 x 10 inches or 8 x 10 inches, or the cover of a hard-backed book, or one part of a plastic folder (the type you get in W H Smiths) – any of these will suffice. Also, if you don't have anyone to help with taking your leg measurement, it can be helpful to buy a long metal ruler about 2½ to 3 feet long, which will make the job easier if you're doing it single-handed. I bought one from B&Q just for this alone, and thoroughly recommend it. So that is the way I get my seat height.

I also recommend that before you do anything, you ensure your saddle is sitting straight by using a small

spirit level; if you don't have one, it is worth your while getting one for this job alone. You may find that you will need it quite frequently as you adjust saddle height and fore aft position, which we will deal with shortly. Next I recommend you set your cleat position on your shoes first, and then adjust your saddle's fore and aft position.

CLEAT POSITION

One of the most important things to get correct nowadays is the position of your cleats on the bottom of your cycling shoes. I will give another simple method of getting a good starting position, which – like all the other adjustment techniques in the book – requires no previous experience, special training, or specialised expensive equipment to enable a successful operation.

Once the basic set-up position is achieved, I will also talk about a more advanced position, courtesy of Mr Steve Hogg, that dynamic Digger (Aussie) whose advice is always worth having. This operation is probably made a little bit easier if you have an indoor trainer to sit you and the bike on, but it can just as easily be performed when sitting on the bike and using one hand to lean against a wall. So once again, here goes.

The idea is to position the cleat on the shoe, so that the ball of the foot sits over the pedal axle when riding. For expediency, this position will from now on be referred to as BOFOPA. The easiest way to do this is to first remove your shoes and socks, then locate what is known as your 1st MTP (metatarsophalangeal) joint. This is the big, bony, first knuckle joint that sits between the foot and big toe. Mark a small line across this (photo 1). The ball of your foot is obviously on the bottom of your foot, but the 1st MTP joint sits directly above it on the top, so we use it as our guide to make the job easier.

Now we want to mark the part of the outside of the cycling shoe which has the 1st MTP joint right below it.

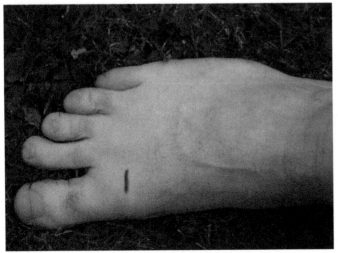
Photo 1

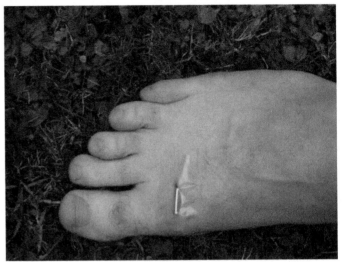
Photo 2

You could just put your shoes back on, without wearing your socks, and try and feel for the joint from the outside then mark the shoe at that point. However to make finding the 1st MTP joint easier, it helps to sticky tape a small metal cable end/nipple (the type you have at the end of your brake and gear cables) to the line you have marked on your foot, then put your shoes back on, again without any socks (Photo 2). You will feel this from the outside of the shoe much easier, and can mark this point with a felt tip pen or a slither of tape or white adhesive paper (Photo 3). If you don't have any cable ends/nipples, then just something small and hard will do.

Once you have marked the shoe, attach the cleats to the bottom of the shoe and tighten them up, but not fully at this point, as there is still some adjusting and manoeuvring to do. Now get back on the bike, click into your pedals and position the cranks horizontally. Then manoeuvre your forward-facing shoe so that the mark on the shoe is in line with the pedal axle. Climb off and tighten the bolts on your cleats, then do the same with the other foot.

It is usually easier to take your foot out of the shoe and leave it in the pedal at this point, as this part of the operation can be a bit higgledy-piggledy, if you are doing it on your own. It is easier if there is someone to help you, but for most of us, it's a one man job.

The final slight adjustment is to ensure that your cleat is facing straight forward. So after you have removed it from the pedal, you may have to loosen the cleat very

Photo 3

SHOE SIZE	APPROX. POSITION
36-38	7-9mm
39-41	8–10mm
42-43	9-11mm
44-45	10-12mm
46-47	11-14mm
48-50	12-16mm

slightly at this point, ensure it stays more of less where it is, then line it up with the marker lines on the bottom of the shoe. *Voilà*! Job done.

If you have a computer and are online, it may be worth your while to have a look at a website run by an Australian bike-fitter called Steve Hogg. He is a very well-known and respected man in the world of cycling. If you are not online (and many of us aren't), I will give you Steve's thoughts on cleat position. Steve says that the foot in cycling is a lever and not a very efficient one. That's because the piston (which in this case is the leg), is positioned at the end of the lever (foot). Problems can arise when you are cycling hard and applying a lot of force to the cranks, because then the heel can drop more than usual and you lose the BOFOPA position, as the foot tends to slide back.

He therefore advocates actually moving your foot forward of BOFOPA position when setting up your cleats, so as to counteract this movement by the foot under pressure. Steve also goes on to explain that some people are toe-down riders while others are heel-down riders. For each size of shoe he gives a range of adjustments. If you are a heel-down rider, he advises to use the greater length of adjustment. It will, of course, take you a little time to figure out what is your own personal pedalling style, and so BOFOPA is still a good place to start. Steve's recommended adjustments are as follows:

Remember, we are moving the cleat back in the shoe, which in essence means we are moving the shoe forward to make our foot a more efficient lever. I am a size 43 and have moved my cleat back by 10mms. Again, the guidelines on the bottom of your shoe should help you achieve an accurate adjustment. Just get your BOFOPA positon first and take it from there.

SADDLE FORE-AFT POSITION

Getting your saddle in the correct fore-aft position comes next, and it will usually mean with most saddles (with only one exception I know) that the saddle height will need to be checked and most likely adjusted again.

Fore-aft is also easier (just like cleat position) to get right if you have an indoor trainer to put the bike on and then sit on, but it is more than doable with you just sitting on the bike and using one hand to lean against a wall, preferably indoors. The only piece of equipment you need is a plumb line, or as some call it a plump bob. If you don't have the real McCoy, you can make one with a piece of string and some metal washers. It only has to be about 3 feet long to do the job.

So get on the bike and do a few turns of the cranks (if you're on a trainer) just to get your feet settled in the right position. Then position the cranks horizontally. Try and put, then keep, your foot in the position it would be in during a normal pedal stroke. This is where the trainer is handy because you can concentrate and watch how your feet move before stopping to do the adjustment.

Now drop the plumb off the front of your forward protruding kneecap and let it fall to the inside of your shoe. Ideally it should just touch the end of the crank arm. If it doesn't, then adjust the saddle forwards or backwards till it does. That's it. This is a very good starting positon for most riders.

However, don't forget that this is only a *starting* position. Some guys, usually time triallists, will sit further forwards, whereas others may want to sit further back. Once the fore-aft position is set, once again check and re-adjust the saddle height if necessary. This will need to be done with most saddles unless you are using a Selle SMP saddle. I will deal with saddles themselves next.

STEM AND HANDLEBARS

STEM

Once saddle height, cleat position, and saddle fore-aft position have been adjusted, it's time to check the length of your stem. I use a very simple on-bike method to check if my stem length is correct, and so far it has served me well and I've had no back problems or shoulder pain.

First, get on the bike and ride along, either on a turbo trainer or out on the road, and put your hands into the hooks of the handlebars. Now tilt your head down at an angle of about 45 degrees, and try and see the hub in the centre of your front wheel. If your stem is the correct length for you, the hub should be obscured by your handlebars. If the hub can be seen in front of the bars, it means your stem is too short. If the hub can be seen behind the bars, it means the stem is too long. Replace accordingly.

HANDLEBARS

I will only go as far as to say that handlebar style and width are very much a matter of personal preference. I personally prefer a narrower bar, measuring about 40 centimetres from centre to centre. My advice is that if you are thinking of trying a different width and style from the one which came with your bike, buy cheap at first to find out what suits you best before digging deeper for a more expensive one. Carbon bars are really pricey. Aluminium is very cheap by comparison. Just remember, a lot of the pros prefer aluminium.

SADDLES

All I can do on saddles is to give some general advice, mostly based on personal experience. That's because finding the right saddle can be a very unique and personal thing. However, generally speaking, the more padding a saddle has the more comfortable it will be. You may find that some manufacturers do a specific saddle in more than one weight. If you are not racing, don't need to save weight, and are planning to do fairly long runs, then it's a good bet to go for the heavier, more padded one in the range. That said, padding isn't the be-all and end-all of more comfortable riding.

That's because you may suit a narrower or broader saddle, depending on the width of your pelvis. This won't be obvious until you have tried out a few for yourself. Again, you can go online and read horror stories of guys and girls who have spent a small fortune in search of the perfect saddle. I advise you to buy cheap at first til you find out what suits you best, then buy a better quality model in that style when you are sure you know what you are about – and have the funds, of course.

I am of quite stocky build, yet it seems that a narrow saddle suits me best. I found this out by accident when the saddle that came with my Trek mountain bike was narrow and padded. As I used the Trek for a bit of rare cycle touring (the battlefields in France), I soon became aware that even after days of riding, my bum still wasn't sore. About the same time, an expensive, lightly padded and broad Selle Italia saddle which I bought for my Eddy Merckx road bike, started to hurt like hell after about 60 miles. Through that, I learned the narrow job was for me.

Even Steve Hogg in his blog admits that he is wrong about people's pelvic size in about 25% of the cases he deals with. So it will come down to a bit of trial and error, especially when you start riding long. At the moment I am using a Selle SMP saddle on both my bikes. On the Merckx I am using the SMP Evolution, which is about the narrowest in the range. On my training bike I'm using the SMP Stratos, which is just the Evolution with more padding. Without any financial inducements, Steve Hogg recommends the Selle SMP on his website, and he rides one himself.

That said, they are not overly comfortable, as the whole centre section is cut out, and you literally ride on two rails. The nose on the SMP dips down noticeably, and it's one of the few saddles that is designed not to be set up horizontally, but to be tipped slightly nose down, anywhere between 1 and 5 degrees. If you do decide to invest in one, it's worth your while buying a digital spirit level to get the angle of degree of drop correct (this also requires some trial and error).

The SMP also has the advantage of being designed so that you do not need to readjust saddle height if you are adjusting fore-aft position. They are not cheap, costing well over £100 for the top ones, and they do take some getting used to, but at the moment that's my personal choice.

I am about to give some general and also very specific information about using heart rate monitors. But before I do, I want to stress that you do not need to know this or even to use a heart rate monitor if you don't want to. It is not essential or even necessary that you do. Some, however, may be interested in using one as they find they are getting into their bike riding and would like to know more about the benefits of using one. So here it is.

As we are doing a lot of long endurance runs in the book, it helps to pace yourself well, so as not to run out of steam halfway there. It is actually easier to do this on your heavier training bike than your top-end machine (if you have one), as the extra weight keeps you from getting carried away and going too fast too soon. The main device for keeping yourself in check is the heart rate monitor, though power meters are becoming much more common. Now as I mentioned at the start, I know plenty of guys who ride long and never use one; that's fine. It's all a matter of personal choice.

I like to use them, and have invested in a fairly upmarket model – the Polar C.S. 600. This gives me plenty of information, though a lot of it I don't need. A basic model of heart rate monitor/cycle computer will suffice, giving you your current heart rate, distance covered, time ridden, current speed, etc., which will do the job for most people, especially if they are riding for recreation, no matter how long the distance. But even for recreational riding, some of the features on a more advanced model are handy and useful, especially if you are a distance man or woman.

The Polar which I have includes a feature which tells you which heart rate zone you are in. This is very useful for people who are racing and want to know what intensity they are training at, but is also handy when you are on a very long run and are trying to pace yourself. In fact, it is a good idea to take your resting heart rate in the morning, before getting out of bed, to judge just how fit and well rested you are on any given day. The fitter you get, the lower it should become. So if you find you're getting into your riding and want to judge your fitness, simply start taking your resting heart rate in the morning so that you have an idea of your resting rate.

As your fitness improves, the amount of heart beats per minute (bpm) should come down. If you start increasing the riding then this will happen and that is good, because it means you're getting fitter. The lower your resting bpm, then the harder and longer you can ride on any given day. However, after a period of long hard riding, you might find your morning heart rate goes up. Warning!!! Time to back off. Your body is telling you you've done too much and you need more rest. Getting fit has a very simple equation, it goes like this.

STRESS THE BODY-------REST AND RECOVER.

Hard training doesn't do you any good on its own; it simply exhausts you and wrecks your muscles. It is resting that rebuilds you and makes you fitter and stronger for the next doing. To improve, you must have both sides of the equation working in tandem. Too much exercise and you burn out. Too little and you become a couch potato.

As you are not a professional bike rider, don't forget to take in the big picture. Stress is stress. The body doesn't know if it's stress from riding, working, DIY, family quarrels, or whatever. It only knows it's getting stressed. So if your morning rate goes up and you haven't been riding a lot, don't forget to take into consideration everything else that's getting lumped onto your plate.

An easier ride on the old machine in those circumstances should reduce the stress levels most of the time, so a run where you stay in your recovery zone should be the tonic. How do you know what is your recovery zone? Well, that's where the old heart rate monitor comes in. Try not to go for the off button here, for this is a good thing to know, although not essential. I've mentioned Aussie Steve Hogg as the main man on the bike-fitting front, but it's Yankee Joe Friel from Boulder Colorado who is the main man on the training front. I first became aware of him when I bought his excellent book *The Cyclist's Training Bible*, though I was unaware it was a book aimed strictly at people who raced. It was the excellent cover photo of Marco Pantani flying up an Alpine bend that caught my eye.

At one time it was thought that the best way to define training zones was to find your maximum heart rate and then work out the zones from there. However, this required you to sprint up a hill at full pelt and almost bring on a heart attack, at least for some (Joe describes it as a gun to the head). There was also the old theory about subtracting your age from some number like 220 (or thereabouts), but this is wildly inaccurate. So Joe explains it's better to work out your training zones based on your lactate threshold (LT).

Here's what's going on. When you are riding at a fairly slow to moderate pace, you are mostly using fat to provide the fuel and oxygen to assist this process, which is called being aerobic.

But once you increase the pace, you start to use more carbohydrate than fat to provide the fuel. When this happens, the muscles produce a by-product called lactic acid. At first the body is still able to flush away the lactic faster than it produces it, so you don't notice this. You are still using oxygen to assist the fuel supply process, and therefore still aerobic at this point. However there comes a point when you further increase your effort and the oxygen supply cannot keep up with demand, and you then cease being aerobic and become anaerobic. This is the point where you produce energy without using oxygen.

This is also the point when you cannot flush away the lactic as fast as you produce it, and it starts to accumulate in the muscles. It's this that gives you the burning sensation in your muscles when you are sprinting hard over a small hill. This is because you are now producing lactic faster than your body can get rid of it. The lactic acid seeps into the bloodstream and becomes lactate, which – being in the bloodstream – is actually measurable. You cannot ride anaerobically for very long as it's too bloody painful. You are riding at your maximum sustainable output just at the point where you are on the threshold of going from being aerobic to anaerobic. This is your lactate threshold (LT). Your heart rate at this point is what we want to find out and then use to determine our heart rate training zones.

 Again, no specialised equipment is required here, only an HRM that records average heart rate. The plan is now to do a short time trial and to go as hard as you can and find out what is your average heart rate for that particular exertion[1]. Once we get the average heart rate, we will divide that by a certain number and this will determine our lactate threshold and from that we will determine our training zones. Joe gives several distances with corresponding numbers by which to divide your average heart rate. This also includes whether you did the time trial as part of a race or as an individual time trial.

As most of you won't probably be racing yet, I'll give the two shortest distances he recommends as an

1 - Recovery	2 - Aerobic	3 - Tempo	4 - Sub-Threshold	5 - Super-Threshold
115-143	144-156	157-163	164-174	175-178

individual time trial – one in kilometres and one in miles, depending on what you prefer to use. Either one will do.

1) Ride a 5 kilometre TT and record your average heart rate then divide this by 1.04.

Or

2) Ride an 8 to 10 mile TT and record your average heart rate then divide this by 1.01.

So, for example, if you did a 10 mile time trial and your average heart rate was 177 BPM, divide this by 1.01 and this would give you 175 as your lactate threshold heart rate. So your corresponding zones would look like this:

If you have bought Joe's book, *The Cyclist's Training Bible*, it now becomes very easy to find out your training zones with the number the calculator gives you, because on page 27 of the version I have, all the corresponding heart rates and zones are given to you in a very well laid-out table. It may be worth buying the book for this alone. However you can work out the zones yourself, which are as follows, with the corresponding percentage heart rates of your lactate threshold heart rate in brackets.

1) Recovery: (65-81%) This is used for easy days after a previous day's hard ride or when you want to de-stress. It is also the zone to be in when recovering between hard training intervals. It is the ideal zone to be in when working on pedalling technique and such like.

2) Aerobic: (82-88%) This is the zone used for building up the endurance base, and the time spent in it is usually measured in hours. It is the most common zone we use when doing the long endurance runs in the book. It is a very valuable zone.

---

1   Make sure you are well rested on the day you do the TT and choose a flat course on a calm   day, if you can manage it.

3) Tempo: (89-93%) A fast form of endurance, but one that is sustainable. It can be handy for building up an endurance base fairly quickly when you haven't got a lot of time to do very long endurance runs.

4) Sub Threshold: (94-100%) This is the fastest you can go and still be aerobic. This zone can be used for several minutes at a time and helps the body deal with lactate build-up and become more efficient at disposing of lactate. This is the highest of the aerobic zones. It is still fairly hard on the body, however, so use this zone wisely. If you are doing training intervals in this zone, it will take at least half to a quarter of the time you spent in the zone to recover before doing the next interval.

5a) Super Threshold: (100-102%)[2] This is you now in the red zone. You are now anaerobic and this is used to help the body deal with lactate build-up. It is very hard on the body, so only short bursts are usual in this zone. Recovery time when doing intervals in the 5a zone are about one to one-and-a-half times the interval time.

Some computers might allow five, three, or one training zone to be pre-programmed. However, even if yours doesn't, as long as you know what your personal numbers are, you can use them for more intelligent and efficient training. This is very useful, especially if training time is limited or you want to take your recreational riding to a higher level and start racing. But remember, none of the above is necessary or compulsory if you only want to ride for fun. That's for sure.

(Main source: *The Cyclist's Training Bible*, by Joe Friel)

---

2   Please note that zone 5 can actually be broken down into 3 separate zones. The other 2 are zone 5b) Aerobic Capacity: (103-105%) and zone 5c) Anaerobic Capacity: 106%+. These are very, very hard training zones, used by experienced athletes.

UNCOMMON KNOWLEDGE

In route 6, the Toward Lighthouse and Loch Striven run, I mentioned a couple of fine fellows, Mark Tyrrell and Rodger Elliot, who along with their associates, call themselves Uncommon Knowledge or Hypnosis Downloads, if you like. They have built up over 800 very effective downloads and CDs to help anyone not only overcome a problem, but to also grow and expand in their lives. I must own about a dozen at least of their CDs and intend to invest in some more in the near future. I thoroughly recommend you give them a try if you need help in any area of your life, and can assure you that you should see quick results for very little outlay.

Each download costs approximately £12, though I prefer the CDs that come in at about £20. They cover just about everything you could think of and I've had a lot of success on a personal basis with most, though not all, of the ones that I've used. They can help in all areas of your life, with things from losing weight to relationships, from overcoming fears to difficult people. This includes sports performance, personal development, and health issues. They even have one to improve your eyesight. I've got that one and there has definitely been an improvement in my vision, especially in my dominant eye, though not quite to prescription glasses standard.

I've noticed that if you string together two or three really important ones, such as Believe in Yourself, General Anxiety Treatment and Self-Esteem Booster, then you will feel a sure gradual build-up of inner strength the more you use them. They will become the most relaxing and enjoyable part of the day, which is just fine, as constant repetition is the key to success here. Using these hypnosis CDs will make a difference; I can say that from experience, a very good experience at that.

I just want to point out that I am in no way connected to or get any financial support from this company, and am only passing on information that I know to be beneficial. So, as already mentioned, you've got nothing to lose, as the guys do a 90-day money back guarantee. I include their address and telephone number at the bottom. Tell them I sent you…Boom, Boom.

Uncommon Knowledge & Hypnosis Downloads
3rd floor, Boswell House, Argyll Square, Oban.
Argyll, UK
PA34 4BD
01273 776 770
www.hypnosisdownloads.com

INJURIES

Unfortunately, injuries from cycling may occur from time to time, either through a collision or a crash of some sort. Obviously we hope nothing too serious, of course, and it's fair to say the benefits outweigh the drawbacks in the vast majority of runs. Broken collarbones are fairly regular in the ranks of the professionals, but not so much with amateurs, and I've never had one in all the years I've ridden. You are more likely to sustain an injury through over-training than anything else and it's usually the poor old knees that give way, as they take all the pounding.

I usually find that easing up for a few days, or even a week or more till things ease off does the trick, but on occasion I've had to seek some professional help. There are many good physiotherapists out there, of course, but ideally it would be better to get one who knows about cycling as well. If you feel that you require the services of a physio, it might be a good idea to ask at your local bike store if they know of anyone who is a cycling-orientated physiotherapist, or even ask fellow riders.

I do know of one who treated me a few years back and who did a very good job, not only on my knee but also on my cleat position which eradicated any further problems. I contacted this gentleman when I was writing the book and offered him some free advertising along with a glowing reference, but he seemed reluctant for any publicity. So, for that reason alone, I did not include his details in this section.

One bit of advice I would give is if you don't have the money for a specialist and you are letting time alone make the repair, try a balm of some sort. Some guys swear by Tiger Balm, which costs about £7 for a small pot, though I have never used that myself. I have used Wood Lock Balm, which cost about £15 for a larger bottle, and acts like a sort of heat balm and massaging it in helps with easing the pain. Both these balms are used in Chinese medicine. I got mine in the Piazza shopping centre, Paisley, where a very helpful Chinese lady has a small store. You may want to give that a try.

DATA

Below the title of every run will be the information and statistics relating to that run, the details of which have been provided by my Polar C.S. 600 cycling computer. Below this again will be the relevant numbers for the Ordnance Survey Landranger maps that cover the area of the run. The details of the information is as follows:

MILES

The mileage for any given run will be from my front door, in Glenburn, South Paisley, to the destination and then back to my front door, unless stated. Obviously this exact distance is only relevant to me, but it should act as a fairly good indicator as to what is involved for anyone wishing to do the run from their home. In the case of starting from a ferry terminal, the distances will be exactly the same for all. I could have used a more central starting point for the runs, such as Paisley Cross or Paisley Gilmour St station, but most riders wouldn't be starting from there either. The mileage given is only meant as a ballpark figure. So if, for example, you live in Renfrew, you can subtract 6 miles from the Stirling run, but would have to add the same 6 miles for the Turnberry run. Adjust to suit.

HOURS

Hours is simply the time taken to do the run. This will be for a run when no photos were taken and stops were kept to a minimum, i.e. toilet breaks, etc. Despite this, these times are of course approximate, as you may ride at a completely different speed from me. I did consider using an average speed for all the runs, say somewhere around 14 mph, but some of the runs were done partly on single track road, which can slow you down considerably, and other runs involved a lot more climbing than ones of a similar distance, so again the time would differ greatly. Also which bike, training or top machine, traffic, weather, and especially wind strength and direction would also play a part in speed and time, as would how many miles you had done the previous day or two. So remember, the time for each run is merely approximate.

ASCENT IN FEET

This is the amount of climbing involved in any given run or variation of that run. The CS 600 will often give a difference of perhaps 80 to 100 feet of ascent in a run covering anywhere from between 60 to 100 miles, so it is a fairly accurate figure that you are given.

CALORIES/BURNED OR CALS

This again is an approximate figure, as the amount of calories burned per mile can vary greatly from individual to individual. Your age, VO2 Max, the speed you ride at, can all affect how many calories you burn. As a useful guide, if you are trying to lose weight by cycling and using a calorie controlled diet, and you don't have a computer that tells you how many calories you've burned, then 40 calories per mile is a good, fairly accurate figure to use to help you know how much energy you are using and burning off. That should be accurate enough to help in your weight loss.

O/S LANDRANGER MAPS

The numbers for the Ordnance Survey maps that will cover the whole run are given. Although it is handy to have these, they are not totally essential and a good road atlas should suffice for the most part. As each map costs about £8 each, you can save quite a few quid by simply using the road atlas. However, the more detailed maps are both handy and interesting to have, and I consider it worth the expense to get them. They will prove beneficial when you are sitting of an evening and looking to plan out runs in the future or, as stated in the text, you may want to see where you took a wrong turn on some small back road after a run has been completed.

PHOTOGRAPHY

I used two cameras to take all the photographs within the book – both compact digitals, small enough to fit into the rear pocket of my cycling jersey. They were the very small and formidable Panasonic Lumix DMC-FT2 (the T stands for tough) and also the slightly larger Nikon Coolpix P-7000. During the countless runs I made while writing the book, I took countless photographs and none have been enhanced in any way. I wanted it to be quite simply what you see is what you get.

Sometimes I have found that when you, say for example, look at a brochure for an area you wish to visit or perhaps to do a long distance ride or walk like the West Highland Way, the photographs in the brochure will have been taken by a very experienced skilful photographer.

They have waited for the light to be right – usually early morning or late evening, when most people will have ended their days walking or riding. And also they have taken up unusual positions and vantage points, sometimes with the aid of a tripod, often when the weather is at its best. So, of course, when you go and do the ride or walk, the area looks nothing like it did in the photos. Well, I didn't want that. All the photos were taken at the time of day most people would be doing the run and in the very weather that nature threw at me at the time. So again, what you will see is what you can expect to get at the time you come to do the ride yourself.

A word to the wise here, if you do decide to start taking photos yourself when you are out on the bike. It is much more time consuming than you would imagine to continually stop the bike and take photos. I am telling you this in case you wish to buy a camera yourself and record your runs as you go along. You probably won't notice when doing a mainland run, but if you are on an island or aiming for a specific ferry, then it is very prudent to watch the clock continuously or you may miss your ferry and end up being stranded overnight. If your computer has an average speed reading, it will be a good indicator of just how much slower you are going when you are using the camera a lot.

To speed things up, I did invest in a bracket to hold the camera in position on my handlebars and save me from continually stopping to take a shot. Although this did save some time, I don't recommend doing this, as too many of the shots were ruined by camera shake. Certainly this set-up could only be used with a tough camera variant, as the non-tough Nikon proved to be totally inadequate on the bracket, but even the majority of shots with the Panasonic turned out to be well below par. The larger Nikon had the advantage of a viewfinder and more powerful lens, but the Lumix had a better metering system, which coped far better with difficult conditions, such as shimmering sunlight on the Clyde.

The photo shows just some (though admittedly, the bulk) of my cleaning and maintenance tools. But as this is not a book on cycle maintenance, I will not go into any great depth on that subject.

However, learning to do your own repairs is very satisfying, convenient, and cost-effective. So I recommend fairly early on in your cycling life to get a good maintenance manual (the two I have are old but still handy), and start to build up the old tool box as you go along. If the worst comes to the worst and a repair goes badly wrong, you can always take it along to your local bike store and you're no worse off than if you had gone there in the first place.

The cleaning kit does not need to be one of the fancy brush sets that you can buy which are specific to bike cleaning. I find a sponge, a rag, and a small brush, will do most of the jobs better than the purpose-built stuff does, though some small specialised brushes are really handy for getting into awkward nooks and crannies. The basic cleaning kit is as follows:

CLEANING KIT

- Bucket
- Fairy liquid
- Sponge
- Rag
- Stiff, small sweeping brush
- Chain cleaner (a must-have)
- Liquid de-greaser for chain cleaner
- Spray degreaser for other parts
- Specialised small brushes for cogs and mechs (optional)
- Old toothbrush (will do in place of small specialised brushes)

WORKSHOP KIT:

- Workstand (optional, but good to have)
- Wheel truing stand (wheels can be trued in situ, but a proper stand is handy)
- Spare tubes
- Spare tyres
- Rim tape
- Puncture repair kit (old glue style)

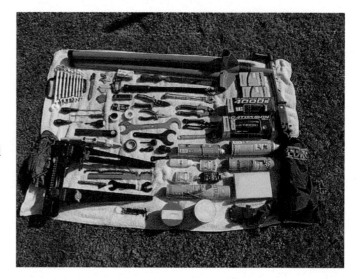

- Handlebar cork
- Spare brake pads
- Brake cables
- Gear cables
- Cable ends
- Cable cutters
- Link pin pliers
- Pliers: normal and long-nosed
- Chain checker
- Chain wrench
- Spoke keys
- Assorted combination spanners and shifting spanner
- Assorted screwdrivers
- Lubes: both wet and dry
- Bearing grease
- Multi-tools
- Bottom bracket tools (various)
- Sprocket removal tool
- Allen keys
- Cone spanners
- Small wire brush (for cleaning bolts, etc)
- WD40 (or equivalent)
- Spirit level
- Digital spirit level (if you have a Selle SMP saddle)
- Torq wrenches (good to have)
- Insulating tape
- Oily rags (last but not least, you'll need one or two)

FURTHER READING

The Secret by Rhonda Byrne

The Cyclist's Training Bible by Joe Friel

The Artist's Way by Julia Cameron

The Secret Code of Success by Noah St John

Steve Hogg's online blog

"Just a guy who does a bit".

Liam is an ordinary bloke. When he decided one night that he needed to change his unhealthy lifestyle, he did so in a spectacular way and found a passion for cycling.

He is a taxi driver with an interest in lots of things; bikes, history, photography, psychology and more. If you are lucky enough to share his cab you could find yourself inspired and entertained by his philosophy. Maybe enough to even start a new journey of your own.

Liam's "bit" has taken him on a journey from his home in Paisley around Scotland on his bike. If you'd like to know more please contact him on his Facebook page at

Liam Farrell - The Circle Game

or e-mail him at

liamfarrellthecirclegame123@gmail.com.

Lightning Source UK Ltd.
Milton Keynes UK
UKOW07f1125260617
304100UK00008B/36/P